COLLIER QUICK AND EASY SERIES

HOME IMPROVEMENT AND MAINTENANCE

IMPROVE PRACTICAL OR VOCATIONAL SKILLS

SUPPLEMENT YOUR FORMAL EDUCATION

GET MORE FUN OUT OF HOBBIES

This Collier guide is designed to offer concise, authoritative information in a clear, readable manner. Carefully prepared with the latest, up-to-the-minute material, it is also valuable as a source for permanent reference. Titles in the Quick and Easy series include—

AMERICAN HISTORY
Robert Sobel, Ph.D.

ARITHMETIC
Simon Dresner

BOOKKEEPING
Morton D. Bluestone, M.A.

PRECISION BOWLING FOR HIGHER SCORES
Hal and Jean Vermes

CARPENTRY IN THE HOME WORKSHOP
Clarence Herisko

CHESS
Richard Roberts

DECORATOR'S GUIDE TO HOME FURNISHING
Richard N. Fried, A.I.D.

DRIVING SAFELY
Edward A. McInroy, M.A.

ECONOMICS FOR BUSINESSMEN AND INVESTORS
George G. Dawson, Ph.D.,
and Russell H. McClain, Ph.D.

EFFECTIVE BUSINESS CORRESPONDENCE
Abraham Ellenbogen

EFFECTIVE SPEAKING
Bernice Loren

ELECTRONICS from Theory to Home Repair
Jesse Dilson

COMPLETE GUIDE TO GOOD MANNERS IN BUSINESS AND SOCIAL LIFE
Dorothy Sara

FAMILY CAMPING
William P. Luce

GOLF
Robert Scharff

HI FI AND STEREO
Richard Roberts

HOME IMPROVEMENT AND MAINTENANCE
Martin Sara

HOME NURSING CARE
Lucille Gidseg, R.N.
and Dorothy Sara

THE HUNTER'S GAME, GUN, and DOG GUIDE
Robert Scharff

INSURANCE
Martin Cornwall

LAW
Jesse Raphael, LL.B.

MAGIC
Hal G. Vermes

MAKING HOME MOVIES
Bob Knight

MOTOR BOATING
Robert Scharff

PHYSICAL FITNESS
Justus Schifferes, Ph.D.

PLANNING AND PAYING YOUR WAY TO COLLEGE
Clodus R. Smith

PLAYING THE GUITAR
Frederick M. Noad

RAPID READING
Myron Q. Herrick,
The Reading Laboratory, Inc.

RUNNING A MEETING
Jack T. Parker

SECRETS OF LOOKING AND FEELING YOUR BEST
Joan Kuehl

SELLING PERSON-TO-PERSON
Hal G. Vermes

SEWING
Dorothy Stepat De Van

SKIING WITH CONTROL
Rick Shambroom and
Betty Slater

SUCCESSFUL SELLING
Hal G. Vermes

TENNIS
Robert Scharff

TV WRITING
George Lowther

WATER SKIING
Glen E. Anderson

WORLD HISTORY
Edwin Dunbaugh, Ph.D.

COLLIER QUICK AND EASY SERIES

HOME IMPROVEMENT AND MAINTENANCE

MARTIN SARA

COLLIER BOOKS
A Division of Macmillan Publishing Co., Inc.
NEW YORK

COLLIER MACMILLAN PUBLISHERS
LONDON

Originally published under the title
The Collier Quick and Easy
Guide to Home Maintenance

Copyright © 1962 by Macmillan Publishing Co., Inc.

Library of Congress Catalog Card Number: 62-16976

First Edition 1962

Fourth Printing 1973

Originally published under the title The Collier Quick and
Easy Guide to Home Maintenance

Macmillan Publishing Co., Inc.
866 Third Avenue, New York, N. Y. 10022
Collier-Macmillan Canada Ltd., Toronto, Ontario

Printed in the United States of America

INTRODUCTION

The attractiveness of a home, and the satisfaction and pride that the members of the family derive from it, depend in no small degree on the way they maintain their house, its equipment and its grounds. Furthermore, care and repair of the house represent an item in every homeowner's budget that cannot be overlooked. The family that makes repairs as they are needed, and performs minor alterations from time to time, is better served by its home than the family that allows such items to accumulate. Failure to make repairs or replacements promptly may lead to deterioration in structural parts of the house and subsequently entail large expense.

The purpose of this book is to explain the kinds of defects that may arise throughout the house and its grounds, some being of an emergency nature and others the result of gradual deterioration due to natural causes. The book tells how to remedy them and, in some cases, how they may be prevented by taking proper precautions.

There may be some repairs that can best be handled by a licensed plumber or electrician, a carpenter or other skilled workman. In some areas there may exist local ordinances that you must follow before attempting any repair projects on your own.

On the market are materials and tools that are made expressly for use in home workshops, and the manufacturers are mindful of this situation in the simplicity and clarity of their directions, which the homeowner benefits by following. Regardless of how much skill and initiative the home handyman possesses, the recommendations of the manufacturers and their local dealers are all geared to help in proper home maintenance.

Grateful acknowledgment is made to the following, from whom information and illustrations were obtained to enable this book to be written with the newest available material in the field of home maintenance: U.S. Department of Agriculture; U.S. Department of Commerce, National Bureau of Standards; U.S. Department of the Army; Cornell University, Extension Department of The College of Agriculture; University of Connecticut, Extension Service of The College of Agriculture; also to DeWalt, Inc., for information about power-tool workshops, and to Stanley Tools and the Masonite Corporation for home workshop material.

MARTIN SARA

CONTENTS

Chapter One

YOUR WORKSHOP

Its location

TO ADD CONVENIENCE and pleasure to the work you do toward the maintenance of your house, create a workshop for yourself that can truly be a "handyman's haven." It can be located in the basement, garage, in a lean-to on your house or wherever there is space to accommodate your workbench and tools. Try to place the workshop so that it will be easy for you to bring materials in and out of the room.

You may want to make your workshop in the attic; however, bear in mind the inconvenience of carrying materials up and down the stairs. You can turn a closet into a satisfactory work spot, or even create a temporary setup in the kitchen, using the kitchen table as a workbench.

Workbench and tool racks

Depending on the space available and on your ingenuity, here are suggestions you might follow:

Buy or make a sturdy worktable, or convert a kitchen table to such use (Fig. 1.1). Nail a wood rack to the back edge of the table, with holes bored in the rack to hold some of your tools. Screw hooks into the front of the rack on which to hang additional tools. At one corner at the front of the table screw a vise, which you will need for holding things securely while you work on them.

The surface of the workbench is left clear, except for the vise screwed down at one corner (Fig. 1.2a). On the wall above the table attach a perforated wallboard (pegboard), into which tools are hung individually on hooks, or, in the case of smaller tools, on racks that are hung

in the perforations. Figure 1.2b is a detail showing how to construct the wallboard over a wood frame for extra strength.

The inside of the closet, as well as the back of its door, provides extra space when there is little space to spare (Fig. 1.3).

If you do not find it feasible to allot space in your house for a workshop, yet want to keep equipment in proper order, a portable tool kit serves the purpose (Fig. 1.4). You can buy or make one. When you have to use the tools, all you do is open up the kit and set it on a table against the wall. (The foregoing refers to work-

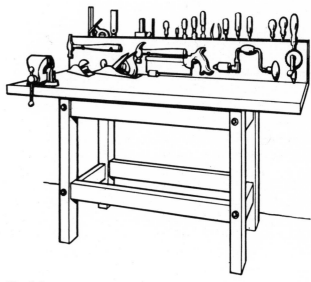

Fig. 1.1

11

Fig. 1.2a

shops accommodating hand tools; the inclusion of power tools is discussed in Chapter 3.)

Whichever kind of workshop you have, it is advisable to have a work surface at a height comfortable for you. You may need to stand a good deal at the workbench, and unless you are relaxed and in a position to use your hands and arms freely, you may tire easily and not do your best work. If you find it more convenient to sit

while working, provide a swivel chair that you may adjust to varying heights when working at different surface levels.

Rack for screws and nails

Screws and nails of varying sizes and kinds should be kept separately in screw-top jars, so that you can see when the supply is running low. If you can get transparent plastic jars for the purpose, they are preferable because less prone to breakage. As shown in Fig. 1.5, the jar covers are nailed to the underside of the rack shelf, and the jars screwed into the covers. This rack serves a double purpose, since items can be stored on top of the shelf.

Sawhorses

A pair of sawhorses is a helpful and versatile aid to the home handyman. When you need an extra table, simply place the sawhorses apart and lay a board across them to give you added working surface. This device is also useful when you measure and paste the back of wallpaper before hanging it on the wall, or when you need a scaffold.

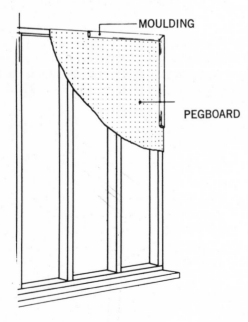

Fig. 1.2b

Fig. 1.3

Fig. 1.4

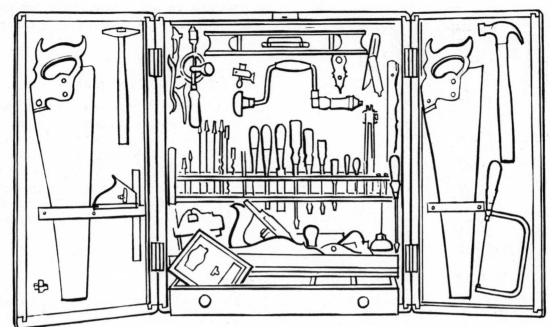

A single sawhorse is used when sawing wood; the board can be placed on top of the sawhorse at whatever angle is most convenient for you.

Fig. 1.6 shows the simplicity of construction, as well as the method, which you can easily follow. Make sure the lumber is strong and the legs braced properly, since they may need to carry heavy weights.

Workshop floor

If the workshop is located in a garage or basement that has a damp concrete or cement floor, lay a wood flooring over the existing floor so that neither you nor the materials in the workshop will be affected by the dampness.

If the workshop is placed on a wood floor, inspect the flooring to be sure it will not crack under the strain of heavy hammering or any other work you may do. If the flooring is insufficiently strong, it may be necessary to lay an extra layer of wood flooring over the existing one.

To permit easy cleaning, lay linoleum over a wood

floor surface. Then all you need do when your work is completed is clean the floor with a damp cloth.

Providing good lighting

Natural daylight from a window is the ideal light, and if possible the workbench should be placed near the window. But if you spend evening hours in your workshop, or if it is located in a place where natural lighting is not adequate, provide sufficient electric lighting to avoid eyestrain and help you achieve the best work results.

A bright ceiling or wall light is essential to give good over-all lighting in your work area. But if you have no ceiling or wall fixture, use a sturdy floor or table lamp that has a flexible gooseneck top so you may raise or lower the light as required. For very close work done by the light of a lamp on an electric cord from the ceiling or on a side fixture, buy the type of cord which allows you to lower or raise the light.

Fig. 1.5

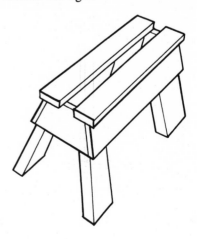

Fig. 1.6

Water supply

If possible, a water faucet should be available in the workshop area, for such purpose as cleaning tools and washing your hands. Should there be no faucet, you can attach a garden hose to the water supply if the workshop is situated in the garage or basement. If it is nowhere near running water, you may find it convenient to have a metal pitcher of water and basin near your workbench.

Correct temperature

Not only must you have warm fingers to do your best work, but when working with wood and glue, the glue must not get chilled and thereby cause faulty results. If the heating system does not extend into your workshop, you may need to use a portable electric, gas or oil heater. If the heater is to stand on a wood floor, place a sheet of metal or asbestos beneath it. Also place a wire screen around the heater to prevent its setting fire to you or to the materials with which you are working.

Preventing fire hazards

You may use combustible materials in your workshop, such as oils and paint. Install a metal fireproof cabinet or box in which to store inflammable materials when not in use. When you finish your work, put oily cloths and anything else that is combustible into this container. Do not leave a littered floor; sweep up sawdust, wood shavings and loose papers or rags, and dump them into a tightly covered metal trash can.

If you are a smoker, or if you have visitors who smoke, have enough metal ash trays on hand. Do not leave cigarette or cigar stubs, or your pipe, on a wood or plastic surface.

When you are using inflammable liquids, make sure that no matchboxes or matches are lying around. Matches should be kept in a tightly covered metal container.

If you have an electric hot plate or a one-burner gas stove in your workshop, for heating glue or for the soldering iron, or perhaps for boiling water for coffee or tea, place that heater on a sheet of metal or asbestos. Never stand it directly on a wood or plastic surface.

Chapter Two

BASIC HAND TOOLS

THE HOME HANDYMAN, or handywoman, does not need a complete set of carpentry or plumbing tools; there are many tools on the market that are too intricate for any but the professionally skilled workman, and many are in the gadget class and not worth buying. It is wise to start off with tools of good quality and, whenever possible, to select those that can be used for more than one purpose. As your skill and interest increase, you can purchase additional tools for more complicated types of work.

The next chapter discusses the power tools you may want to get; but here is a suggested starting list of manual tools and supplies for your workshop.

Choosing tools and supplies

GENERAL TOOLS

The tools most frequently needed to enable you to perform the usual tasks in the upkeep of a house are the following:

Brad awl	Mason's trowel
Carpenter's level	Metal shears
Claw hammer	Monkey wrench
Cold chisel	Nail set ($\frac{1}{16}$-inch)
File (3-cornered)	Oilcan
Flashlight	Oilstone
Folding rule	Paintbrush (small, flat)
Funnel	Plumb bob
Gimlet	Plunger (plumber's friend)
Glass cutter	Putty knife
Hacksaw	Screw drivers (one large, one
Handsaw (crosscut)	small)
Hatchet	Smoothing plane
Jackknife	Soldering iron
Marking pencil	Steel square

Stepladder (6-foot)	Wire-cutting pliers
Stillson wrench	Wood chisels ($\frac{1}{4}$- and $\frac{7}{8}$-
Washtub (small)	inch)
Water bucket (galvanized)	

SPECIAL TOOLS

Tools that are very useful, but not required as often as those in the preceding list, include the following:

Auger (coil, spring-steel,	Miter box
pipe-cleaning)	Paintbrush (3-inch, flat)
Brace and bit	Plasterer's trowel
Drills (hand, $\frac{1}{4}$-inch; twist;	Ripsaw
assorted)	Straight ladder (12-foot)
Jackplane	Vise

SUPPLIES

The following supplies will be found useful in many cases and may be kept on hand to meet emergencies:

Candles	Sandpaper
Electric fuses	Screws (assorted)
Liquid glue	Seat washers
Lubricating oil	Soft solder
Nails (assorted)	Sponge
Nuts and bolts	Tape (friction; rubber)
Rubber tubing (narrow)	Wire (copper and iron)

Care of tools

Rust and abuse are two of the worst enemies of tools. To prevent rust, occasionally put a few drops of light machine oil over metal surfaces and rub the oil dry before storing the tool. If the tool is already rusty, rub it with very fine steel wool and a little kerosene. Be sure to wipe off the kerosene before putting the tool away.

To safeguard the tool, use it only for the job for which

15

it was intended. Always keep the cutting edges sharp, since dull tools are dangerous tools.

Rules and squares

Measuring and marking must be accurate if the job is to be well done. Any piece of wood on which you work should be squared on one side, or end, as described below. All measurements are made from the squared line.

The folding rule is good for general measuring.

The steel tape is flexible and handy for taking inside measurements, as in cupboards for example.

There are several kinds of squares: steel square, try square and combination square (Fig. 2.1). Any of these may be used for measuring or squaring wood. In addition, the combination square may be used as a miter or as a level. The square is used as follows:

1. Measure the desired length or width with the rule. Mark with a sharp pencil.

2. To square a line across the end of a board, put one

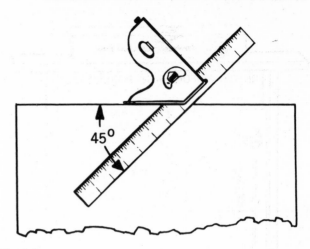

Fig. 2.2

blade of the square along the straight side of the board and move the square until the other blade is in position at the point at which the board is to be cut.

3. Draw a line along the edge of the blade.

4. The combination square is useful in measuring lines at an angle, as shown in Fig. 2.2.

Level

The level is designed to discover whether a plane or surface is true horizontal or true vertical. It is a simple instrument consisting of a glass tube, or vial, in which a liquid has been sealed. The tube is mounted in a frame which may be of aluminum, iron or wood. Levels are equipped with one, two or more tubes. One set of tubes is built into the frame at right angles to the other set, with an air bubble in each tube.

USING THE LEVEL

Figure 2.3 shows how the level is placed against or on a surface.

To check for true horizontal, position the level horizontally on the work and note the graduated tube for proper indication. Ground glass tubes usually have two or more etched lines on the glass. For true horizontal, the bubble should be centered between the lines; on graduated tubes, proper indication is dependent on the accuracy required. The bubble should be centered between the divisions on the tube that indicate the desired position of the work.

To check for true vertical (plumb), place the level vertically against the work and check for true vertical by observing the position of the cross-tube bubble. The bubble should be centered between the lines on the tube.

CARE OF THE LEVEL

Use the level with caution; it should not be dropped, handled roughly or used for purposes other than those

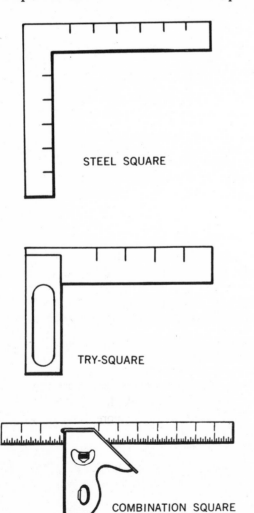

STEEL SQUARE

TRY-SQUARE

COMBINATION SQUARE

Fig. 2.1

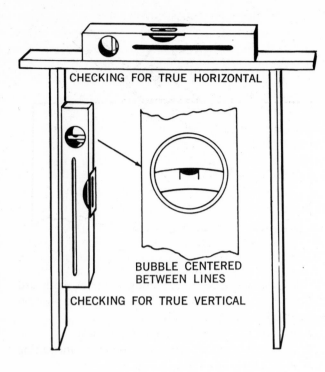

CHECKING FOR TRUE HORIZONTAL

BUBBLE CENTERED
BETWEEN LINES

CHECKING FOR TRUE VERTICAL

Fig. 2.3

intended. When not in use, store the level in a rack or other suitable place to prevent damage. Make certain the storage place is dry. Spread a thin film of rust-preventive compound or oil on all metal parts before storage. Remove rust-preventive compound before using by washing with a suitable cleaning solvent.

Plumb bob

The common plumb bob is used to determine true verticality. It is used in carpentry when erecting vertical up-

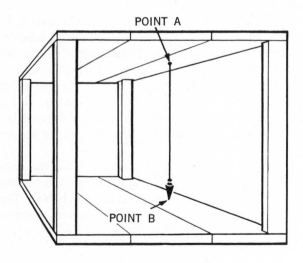

POINT A

POINT B

Fig. 2.4

rights and corner posts of framework. The bob is attached to the end of a strong cord or a steel tape. You may make a substitute plumb bob by hanging a small screw driver, or even a heavy spoon or fork, at the end of the cord.

To locate a point that is exactly below a particular point in space, secure the cord or tape to the upper point, such as A in Fig. 2.4. When the plumb bob stops swinging, its point will indicate point B, which is exactly below A.

Hammer and nail set

There are many types of hammers. A ten- to fourteen-ounce drop-forged claw hammer is suitable for driving and drawing nails. This hammer and the way to hold it are shown in Fig. 2.5.

The hammer handle should fit tightly into the hammer head. If the handle loosens, drive a wooden or metal wedge into the center of the handle where it comes through the head.

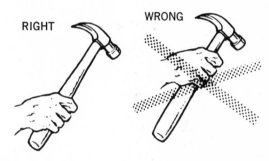

RIGHT

WRONG

Fig. 2.5

DRIVING A NAIL

1. Grasp the hammer as shown in Fig. 2.5. Hold the handle of the hammer parallel with the surface into which the nail is being driven and strike the nail squarely on the head to avoid bending it.

2. When driving large nails grip the hammer handle firmly at the end to obtain more power and to force the nail in straight. Use short light strokes to drive small nails.

3. Use wrist motion and let the hammer drop, thus letting gravity do the work. It may be necessary to use arm movement to apply more force when driving a very large nail.

4. Finish driving the nail with light strokes so the wood surface will not be marred. On fine work use a block of wood over the nailhead to avoid hammer marks on the wood surface.

NAIL SET

The nail set has a concave tip and is used to drive

finishing nails below the surface of the wood (Fig. 2.6).

Place the tip of the nail set on the nail and tap it with the hammer until the nailhead is below the surface of the wood.

Fill the resulting holes with wood putty or plastic wood. When the putty or plastic wood is dry, smooth the surface with a file or sandpaper.

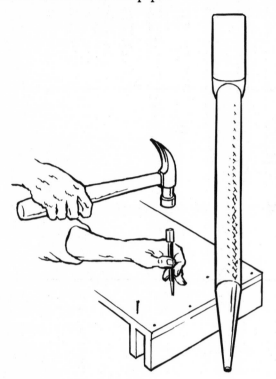

Fig. 2.6

Nails

Nail sizes are designated by the use of the term "penny." This term designates the length of the nail (one penny, two penny and so forth), which is the same for all types (Fig. 2.7). The approximate number of nails per pound varies according to the type and size. The wire gauge number varies according to type. The table with Fig. 2.8 provides the information implicit in the term "penny" for each of the types of nails referred to in this section. The "d" adjacent to the numbers in the *Size* column is the accepted abbreviation of the word "penny" as used in nail sizing and should be read "2 penny," "3 penny" and so forth.

Screw types and uses

The use of screws, rather than nails, as fasteners may be dictated by a number of factors. These may include the type of material to be fastened, the need for greater holding power than can be obtained by the use of nails, the finished appearance desired and the fact that the

number of fasteners that can be used is limited. The main advantages of screws are that they may be easily tightened to draw the items being fastened securely together, are neater in appearance if properly driven and may be withdrawn without damaging the material.

Wood screws are designated according to head style. The most common types are flathead, ovalhead and roundhead (Fig. 2.9a). To prepare wood for receiving the screws, bore a pilot hole the diameter of the screw to be used in the piece of wood that is to be fastened (b). Then bore a smaller, starter hole in the piece of wood that is to act as anchor or hold the threads of the screw. The starter hole should have a diameter slightly less than that of the screw threads and be drilled to a depth one-half to two-thirds the length of the threads to be anchored. The purpose of this careful preparation is to assure accuracy in the placement of the screws, to reduce the possibility of splitting the wood and to reduce the time and effort required to drive the screw. Properly set slotted and phillips flathead and ovalhead screws are countersunk sufficiently to permit a covering material to be used to cover the head. Slotted roundhead and phillips roundhead screws are not countersunk, but are driven so that the head is firmly flush with the surface of the wood. The slot of the roundhead screw is left parallel with the grain of the wood.

Lag screws (c) are often required in construction carpentry. They are longer and much heavier than the common wood screw and have coarser threads, which extend from a cone or gimlet point slightly more than half the length of the screw. Squarehead and hexagon-head lag screws are always externally

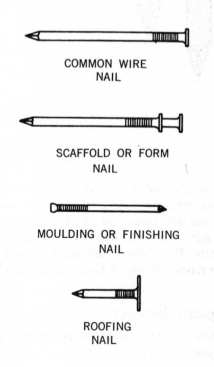

COMMON WIRE
NAIL

SCAFFOLD OR FORM
NAIL

MOULDING OR FINISHING
NAIL

ROOFING
NAIL

Fig. 2.7

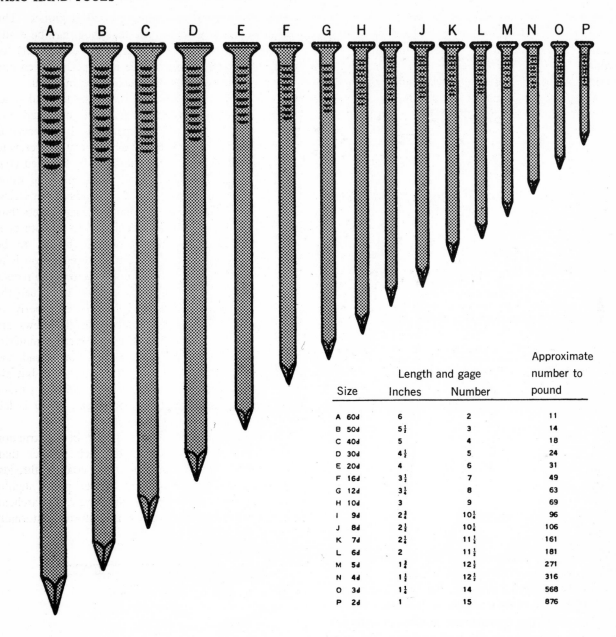

| Size | Length and gage | | Approximate number to pound |
	Inches	Number	
A 60d	6	2	11
B 50d	$5\frac{1}{2}$	3	14
C 40d	5	4	18
D 30d	$4\frac{1}{2}$	5	24
E 20d	4	6	31
F 16d	$3\frac{1}{2}$	7	49
G 12d	$3\frac{1}{4}$	8	63
H 10d	3	9	69
I 9d	$2\frac{3}{4}$	$10\frac{1}{4}$	96
J 8d	$2\frac{1}{2}$	$10\frac{1}{4}$	106
K 7d	$2\frac{1}{4}$	$11\frac{1}{2}$	161
L 6d	2	$11\frac{1}{2}$	181
M 5d	$1\frac{3}{4}$	$12\frac{1}{2}$	271
N 4d	$1\frac{1}{2}$	$12\frac{1}{2}$	316
O 3d	$1\frac{1}{4}$	14	568
P 2d	1	15	876

Fig. 2.8

driven, usually by means of a wrench. They are used when ordinary wood screws would be too short or too light and spikes would not be strong enough.

Sheet metal screws (d) are used for the assembly of metal parts. These screws are made of steel or brass, with four types of heads: flat, round, oval and fillister.

Corrugated fastener

This fastener is often used to strengthen wood or to hold mitered joints together.

Center the corrugated fastener over the parts to be connected to give the greatest holding power, as shown in Fig. 2.10. Hammer the fastener into the wood until it is flush with the surface.

Brad awl

This tool resembles an ice pick and is used to punch small holes for screws and nails. Nails that would ordinarily split a piece of wood may be driven safely after a brad awl has been used to start the hole.

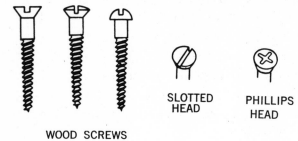

WOOD SCREWS

SLOTTED HEAD

PHILLIPS HEAD

Fig. 2.9a

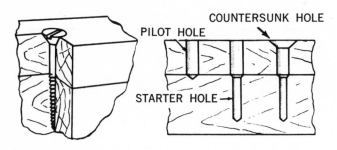

PILOT HOLE

COUNTERSUNK HOLE

STARTER HOLE

Fig. 2.9b

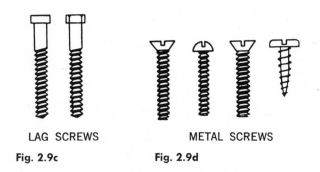

LAG SCREWS

Fig. 2.9c

METAL SCREWS

Fig. 2.9d

Hold the awl at the handle and place its sharp point at the spot where you want to make the hole. Use a twisting motion to the right and to the left, pushing on the handle to force the awl into the wood. Make the hole slightly smaller than the nail or screw you will use.

Awls are very sharp and should be used with extreme caution. Do not carry an awl in your pocket or place it on a workbench or table where others may be hurt by its sharp point. When not in use, hang the awl on a rack or, if it is to be stored in a toolbox, stick a cork on its point.

Gimlet

The gimlet is another tool with which to start the hole into which a nail or screw is to be placed. It has a long pointed metal piece, like an ice pick, but is threaded at the end of the point. The handle is generally a horizontal, round bar, on which the hand may obtain a good grip. Place the point of the gimlet on the spot where the nail or screw is to go; press down hard on the handle,

and then turn the gimlet round and round in the same manner as you would a corkscrew. Do not bore the hole too long or too wide, but just enough to give the nail or screw a good, firm start.

Pliers

Pliers are used for gripping, cutting, bending, forming or holding work, and for special jobs. Pliers basically consist of a pair of jaws designed for a specific purpose, a pivot or hinge and a pair of handles. They are made in many shapes and sizes to handle a variety of jobs. The size is determined by the over-all length, which usually is five to ten inches.

When using pliers, keep your fingers away from the jaws and cutting edges. Make sure the hinge or joint is tight before using the pliers. Insulate handles of pliers, when using them in electrical work, with several thicknesses of friction tape, rubber tape or specially manufactured rubber grips.

Chisel

WOODWORKING CHISEL

There are many chisels available on the market, but the socket and tang types are preferable for working on wood. When in use the chisel should always be held with the flat side, or back of the chisel against the work for smoothing and finishing cuts. When avoidable, it should not be pushed straight through an opening, but should be moved laterally at the same time that it is pushed forward, as shown in Fig. 2.11. This method insures a shearing cut, which, with care, even when the work is cross-grained, will produce a smooth and even surface.

On rough work, use a wooden mallet to drive the socket-type chisel. On fine work, use your hand as the driving power on tang-type chisels. For rough cuts, the beveled edge of the chisel is held against the work.

Whenever it is feasible, other tools such as saws and planes should be used to remove as much of the waste

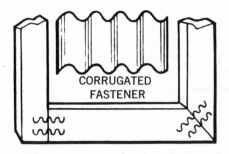

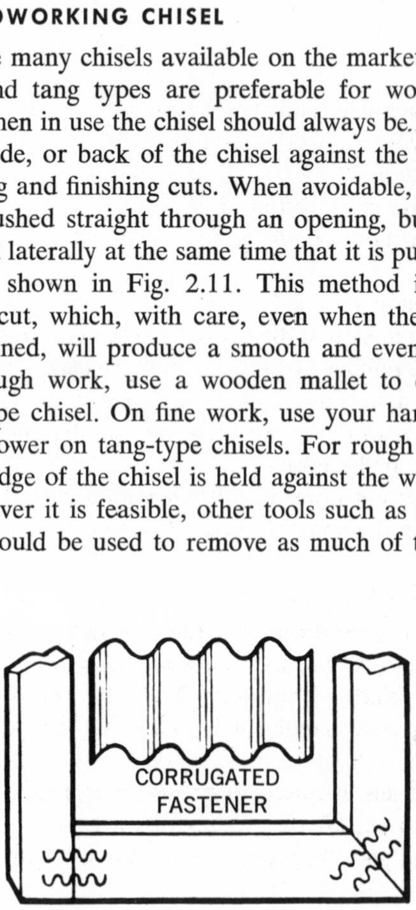

CORRUGATED FASTENER

Fig. 2.10

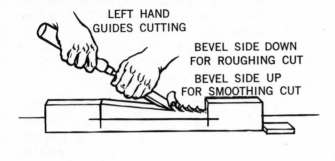

LEFT HAND GUIDES CUTTING

BEVEL SIDE DOWN FOR ROUGHING CUT

BEVEL SIDE UP FOR SMOOTHING CUT

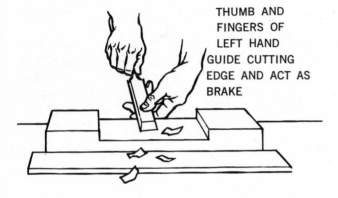

THUMB AND FINGERS OF LEFT HAND GUIDE CUTTING EDGE AND ACT AS BRAKE

Fig. 2.11

wood as possible, and the chisel used for finishing purposes only.

Precautions:

1. Secure work so that it cannot move.

2. Keep both hands back of the cutting edge at all times.

3. Do not start a cut on a guideline. Start slightly away from it, so that there will be a small amount of material to be removed by the finishing cuts.

4. When starting a cut, always chisel away from the guideline toward the waste wood, so that no splitting will occur at the edge.

5. Never cut towards yourself with a chisel.

6. Make the shavings thin, especially when finishing.

COLD CHISEL

This chisel is used on cast iron, steel, brass and other metal pipes and surfaces, as well as on brick, concrete and other kinds of masonry. The cold chisel does not have a separate handle; it is made of a single piece of alloy steel.

Cold chisels are used to break up masonry or metal surfaces, to cut off rivet heads or to demolish nuts and other metal parts that cannot be removed with a wrench or pliers.

When working with the chisel, hold it with one hand and place its point on the spot to be cut; with the other

hand hit the top of the chisel with a hammer. Be sure to handle the chisel carefully, to avoid injury to your fingers.

Types and uses of wrenches

Wrenches are used to tighten or loosen nuts, bolts, screws and pipe plugs. They come in two types, as shown in Fig. 2.12:

Open-end wrenches (a) have varying shapes and sizes of openings; although most of them are double-ended there are some with a single end. The size of the item you wish to loosen determines the selection of the size of the opening at the end of the wrench.

Boxed-end wrenches (b) either have a double-ended box or have a box at one end and are open at the other end.

Fig. 2.12a

Fig. 2.12b

OTHER WRENCHES

The monkey wrench, or auto wrench (c), has an adjustable jaw. Place the wrench on a nut or bolt so that the force used to turn it is applied to the stationary jaw side of the wrench. After placing the wrench in position, tighten the knurled adjusting nut until the wrench fits the nut or bolt head as tightly as possible. If it does not fit tightly, it will slip, which may cause injury to your hand and also may round the corners of the nut or bolt head.

The Stillson wrench, or pipe wrench (d), will work in one direction only. Always turn the wrench in the direction of the opening of the jaws. Apply force to the back of the handle; since the top jaw is capable of a slight angular movement, the grip on the work is increased by pressure on the handle.

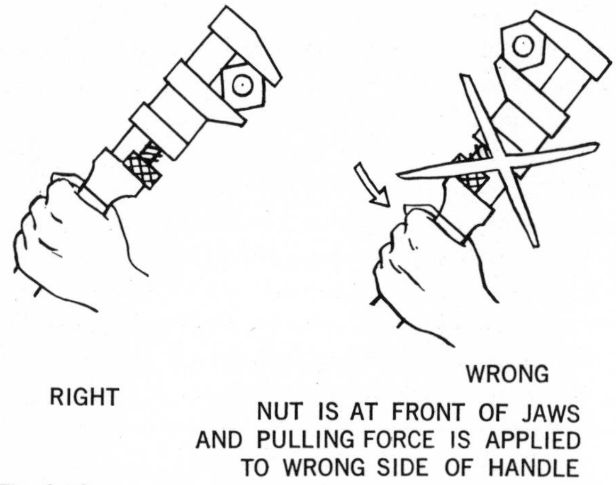

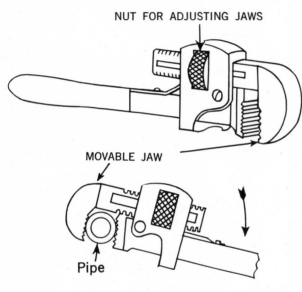

RIGHT

WRONG
NUT IS AT FRONT OF JAWS
AND PULLING FORCE IS APPLIED
TO WRONG SIDE OF HANDLE

Fig. 2.12c

NUT FOR ADJUSTING JAWS

MOVABLE JAW

Pipe

APPLY FORCE TO BACK OF
HANDLE IN DIRECTION INDICATED

Fig. 2.12d

Screw driver and ratchet

The purpose of a screw driver is to drive or remove screws or bolts with slotted or special heads. The tip of the screw driver should fit the slot of the screw. It is desirable to have several screw drivers to fit screws of different sizes.

Do not abuse the screw driver. It is designed to set screws and should not be used to pry open cans.

SETTING A SCREW

1. Make a hole in the wood with an awl or drill the depth of the threaded part of the screw. The hole should be slightly smaller than the thickness of the screw.

2. Hold the screw driver with the handle in the palm of the right hand. Guide the tip of the screw driver with the left hand.

3. Place the screw driver squarely in the groove of the head of the screw and turn it until the screw is in place. Hold the screw driver firmly in the slot to avoid burring the head of the screw.

4. If the screw does not fit in easily, apply a bit of soap to the threads. Never force the screw into place; instead, remove the screw and enlarge the hole in the wood.

RATCHET SCREW DRIVER

The ratchet is used to drive or remove small screws rapidly, and comes in spiral or common type (Fig. 2.13). The spiral ratchet automatically drives or removes screws. It can be adjusted to turn left or right, or locked to act as a common screw driver. It has a knurled sleeve with a spiral chuck and a control-locking device that has three positions: right and left ratchet, and rigid. Some spiral ratchets have a spring in the handle that automatically returns the handle for the next stroke. Another style of ratchet screw driver has a knurled collar so you can rotate the blade with your fingers. The spiral type has separate blades that are inserted in the chuck. The common ratchet is made with one integrally built blade.

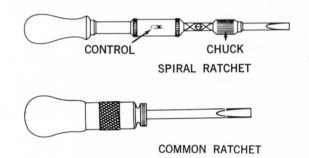

CONTROL   CHUCK
SPIRAL RATCHET

COMMON RATCHET

Fig. 2.13

Types and uses of hand drills

A hand drill is used to bore small holes, especially at the point where a screw is to be driven; it is also used in some cases as a starter before using a keyhole or compass saw for cutting through wood. There are two common types of hand drill:

ROTARY DRILL

The rotary drill operates on the same principle as a rotary egg beater. Instead of the paddles at the end there is a device called the chuck, which holds the drill point in place. Drill points ranging from $\frac{1}{32}$ to $\frac{1}{4}$ inch will serve most purposes. The drill is used as follows:

1. Select a drill point slightly smaller than the diameter of the nail or screw.

2. Open the chuck of the drill and insert the drill

point. Grasp the chuck and turn the wheel handle to the right until the point is firmly in place.

3. For drilling, hold the knob of the drill in the left hand and turn the handle with the right hand, as shown in Fig. 2.14.

4. To remove the drill point from the wood, continue to turn the handle to the right and pull the drill gradually upward with the left hand.

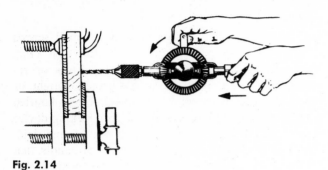

Fig. 2.14

PUSH DRILL

This drill, which operates in a rotary motion at the spot where hole is to be made, works by pushing. To make a hole in a horizontal surface, push the drill with up and down strokes, as shown in Fig. 2.15a. To make a hole in a vertical surface, secure the wood in a vise as shown in Fig. 2.15b, and push the drill back and forth. If you have no vise or other method of holding the wood securely, and must use your hand for this purpose, keep it as far as possible from the spot where the drill is drilling.

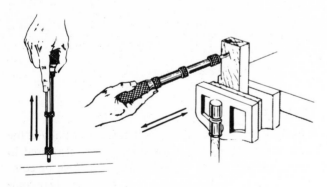

Fig. 2.15a   **Fig. 2.15b**

Types and uses of saws

There are many kinds of saws for sale, for all sorts of wood cutting, but the most common ones for use in your household are the following:

CROSSCUT SAW

The best size for all-round use is a twenty-four or twenty-six inch saw, which has about eight or ten points to the inch (Fig. 2.16). The number of points is stamped on the blade of the saw. For work in the average household the crosscut saw may be used to cut either across or with the grain of the wood, as follows:

1. If you are using old lumber, be sure to remove nails before you begin to saw.

2. Use a square to determine the line you wish to saw. Mark the line with a pencil.

3. Lay the board on a sawhorse or box. Keep the line to be sawed as close as possible to the box so the board will be firm. Steady the board with the left knee and left hand. Grip the handle of the saw firmly with the right hand.

4. Hold the saw so that the blade is at a 45° angle to the wood. Use the knuckle of the left thumb as a guide for the saw.

5. Make a few light upward strokes to start the cut. Then take long even strokes with pressure on the downward stroke. Do not force the saw.

6. As you near the end of the cut hold the free end of the board to prevent splintering.

7. To protect the cutting edge do not lay the saw on metal objects.

COPING SAW

This saw (Fig. 2.17) is used for cutting curves and irregular shapes in thin wood, as follows:

1. Insert the blade in the saw, with the teeth slanted toward the handle.

2. Be sure that the blade is in straight. The angle of the blade on some coping saws may be adjusted. The thumbscrew holds it in the desired position.

3. Clamp the board in the vise, with the line to be cut as close to the jaws of the vise as possible. If a vise is not available, the board may be fastened firmly to a table with a C clamp.

4. Grasp the saw with the right hand and steady the board with the left hand.

5. Start the cut on the pull stroke and allow the frame of the saw to follow the direction of the marked line.

6. Use the whole length of the blade when sawing, because short strokes tend to heat the blade and cause it to break.

KEYHOLE OR COMPASS SAW

When you need to cut within a small area through thin wood, or to cut special curves and angles, the coping saw may sometimes be too large to handle. In that case, use a keyhole or compass saw (Fig. 2.18) (these are similar, except that the compass saw has a longer blade). Before using the saw, drill a hole at the point where you want to start the cutting, then insert the blade of the saw into that hole and saw with the blade at an angle or curve.

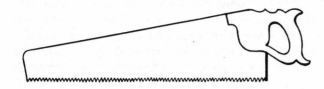

Fig. 2.16

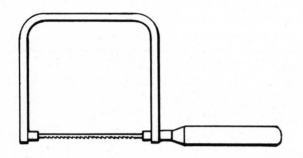

Fig. 2.17

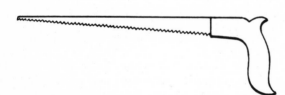

Fig. 2.18

Plane

Planes come in various sizes and types, and it is advisable to ask your hardware dealer to suggest what you need for your purposes. The plane is used to shave board edges and surfaces to make them smooth and even, using the following method:

1. It is desirable to use a vise or other device to hold securely the board to be planed.

2. Determine the grain of the wood. Clamp the board in a convenient position so as to plane with the grain.

3. Test the plane on a piece of scrap wood before you begin work. A well-adjusted plane should take off a long, thin shaving. The cutting depth is controlled by the adjusting nut. For a deeper cut turn the nut clockwise.

4. Hold the plane in the right hand and place the left hand on the knob at the front of the plane.

5. Keep the plane straight and push it with the grain of the wood.

6. Apply pressure on the knob of the plane at the beginning of the stroke and on the handle when finishing the stroke.

7. Test the planed board for evenness by holding the

edge of the square against it. If light shows beneath the blade of the square, the board needs further planing.

8. Lay the plane on its side when not in use, to avoid dulling the blade.

Clamping devices

There are two ways to hold work on a bench or table when it is being planed, drilled, sawed, shaped, sharpened or glued.

VISES

Vises come in various types and sizes, depending on whether you need one for a small worktable to use for light work, or a large one for handling larger pieces or pipes in a power-tool workshop.

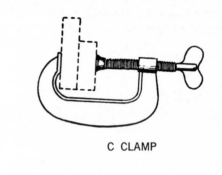

C CLAMP

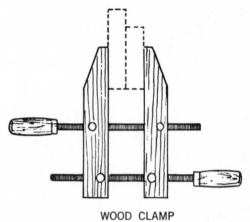

WOOD CLAMP

Fig. 2.19

CLAMPS

Clamps are generally used for holding work that cannot satisfactorily be held in a vise because of its size or shape, or when a vise is not available (Fig. 2.19). Clamps are generally used for light work. They come either in the metal C-clamp type, which has openings of from two to twelve inches, or in wood, with parallel jaws. Wood clamps are useful for holding together small wood pieces that have been glued together.

Soldering

Soldering is the joining of two pieces of metal by adhesion. The soldering iron (or soldering copper) is the source of heat for melting the solder and for heating to the proper temperature the parts to be joined.

There are two general types of soldering iron, the electric-heated and the nonelectric-heated (Fig. 2.20); each has a copper tip. Before any soldering iron can be used, the faces of the tip must be treated in the following manner:

1. Clamp the iron in a vise and file the tip faces bright while the iron is cold, as shown in Fig. 2.21.

2. Remove the soldering iron from the vise. Plug the electric cord into an outlet (or, if the iron is not an electric-heated type, heat it with a gas flame, charcoal fire or blowtorch), and as the iron heats up rub flux core solder over the tip faces every fifteen or twenty seconds. At first the iron will not be hot enough to melt the solder.

3. As soon as the temperature has risen sufficiently,

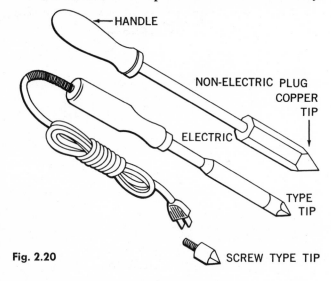

HANDLE

NON-ELECTRIC PLUG

COPPER TIP

ELECTRIC

TYPE TIP

SCREW TYPE TIP

Fig. 2.20

the solder will spread smoothly and evenly over the faces. The purpose of this procedure is to do the tinning as soon as the copper is hot enough to melt the solder and before it has had a chance to oxidize.

4. When the tinning is completed, wipe the tip with a rag while the solder is hot and molten. This will expose an even, almost mirrorlike layer of molten solder on the tip faces.

APPLYING SOLDER

There are many rules to follow in order to perform a successful soldering job, but the six most important follow:

1. The work that is to be soldered must be perfectly clean. All oxide, corrosion, paint, grease, dust and foreign matter must be scraped off, or the solder will not stick. A steel scratchbrush, emery paper, steel wool, file, knife, emery wheel or scraper may be used, whichever works best for the particular job, to clean the metals and produce the required bright surface.

2. The proper flux must be used; it must wet the entire surface to which the solder is to adhere. Too much flux will interfere with soldering. Rosin flux may be applied in the form of a powder, which is sprinkled on or dissolved in alcohol and applied with a brush. In soldering small brass, copper or tin-plated items, rosin core solder can be used. In heavy work it is necessary to apply flux separately. Zinc chloride, or any fluid flux, should be swabbed on. After soldering, all traces of acid and zinc chloride fluxes should be removed by washing with a solution of soap and washing soda in water.

3. The work must be properly and rigidly supported so that it does not move while the solder is setting. If a joint is moved while the solder is cooling and setting, the solder will be broken or weakened. When holding work in clamps or vises, make sure that the heat is not conducted to the jaws of these devices. In most cases, several layers of newspaper or asbestos paper placed between the jaws and the work will provide an effective insulator, which will prevent the heat from escaping. The best method of securing the work will vary with each job.

4. The iron must be the right size for the job and must be of the proper temperature. An iron used to melt solder and heat the work loses its heat very rapidly. If an electric iron becomes too cold to solder, it is too small and a large iron should be used. Soldering small, light objects does not draw a great deal of heat from the iron, but large castings, pipe fittings and so forth, will cool an iron very quickly, so that a torch or flame must be used to preheat the work before the iron is applied. In some cases soldering can be done with a torch alone, eliminating the iron.

5. The iron must be kept well tinned and clean. An electric iron must be wiped frequently with a rag and a nonelectric iron wiped clean after it is removed from the flame.

6. The work must be heated by the soldering iron so

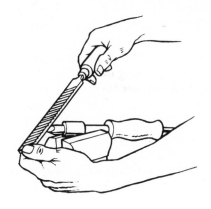

Fig. 2.21

that the solder flows or sweats into the joint. To pass heat quickly to the work, the iron should be held so as to establish sufficient contact surface. When soldering splices in wire, the solder should be placed on top of the splice and heated by the iron held under the splice.

Oilstone for sharpening

The stone has a coarse surface on one side and a fine surface on the other. If the edge of a tool to be sharpened (such as the edge of a woodworking chisel) is nicked or very dull, it should be rubbed on the coarse surface of the oilstone, in a back and forth motion, as shown in Fig. 2.22a.

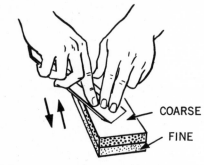

Fig. 2.22a

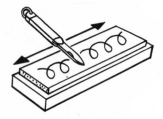

Fig. 2.22b

If the edge to be sharpened is smooth (such as the blades of scissors and knives), first put a few drops of a light oil on the fine surface of the stone and rub the blade along the stone in a circular motion, as shown in Fig. 2.22b. When sharpening a knife, rub one side of the blade on the stone, then turn the knife over and repeat the rubbing on the other side of the blade.

After each use, wipe the oil off the stone. If the stone becomes gummy, clean it with ammonia and water, or with a dry-cleaning solvent like carbon tetrachloride.

Steel wool, abrasives and sandpaper

When carving in woodwork or when other fine wood finishes need to be smoothed before refinishing, steel wool is a fine abrasive. Rottenstone or powdered pumice may also be used for fine smoothing.

Emery cloth and other abrasive cloths and papers are available for various surfaces. Sandpaper is a good all-purpose abrasive for final smoothing of a wood surface. A coarse sandpaper, No. 1 or No. ½, is usually used first; the final sanding is done with a No. 0 to No. 3/0. Sandpaper is sold in 9 by 11 inch sheets and in packages of small sheets of various degrees of fineness. Emery cloth also comes in different size sheets.

Sandpaper or emery cloth is used as follows (Fig. 2.23):

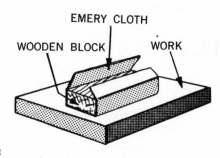

Fig. 2.23

1. Tear the sheet into four equal parts.
2. Fold a piece around a block of wood, for easier handling.
3. Rub the surface with the grain of the wood.

Some small pieces of wood may be sanded more easily if the sandpaper is laid (smooth side down) on a flat surface and the wood piece is held in the hand and rubbed against the exposed rough side of the sandpaper.

Gluing wood

Plastic resin powder glue is satisfactory for gluing wood. It is mixed with water, spread thinly on the surface and allowed to dry thoroughly.

When two pieces of wood are fastened together, glue is often used to give the joint added strength. The glue should be allowed to become sticky before the boards are fastened. If work is done in cool temperature, you may need to heat the glue pot to get best gluing results.

After glue has been applied, remove all traces of excess with a damp cloth before the glue hardens.

Plastic wood and wood putty

Plastic wood and wood putty are used for filling nail holes, dents and other imperfections in the wood. After the filler has been applied and when the surface is thoroughly dry, the area should be smoothed with sandpaper.

Be generous when filling the holes, since filler sometimes shrinks when it hardens. Also, you may want to keep such material on hand in various colors in case it becomes necessary to match different wood surfaces.

Chapter Three

BASIC POWER TOOLS

Power shop

THE GRADUATION from a workshop based on hand tools to one that includes power tools is a big step toward making your house-maintenance chores more interesting. The power-tool workshop is also an incentive to the pursuit of a creative hobby in woodwork.

It is not necessary to install many heavy pieces of power equipment or to give up much space to have a power-tool workshop. Buy the tools slowly and carefully; study manufacturers' catalogues and ask your hardware dealer for information. You may model your power-tool shop on one of the following types:

The universal shop is based on one major tool, the radial arm saw. This tool is a power shop in itself, since it fulfills the multipurpose functions of shaper, disc and belt sander; lathe; router; grinder; horizontal borer and aluminum cutter. Because of its versatility, the radial arm is ideal for locations where space is restricted. To harbor this radial arm saw, a suggested workbench is shown in Fig. 3.1a. It becomes a complete workshop in itself, permitting maximum storage and operation flexibility because of its double use. The workbench not only houses the "power shop" but also serves as a worktable for other uses when the radial arm is swung back against the tool board in the out-of-the-way position. Handy drawers and doors, and a perforated wallboard (pegboard) attached to the back of the workbench, offer convenient storage area for accessories to the radial arm saw as well as for hand tools. The space under the workbench provides storage area for spare lumber and unfinished parts. The detailed drawing (b) shows the way the radial arm saw swings out when in use.

The combination shop is a variation of the universal shop and is a combination of table saw, drill press,

sander and jointer, all using a common motor. This shop does not take much space either and provides a convenient way of working with power tools.

The traditional shop is built around the tools, which are bought piece by piece. Of course, it takes up more space and eventually may result in a greater expenditure of money than either the universal or the combination

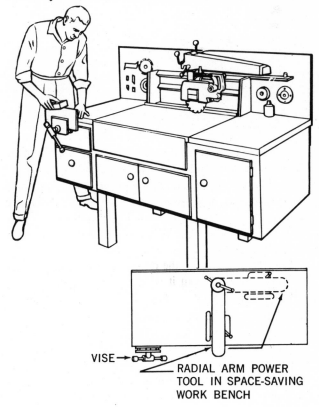

VISE→

RADIAL ARM POWER
TOOL IN SPACE-SAVING
WORK BENCH

Fig. 3.1a **Fig. 3.1b**

27

shop. The power tools that may be bought individually (in the order given) and the work they do are as follows:

1. Your first purchase should be a multipurpose tool for cutting operations. Get a table saw to work the wood with the grain or against it; a tilting arbor type is good, because the blade can tilt for cutting wood at an angle. Such a saw also cuts miters and rabbets; with attachments it cuts grooves or dados and shapes edges as well.

2. The next tool to buy is a drill press, which drills holes through wood. With attachments it can also cut square holes, shape edges and plane surfaces.

3. The planer-jointer is a precision tool that makes edges square and smooth and is helpful in fine woodworking.

4. The jigsaw (or scroll saw) is the right tool for cutting curves. In addition to its utility for household repairs, it is a safe tool for children who want to develop a hobby in woodwork.

5. The band saw is a larger version of the jigsaw; although it does the same kind of work on wood, it has more power and is used for cutting larger pieces of lumber.

6. The lathe is the last tool to add to your workshop and is regarded as the one that gives work a professional touch. It is used for wood turning and to produce extra effects such as curves and decorations on railings, furniture legs, and so forth.

The compact shop is usually built around the electric drill as its basic tool. This tool has attachments to enable you to use it as seven different tools: lathe, horizontal drill, vertical drill, shaper, bench saw, disc sander and portable drill. The important factor for this compact shop is that the electric drill with which you start be of the finest quality; a drill of inferior grade will not be able to withstand the strain the various attachments and their work put upon it.

Guide to the use of power tools

1. To saw a straight line, use the circular or band saw, the jigsaw or the electric drill with its attachments.

2. To cut a curve, use the circular saw with attachments, the band saw or jigsaw or the electric drill with its attachments.

3. To cut a groove, use the circular saw, or the drill press or electric drill with their respective attachments.

4. To drill a hole, use the drill press, lathe or electric drill.

5. To make a turning, use the lathe, or the electric drill with its attachments.

6. To smooth a surface, use the jointer, the circular saw or the drill press or electric drill with their respective attachments.

7. To sand a surface, use either of the following with their attachments: circular saw, drill press, lathe or electric drill.

8. To sand an edge, use either of the following with their attachments: circular saw, drill press, jigsaw, lathe or electric drill.

9. To shape an edge, use either of the following with their attachments: circular saw, drill press or electric drill.

Care and safety

To keep your power tools in first-class working order, follow manufacturers' directions on how to oil them, keep them clean and adjust them when necessary.

Although the tools you place into your power shop are safe to use, there is always an element of risk in handling power-driven equipment, regardless of how cautious you are. It is essential that extra measures be taken.

1. Take fire-prevention precautions, as explained in Chapter 1.

2. If you have visitors while you are working, don't let the conversation distract you from your work while you are operating a machine.

3. Don't wear a necktie, since the ends might be caught in the tool, and don't wear any loose-fitting clothes that might also be caught. Loose sleeves should be rolled up.

4. Be sure the tools are always in finest condition, because a dull saw blade or any other dull edge may cause defective work as well as harm to yourself.

5. Periodically inspect the electric cords, plugs and switches to see they are in best condition.

6. Put a lock switch or similar device on the motors if children have access to your workshop.

7. If you must make any adjustment to the machine, stop the motor before you do so.

8. When you have to go out of your workshop, even if only for a few minutes, do not leave a machine running. Stop the motor.

Chapter Four

HOW TO INSPECT YOUR HOUSE

A SYSTEMATIC CHECK of the house and its equipment should be made at regular intervals so that you may see what defects exist and take the necessary measures to correct them. Do not wait until an emergency such as a leaking roof or a burst pipe, occurs. You will avoid much inconvenience and save money by anticipating such occurrences.

Sometimes it is necessary to call in an experienced workman to help you make the inspection, especially if it is your first one. For your own knowledge of the essential parts of a house, see Fig. 4.1.

Check list

When you make a survey of the possible repairs or improvements of your house, use the following list as a guide.

FOUNDATION WALLS

Masonry walls, for cracks or broken portions that may require filling.

Mortar joints, to see if pointing is needed.

Walls, for leaks that may require dampproofing.

Eaves or tops of walls, for leakage and to see if repairs or coping are needed.

Masonry walls, for efflorescence or scum that may need removal.

Stucco walls, for cracks, discoloration or damaged portions that may need pointing, cleaning or replacing.

Frame siding, for loose or decayed boards or open joints that may need repair or replacement.

Painted surfaces, to see if blistering, cracking or peeling has occurred and if repainting is needed.

Wall surfaces, to see if they need replacement or re-covering.

Grading around foundation, for proper drainage.

EXTERIOR WINDOWS AND DOORS

Window caps, to see if new flashing or repair of existing joints is required.

Window frames, for holes and cracks and to see if calking or repair is needed.

Windows, for broken glass panes that may need replacement.

Putty around panes, to see if reputtying is necessary.

Screens, to see if repair or repainting is needed.

Storm doors and windows, to see whether or not they need repair or repainting and if additional ones should be provided.

Blinds and shutters, to see if repairs are needed.

Awnings, to see if repairs or replacements are necessary.

Balconies and railings, to see whether or not they need repairs or painting.

Windows, to determine whether or not additional ones should be installed.

ROOF, FLASHING, GUTTERS AND DOWNSPOUTS

Shingle slate or tile roofing, to see whether or not repair or replacement of broken, loose or missing units is necessary.

Metal or roll roofing, for cracks, open joints or worn coatings that might need repair or the application of waterproofing materials or paint.

Flashing, for rust or defects and to determine whether or not repair, replacement or repainting is necessary.

Gutters or conductor pipes, for leaks and to see whether or not they need repainting or replacement.

Skylights, for leaks or defects that might require glazing, flashing, repairing or repainting.

Trapdoors, scuttles or other roof openings, for leaks that might need flashing, repair or repainting.

Chimney, for defects and to see if pointing or replacement of brick is necessary or if there is a need for chimney cap or chimney pots.

Fig. 4.1

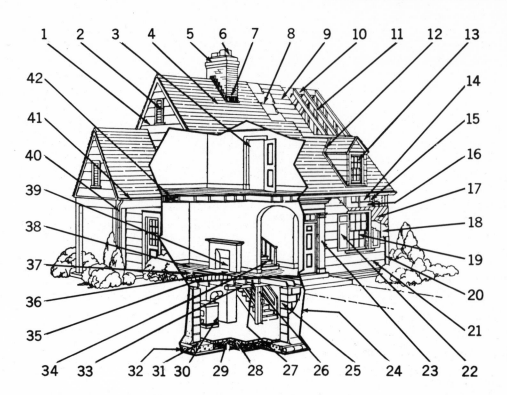

1. Gable end.
2. Louver.
3. Interior trim.
4. Shingles
5. Chimney cap.
6. Flue linings.
7. Flashing.
8. Roofing felt.
9. Roof sheathing.
10. Ridge board.
11. Rafters.
12. Roof valley.
13. Dormer window
14. Interior wall finish.

15. Studs.
16. Insulation.
17. Diagonal sheathing.
18. Sheathing paper.
19. Window frame and sash.
20. Corner board.
21. Siding.
22. Shutters.
23. Exterior trim.
24. Waterproofing.
25. Foundation wall.
26. Column.
27. Joists.
28. Basement floor.

29. Gravel fill.
30. Heating plant.
31. Footing.
32. Drain tile.
33. Girder.
34. Stairway.
35. Subfloor.
36. Hearth.
37. Building paper.
38. Finish floor.
39. Fireplace.
40. Downspout.
41. Gutter.
42. Bridging.

Chimney draft, to see whether or not it is effective or requires lengthening of the chimney or installation of metal hoods.

Lightning arrestors.

Downspouts, to see whether or not splash blocks need to be provided at the outlet end or if downspouts should be connected to a drain line.

PORCHES AND STEPS

Column bases, for possible decay and need for repair or renewal.

Banisters, to see that none are broken, loose or have rails missing.

Railings and posts, to see that none are broken, loose and need repair or strengthening.

Floorboards, to see that none are decayed, broken or loose.

Floor supports, for decay and to see whether or not they need replacement or strengthening.

Steps, to see that none are broken, loose or worn.

Advisability of installing latticework to screen spaces under the porch.

Advisability of enclosing porches with glass or screening.

Floors, to see if they need refinishing or repair.
Masonry, for open joints or cracks that might need pointing.
Floor tile, for loose tile.
Other masonry material, for damage that might need repair.

BASEMENT

Foundation walls, for large cracks or broken places that might require filling.
Walls, for smaller cracks or mortar joints that might require pointing.
Walls and ceiling, to see if they need brightening with new and lighter paint coatings.
Walls and floors, for leaks that might require waterproofing or provisions for drainage.
Wood sills and walls, for joints between them that might require calking.
Floor joists at the sills, for spaces or holes around pipes that might need firestopping.
Floor joists, for sagging and warping that might require additional support or bridging.
Basement floor, for cracks or disintegrated places that might need repair or resurfacing.
Need for additional partitions to provide space for special purposes.
Unfinished walls and ceilings, to determine desirability of finishing them.
Floors, for painting or installation of asphalt tile.
Storage facilities such as shelves, closets, cupboards, and bins, for adequacy and advisability of constructing additional facilities.
Advisability of constructing a basement garage.

HEATING AND VENTILATING

Smoke pipes or flues, to see whether or not cleaning is necessary.
Boiler coils or baffles, to see if they require cleaning.
Grates, to see if they are warped or broken.
Firebox, to see if it is cracked.
Boilers, for cracks or leaks that might need repair or new parts.
Chimney masonry, for cracks that might require pointing.
Woodwork adjoining pipes and heating system, to see that fire protection is adequate.
Coating on boilers, to see if patching or re-covering is needed.
Heating pipes, to see whether or not repairs to covering are needed.
Advisability of installing automatic stokers, ash conveyors or similar labor-saving devices.
Radiator valves, for leaks that might require repacking.
Radiators, to see that they are painted properly to increase efficiency.
Need for installation of additional radiators.
Need for radiator covers and radiator tops.
Thermostatic heat-control system, to see that it is operating properly.
Advisability of installing air conditioning and humidifiers.
Advisability of building new or additional fireplace.

Advisability of installing an ash dump for the fireplace.
Need for installation of room-heating device in existing fireplace.
Fireplace screens, andirons and similar equipment, to see whether or not repair or replacement is needed.
Gas or electric log, to see that it is operating properly.
Fireplace hearth, fireback and dampers, for possible repair.
Mantel or fireplace front, for possible remodeling.
Ventilating devices in kitchen, to check efficiency and need for additional ones.
Walls and ceiling, for installation of insulating material.

PLUMBING

Drains, to see that they are open.
Faucets, for leaks that might require new washers, tightening or new parts.
Flush valves in water closets, to see whether or not they need repair or replacement.
Covering for water pipes, for adequacy and advisability of taking other precautions to prevent freezing.
Water-pipe fittings, to see whether additional shut-off cocks or valves are needed.
Water-heating equipment, to see that it operates properly.
Piping, for possible repair or replacement.
Fixtures, for repair or replacement.
Advisability of installing additional bathrooms, lavatories and toilets.
Advisability of providing toilet and shower in basement.

LIGHTING AND POWER

Wiring, to see whether rewiring is needed.
Exposed wires, to see that insulation is not worn or damaged.
Appliance cords, to see whether or not they need to be replaced.
Electric outlets, to see if additional convenience outlets, such as floor and base plugs, are needed.
Supply of fuse plugs for fuse box.
Chimes, buzzers and doorbells, to see if repairs or additional installations are needed.
Advisability of installing transformers for bells to replace batteries.

INTERIOR DOORS AND WINDOWS

Doors and windows, to see whether or not they need refitting, adjustment or repair.
Doors, for advisability of replacing wood panels with glass.
Locks, chains or bolts, to see if they are defective and need repair or replacement.
Supply of extra keys for various locks.
Window cords and pulleys, to see if they are broken or defective and need replacement.
Window latches or other window-fastening devices, to see if they are broken and need replacement.
Window sash and doors, to see if cracks around them need weather stripping.

WALLS AND CEILINGS

Plaster, for cracks or holes that may require patching or replastering.

Advisability of installing more partitions, either temporary or permanent, to provide additional rooms or closets.

Partitions, for removal to afford additional space.

Doorways, for width and to see if plastered arches or similar larger openings should replace them.

Walls and ceilings, for refinishing or redecorating and need for painting, papering or installation of wall tile.

FLOORS

Floors, to see that they do not creak or need renailing, additional supports or joists stiffened by bridging.

Need for refinishing.

Advisability of laying new flooring over old.

Floor coverings, to see if they need repair or replacement.

Baseboard and molding, for shrinking and settling and to see if adjustment or replacement is needed.

Tile, for repair or replacement.

STAIRS AND STAIRWAYS

Stairs, to see that they do not creak or need strengthening.

Treads on stairs, to see if replacements are needed.

Rubber or composition treads, for slipperiness.

Basement stairs, to see if repairs or additional supports are needed.

Railing on basement stairs, to see that it is structurally sound.

Advisability of changing closed stairways to open ones by the removal of a wall on one side.

Posts and railings, for stiffness and need of replacement.

Method of access to attic and advisability of providing disappearing stairs.

ATTIC

Walls, floor or underside of roof, to see whether or not insulation is needed.

Ventilation and need for installation of louvers or additional windows.

Mortar joints in chimney, to see whether or not they require repointing.

Chimney and side walls, for cracks between them that may need filling.

Studs at floor line, for firestopping.

Possibilities for changing attic space into a finished room or rooms.

Need for additional partitions.

Flooring, for stability and smoothness as well as need for refinishing.

GARAGE

Advisability of installing insulating material.

Roof, for cracks, open joints or worn coatings that may need repair.

Doors, for adjustment.

Windows, for replacement of broken panes.

Advisability of laying concrete floors.

Advisability of installing heating equipment.

Inside and outside surfaces, to see if painting is necessary.

GROUNDS

Walks and driveways, to see if they need repair, replacement or if additional ones are necessary.

Fences, trellises and latticework, to see if repairing or painting is necessary.

MISCELLANEOUS

Lining of existing closets, to check for adequacy and need for additional closets.

Need for additional shelves, bookcases and cupboards.

Advisability of providing clothes chute, telephone cabinet or other built-in conveniences.

Chapter Five

WOODS, JOINTS AND MOLDINGS

WHEN THE AMATEUR HANDYMAN goes out to buy lumber it is wise to recall the old "beauty is only skin deep" adage, and to consider that the outer surface of the wood is no indication of its basic quality. It is always wise to deal with a reliable lumber-yard when making your selections.

Facts about lumber

Woods come in varying degrees of hardness and softness. To distinguish between hard and soft woods, remember that generally hard wood is from trees that shed their leaves annually, such as mahogany, cherry, black walnut, maple, cypress, ash, poplar (called white wood), redwood, birch and oak. Soft wood comes from evergreen trees, such as pine, hemlock, spruce, fir, basswood and Southern yellow pine.

You may buy either rough or surfaced wood. It is called *rough* when bought as it comes from the sawmill without any finished surface. It is called *surfaced* when either one or both sides of the wood has been planed, and you will find surfaced wood much easier to work with than rough wood.

Lumber is either seasoned or green. When it is cut, lumber contains much moisture, and it is stacked in such a manner that air circulates through all sides of the wood and dries it; wood dried in this way is termed *seasoned*. If the lumber did not have sufficient time to dry out, it is called *green*, and if you use it in your work you will discover that it will shrink and perhaps warp after it has fully dried out. A good way to test wood is to weigh a piece when it is dry, then put it in a warm oven and let it remain there for a few hours. Weigh the wood when you remove it from the heat. If it has lost much weight, the wood is green; if not, you may work with assurance that it is seasoned.

Lumber is bought by the board foot, and the price is usually figured on the basis of one thousand board feet. To arrive at the amount of board feet in a piece of lumber, using inches as your unit of measurement, multiply the length of the board by its width and its thickness, then divide by 144. For instance, a board 12 by 12 by 1 inches equals 1 board foot of lumber.

The abbreviations used in the building trades to designate types and measurements of lumber are given after the Glossary, at the end of the book.

You may be able to get odd pieces or second-hand board at the lumberyard if you need to use the wood for minor purposes. Inspect the board to see that it is in good working condition and that it doesn't have nails or other metal pieces in it that can cause damage to the board or the saw when the wood is cut.

LUMBER GRADES

Lumber as it comes from the sawmill is divided into three main classes: yard lumber, structural material and factory and shop lumber. The dealer will tell you which class of wood is needed for your purpose; the following listings will show how yard lumber is classified, as either *select* or *common* lumber, the classifications most generally used.

Select lumber is of good appearance and finish, and is graded as follows:

Grade A, suitable for natural finishes and practically clear.

Grade B, suitable for natural finishes, of high quality and generally clear.

Grade C, adapted to high quality paint finishes.

Grade D, suitable for paint finishes between higher finishing grades and common grades, and partaking somewhat of the nature of both.

Common lumber is suitable for general construction and utility purposes, and is graded as follows:

No. 1 common, suitable for use without waste; it is sound and tight-knitted; it may be considered watertight lumber.

No. 2 common, less restricted in quality than No. 1, but of the same general quality. It is used for framing, sheathing and other structural forms where the stress or strain is not excessive.

No. 3 common, permits some waste and has prevailing grade characteristics more prominent than in No. 2. It is used for such rough work as footings, guardrails and rough flooring.

No. 4 common, permits waste and is of low quality, admitting the coarsest features, such as decay and holes. It is used for sheathing, subfloors and roof boards in the cheaper types of construction.

PLYWOOD

This wood is generally recommended for interior use only, since although it is strong and durable, it is not of sufficient sturdiness to withstand exterior exposure to bad weather. Plywood is a composite board made up of several thin sheets of wood that are stuck together with glue or a plastic adhesive. The alternate layers are placed with the grain at opposite angles, although in the two outside layers the grain runs in the same direction.

Plywood comes in large sheets and is bought by the square foot. It may be available at your hardware dealer or handyman's shop, as well as at the lumberyard.

Molding

Molding is made of narrow strips of wood machined into a special design and is used to finish the top of a baseboard, as interior trim around windows and doors, high on the wall to hang pictures and mirrors and as a trim under the ceiling. The molding most commonly used is the *quarter round*, to trim the top of a baseboard or to round off square corners. Molding is not an expensive item, and a good choice of design may be found at the lumberyard.

APPLYING MOLDING

When molding is used as a trim around doors, windows or any other place you wish to use it, it should fit tightly against the object it is trimming and be hammered down securely with appropriate small nails.

To put up a picture molding or to apply a baseboard molding on a wall covered with lath and plaster, you must first locate the wooden studs so you may drive the nails into them. To do this, tap wall lightly with a hammer and when you hear a more solid sound you have found the stud. As most studs are spaced sixteen inches apart, you should not have difficulty in finding the rest once you have located the first one. Nail the molding to the studs.

If you have special type walls, with no wood framework and studs into which to drive nails, you may need to put expansion plugs into the wall and then fasten your molding to them. (Expansion plugs are hollow cylinders, made in a mortar by special expansion-plug tool.) Measure and cut the strip of molding, drill a hole near each end of it and then place your bit into the hole and tap it lightly with a light hammer. Measure and mark the position on the wall; place the plug holes over the marks on the wall surface, tapping the expansion plug tool in place. With the drill, bore the holes in the proper places and, when the holes are sufficiently large, insert the plug into the wall. Screw the molding into place through the plugs.

Miter box

These boxes come in wood or sometimes metal and may be bought in all sizes; however, they are easy to make if you prefer to do so. The miter box (Fig. 5.1) is used for sawing molding or any other wood strips where diagonal cuts are needed. The diagonal slits in the box are usually cut at an angle of $45°$ or in some cases at $90°$.

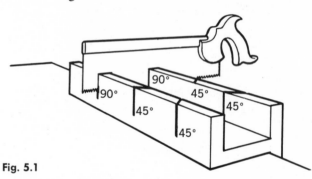

Fig. 5.1

To make the box, use three pieces of board three-quarters to one inch thick and eighteen inches long by four inches wide. Use a square to mark off the $45°$ angles (or other special angles you may require) on the two side boards, then saw these diagonal slits halfway down each board. Screw the two uprights to the bottom board, making sure that all edges are flush.

Joints

All connections between pieces of wood are classified either as joints or splices. Joints are connections between two pieces that come together at an angle. Splices are connections between two pieces of wood that extend in the same line.

BUTT JOINTS

The most common type of joint used in carpentry is the butt joint (Fig. 5.2). It is constructed by placing the end of one board on another board in such a manner that the boards are at an angle (usually a right angle) forming a corner.

Straight Butt Joint. The straight butt joint (a) is formed by bringing the square-cut end of one board against the square face of another. The butt end of one board should be square and the face of the other smooth so that the pieces fit properly and are perpendicular to each other. Nails or screws are used to hold the two pieces together. Properly selected screws will hold such a joint securely. However, for framing, butt joints are secured by eight- or ten-penny nails that are toenailed to strengthen the joint. Toenailing is done by driving a nail diagonally through both pieces. End grain is the weakest part of a piece of wood when used in joint connections. Since a butt joint connection is made at either one or two end-grain parts, the connection will be no stronger than the characteristics of the end-grain parts. A butt joint is, therefore, the weakest type of joint. This is especially true if the joint consists only of two pieces of wood.

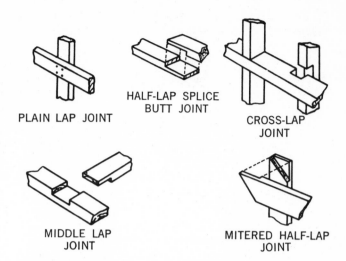

Fig. 5.3

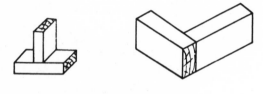

STRAIGHT BUTT JOINTS

Fig. 5.2a

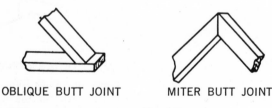

OBLIQUE BUTT JOINT   MITER BUTT JOINT

Fig. 5.2b   Fig. 5.2c

Oblique Butt Joint. The oblique butt joint (b) is formed by bringing the end of one board, cut on the oblique to form the desired angle, against the face of the board with which it is to be joined. Bracing is a typical application for this joint. This joint should not be used where great strength is required. The strength of the joint depends upon the nailing; the size of the nails used depends entirely upon the size of the timber. Nails should be toenailed as in the case of the straight butt joint, and the use of too many nails should be avoided.

Miter Butt Joint. The miter butt joint (c) is formed by bringing the mitered ends of two boards together to form the desired angle. It is usually used at corners where the straight butt joint is not satisfactory. To make

a miter joint, the angle of cut is the same for both pieces. To form a right-angle miter joint (the most commonly used miter joint), each piece is cut at a 45° angle so that when the pieces are joined they will form a very weak joint, which should not be used where strength of joint is an important factor.

LAP JOINTS

The lap joint is constructed by overlapping two pieces of wood and securing them to form a joint, or by cutting away corresponding portions (usually half) in equal lengths from the thickness of two boards and then joining them in such a manner that the cut-away portions overlap and form a corner. The various types of lap joints are discussed in the following paragraphs and shown in Fig. 5.3.

Plain Lap Joint. The plain lap joint is formed by laying one board over another and securing the two by means of screws or nails. This is the simplest and most often used method of joining in framing and construction. The joint constructed in this manner is only as strong as the fasteners and material used in its support.

Half-Lap Splice Joint. The half-lap splice joint is constructed by cutting away portions (usually half) in equal lengths from the thickness of two boards and joining them in such a manner that the cut-away portions overlap in a complementary manner to form the joint. The half-lap is a relatively strong, easily made joint. Overlapping surfaces must fit snugly and smoothly. Saw on the waste side of the gauge line when cutting out the lap. In this category are dado, rabbet, dado-rabbet and stopped dado joints (Fig. 5.4).

Dovetail, Mortise and Tenon and Tongue-and-Groove. Locked joints give added strength at the cost of added work and workmanship, and are not used unless particular strength is required at this joint. The most com-

Fig. 5.4

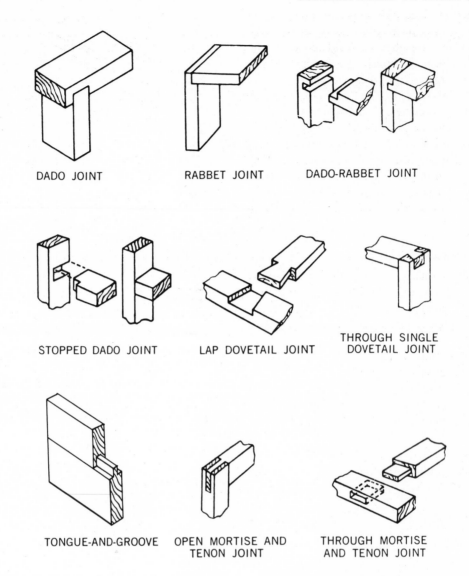

DADO JOINT   RABBET JOINT   DADO-RABBET JOINT

STOPPED DADO JOINT   LAP DOVETAIL JOINT   THROUGH SINGLE DOVETAIL JOINT

TONGUE-AND-GROOVE   OPEN MORTISE AND TENON JOINT   THROUGH MORTISE AND TENON JOINT

mon locked joints are lap dovetail, through single dovetail, open mortise and tenon, through mortise and tenon, and tongue-in-groove (Fig. 5.4). The dowel joint is also a strong joint; it is discussed later in this chapter.

Splices

The function of a splice is to connect two or more pieces of wood in such a way that, when joined, they will be as strong as a single piece of wood of equivalent length and the joint will be as strong as the unjoined portions (Fig. 5.5). The type of splice utilized is determined by the way in which the spliced wood is to be subjected to stress and amount of strain it must support. Wood subjected to direct longitudinal stress, through acting as a vertical support or in exerting pressure, requires splices designed to resist compression. Wood subjected to transverse and angular stresses when used as trusses, braces, or joists, requires splices designed to resist tension. Wood used as

a horizontal support requires splices designed to resist bending. Splices efficient in resisting compression are usually worthless for tension or bending; therefore, splices should be made to meet the conditions for which they are to be used.

COMPRESSION-RESISTANT SPLICES

Compression-resistant splices are designed to support weight or exert pressure, and will effectively resist compression stress only. The butt splice and the halved splice are the most common types.

Butt Splice. This splice (Figs. 5.6a and b) is constructed by butting the squared ends of two pieces of wood together and securing them in this position by means of two wood or metal pieces fastened on opposite sides of the wood. The two short supporting pieces keep the splice straight and prevent buckling. Metal plates used as supports in constructing a butt splice (a) are called fishplates. Wood plates (b) are called scabs. Fishplates are fastened in place with bolts and screws. Bolts, nails or corrugated fasteners may be used to secure scabs. If nails are used with scabs, they are staggered and driven at an angle away from the splice. Too many nails, or nails that are too large, will weaken a splice.

Halved Splice. This splice (c) is constructed by cutting away half the thickness of equal lengths from the ends of two pieces of wood and fitting the complementary tongues, or laps, together. The laps should be long enough to have adequate bearing surfaces. Nails or bolts may be used to fasten the halved splice. In order to give this type of splice resistance to tension as well as to compression, fishplates or scabs may be used as with the butt splice.

TENSION-RESISTANT SPLICES

In tension members such as trusses, braces and joists, the joint undergoes stress that is exerted in more than one direction and creates a tension tending to buckle the member in a predictable direction. Tension splices are designed to provide the greatest practicable number of bearing surfaces and shoulders within the splice to resist the buckling tension.

Square Splice. The square splice (d) is a modification of the compression halved splice. Complementary notches are cut in the tongues, or laps, to provide an additional locking shoulder. The square splice may be fastened with nails or bolts or may be greatly strengthened by the use of fishplates or scabs.

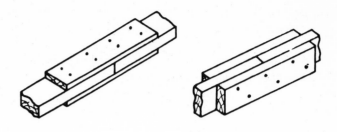

Fig. 5.6a   Fig. 5.6b

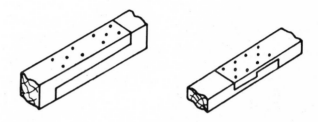

Fig. 5.6c   Fig. 5.6d

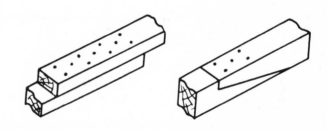

Fig. 5.6e   Fig. 5.6f

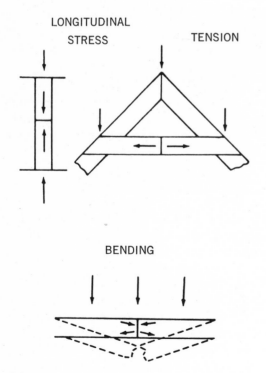

Fig. 5.5

Plain Splice. A hasty substitute for the square splice is the long plain splice (e). A long overlap of the two pieces is desirable to provide adequate bearing surface and sufficient room for enough fasteners to compensate for the lack of shoulder lock.

BEND-RESISTANT SPLICES

Horizontal lengths of wood supporting weight undergo stress at a splice, which results in a compression of the upper part that has a tendency to crush the fibers and in a tension of the lower part that tends to pull the fibers apart. Bend-resistant splices are designed to resist both compression and tension; they combine the features of the compression and tension splices.

Construction. The bend-resistant splice is constructed by cutting oblique complementary laps in the ends of two pieces of timber. The upper tongue (bearing surface) is squared to butt against the square of the complementary lap (f) to offer maximum resistance to crushing, and the lower tongue is beveled. A scab or fishplate may be fastened along the bottom of the splice to resist the tendency of the pieces to separate. In cases where it is not desirable to lap or halve the wood ends for a splice subject to tension, a butt joint secured by fishplates may be used.

Dowel joint

Dowels are pegs made of wood; they may be bought in different sizes, or you may make them yourself (Fig. 5.7). Sometimes they come with vertical ridges cut in the dowel, or a spiral ridge cut into it; the purpose of this is for the glue that is put into the hole to take better hold of the peg when it is inserted, and for any extra glue to be able to run out and not clog.

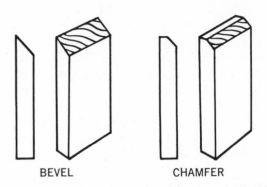

Fig. 5.8

Before joining two pieces of wood with dowels, make sure that the two edges (which will meet) are perfectly even. Use a pencil to mark, on each surface, where the dowel holes are to be made. Use a bit to bore the holes to a depth twice the diameter of the dowel.

Rub the two ends of the dowel pegs (or dowel pins, as they are often called) with sandpaper so they won't slide when put into the holes. Make sure that the boards and the dowels are warmed (if working in a cold place), then warm the glue. Put glue on the dowel ends and into the holes. Slip the dowels into the holes and put glue between the boards. To get best results, place the work in a vise or clamp until thoroughly dry.

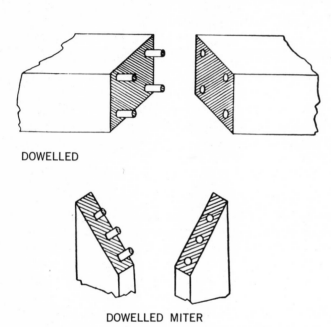

Fig. 5.7

Bevel and chamfer

A bevel is an angled side, and a chamfer is an angled edge, as shown in Fig. 5.8. A bevel or chamfer may be made at a 90° angle or whatever depth you desire. These are used mainly to give a finished and decorative appearance. Sometimes they are used functionally to prevent splintering of the wood edge.

The bevel or chamfer may be cut with either a plane, saw, sander or wood chisel, depending on your preference of tool and the job to be done.

Chapter Six

WOOD FINISHING

THE PREPARATION of the surface is the first step to take before applying new finish or refinish to the wood. There may be scratches, cracks, dents or stains in the wood that need to be remedied to produce a clean, smooth surface.

In Chapter 10 directions are given on how to repair cracks in wood floor surfaces, how to level rough spots and how to finish or refinish after the surface is clean and smooth. These directions also apply for other interior wood surfaces in the house.

Cleaning and repairing finished surfaces

Smoke, steam, house dust and wax all tend to soil wood surfaces. Often a thorough cleaning is all that is needed to revive the luster and depth of an oil, sealer, varnish or lacquer finish.

Shellac finishes are sensitive to water, alcohol and heat, and may be permanently damaged by cleaning mixtures. To test for a shellac finish, apply a small quantity of alcohol to an inconspicuous place on the wood. If the finish becomes sticky or gummy, or is dissolved, do not use the following cleaning solution.

CLEANING MIXTURES

On finishes other than shellac, good results are obtained by cleaning the surface with a cleaning mixture of 1 quart warm water and either 3 tablespoons boiled linseed oil or 1 tablespoon turpentine. Keep the mixture warm in a double boiler. Rub the wood surface with a soft cloth dampened in this mixture; then wipe it dry and polish with a dry cloth.

Dullness is difficult to remove from varnish or enamel of poor quality. To increase the luster, apply a thin coat of paste wax and buff well; or use a light-mixture polish made of 2 parts boiled linseed oil and 1 part turpentine.

DENTS IN WOOD

A small dent is sometimes overcome by steaming. Place a damp cloth over the dented area, then hold a warm pressing iron over the cloth to create steam. The iron must not be too hot; nor must it be set down directly on the cloth. The steam should draw out the dent. However, if this does not occur, it may be necessary to put a paste filler into the dent to bring it up to the surface of the wood (see "Wood Fillers" later in this chapter).

WHITE SPOTS

White spots on natural finishes are caused by heat, moisture or alcohol. In most cases you can remove them by rubbing the finish with a thin paste of powdered pumice stone and light mineral or machine oil. Rub the mixture over the spot, using your fingertips or a piece of felt. Wipe the surface clean with a dry cloth. To remove any oil that remains, wash the surface with a cloth moistened with soap or detergent suds. If the pumice leaves a dull spot, polish it with rottenstone and oil.

Moisture causes white spots on shellac. Let the finish dry thoroughly; the spot may disappear. If it remains, remove any wax with a cloth dampened with turpentine or a nonflammable dry-cleaning fluid; then rewax. Or, remove the wax, rub down the white spot with pumice and oil (as explained in the foregoing) and rewax it.

Commercial preparations for removing white spots may damage certain finishes. It is wise to test these preparations on an inconspicuous part of the surface.

SCRATCHES

If scratches are small, they can often be made less noticeable by applying a cleaning solution. However, if you need to treat scratches of a more serious nature, use one of the following:

1. Rub the scratch with a commercial scratch remover. (Test the reaction of the remover first on an inconspicuous part of the wood.)

2. Rub a small amount of oil color (see "Color Matching" later in this chapter) into the scratch to color it. Allow it to dry, then cover it with a quick-drying varnish applied with a toothpick or fine brush.

3. Mix oil color with the varnish and apply as directed in item 2. More than one application may be necessary.

HAIRLINE CHECKING IN VARNISH

This condition is caused by changes in the moisture content of the wood that make the wood expand and contract, cracking the varnish finish. Sunlight, hot radiators and extreme changes in humidity can be contributing factors.

To prevent this condition from going any further and to improve the appearance of the finish, first wash the finish with the cleaning mixture given at beginning of this section. When it is thoroughly dry, rub the surface with a heavy-mixture polish made of 2 parts boiled linseed oil, 1 part turpentine and 1½ parts of clear varnish.

Warm this mixture before you use it. Apply it to a small part of the surface at a time, and rub it hard, using the palm of your bare hand. When the polish begins to stiffen under your hand, wipe off the polish that remains, using several clean cloths; if you do not take off all this extra polish, the surface will remain sticky. Repeat the treatment as necessary.

This mixture is effective in repolishing very dull finishes and building up worn or damaged places in the finish. It is a treatment rather than a cure. It will seal the surface but will not restore a deteriorated finish. Repeat treatment annually for best results.

SMALL HOLES, GOUGES AND CRACKS

A more extensive filling job is necessary for blemishes that have penetrated the finish and damaged the wood. These depressions can be filled in one of the following ways:

Mix a small quantity of dry spackling compound with water to make a stiff paste. Add oil color until the paste has a workable consistency. To match the finish, choose a color darker than the finish, because the paste will lighten as it dries. Apply this "Swedish putty" to the hole, using a palette knife, putty knife or spatula. Do not worry about using too much, because you can smooth it down easily. After about one hour, when it is dry, smooth the patch with fine steel wool or very fine abrasive paper. The hole should be full and the surrounding area clean. Varnish the patch. Adjust the color, if necessary, with colored varnish and let it dry.

Melt stick shellac with a heated kitchen knife, screw driver or soldering iron. Drop the melted shellac into the hole and press firmly with a moistened finger. (Don't burn your fingertip!) The patch should stand above the surface. When it is hard, shave it down with a single-edged razor blade until it is level. Rub gently with very fine steel wool, or pumice and oil, to smooth the patch and the surrounding surface; apply wax or polish.

CIGARETTE BURNS

Remove the blackened finish and charred wood with fine steel wool wrapped around a matchstick. Rub only on the burned area to avoid scratching the good finish. If the burn seems to have damaged only the finish, the spot may be repaired by using the method given earlier in this chapter for scratches.

Burns that have damaged the wood need more filling, such as outlined in the preceding section.

Color matching

Oil colors used to cover scratches or other wood damages come in the four following classifications:

Reds: Turkey red, rose madder, rose pink, burnt sienna.

Yellows: Raw sienna, French ocher.

Browns: Burnt umber, Vandyke brown, raw umber.

Blacks: Lampblack, ivory black.

WOOD COLORS TO BE MATCHED

Walnut: Use either burnt umber or Vandyke brown; both are rich, dark, warm browns. Raw umber, a yellowish brown, is sometimes added.

Mission Oak: Use raw umber.

Brown Oak: Use burnt umber, or burnt umber and a little raw sienna.

Golden Oak: Use raw sienna and a little burnt umber.

Maple: Use burnt sienna for the redder maples, raw sienna for yellow maples. To obtain a blend, mix both burnt and raw sienna.

Red Mahogany: Use turkey red, rose madder or rose pink; add a little burnt umber or black, if needed.

Brown Mahogany: Use burnt umber, adding a very small quantity of red, if needed.

Dark Mahogany: Use one of the mahogany reds with black added.

Cherry: Use burnt sienna. Add a little burnt umber and one of the mahogany reds, if needed.

Fillers

Paste and wood fillers are available on the market for adding body to porous wood, or for small repairs, and it is well to apply the filler before the wood surface is finished by painting or varnishing. Tell your hardware or paint dealer the type of wood on which you wish to use the filler, so he may provide you with suitable material.

As a rule, an open-grained wood (such as walnut, rosewood, mahogany, ash, elm, chestnut and oak) needs a paste filler, while a close-grained wood (such as pine, poplar, fir, bass, cherry, gum, spruce, birch, cedar and beech) calls for a liquid filler.

Paste filler should be thinned with turpentine, but not too much so, since it may lose its effectiveness for closing the pores and mending the cracks in the wood. Brush the paste filler deeply into the wood surface, going in the direction of the grain. After about 20 minutes, when the filler sticks to the pores or cracks, wipe the surface dry. Then rub with steel wool or sandpaper, and let it dry overnight.

The liquid filler is applied on the wood in the direction of the grain, then rubbed smooth with steel wool or sandpaper.

COLORED FILLER

Filler may be bought in many colors to match wood stains; your dealer may have some of these popular ones: golden oak, brown oak, white, antique maple, golden maple, American walnut, Circassian walnut, red mahogany, brown mahogany, black and gray. Before using a colored filler, test it out on an inconspicuous spot on the wood surface to make sure you obtain the proper shade. If you find a ready-made color, you may experiment with coloring the filler yourself by following the information in the section "Color Matching."

Staining

Ready-made stains are available in many colors and types, and the stain you buy depends on the quality of the wood in your house and the color you wish to achieve. Carefully read manufacturers' directions that come with the product, and ask your paint dealer to assist you in your choice.

Do not apply stain on any wood surface that is not thoroughly smooth and clean. Be sure to give yourself adequate space in which to work, have the room free of dust and provide a good light so you may work under best conditions. Use a thoroughly clean, wide, flat bristle brush for applying the stain, and work with even strokes in the direction of the grain.

You may need to stain a wood surface that does not present large, open working areas, or you may want to give special attention to fine work; in such cases the stain may be applied with a very fine brush or a soft cloth.

Stain may sometimes dry out to a shade lighter than you intended it to be. In such a case, you may go over the stain again to achieve a darker shade.

TYPES OF STAINS

There are five general types of stain:

Oil stains give good results if properly applied. To achieve a more penetrating quality when working on fine-grained wood, add benzol to the stain; but ask your paint dealer about quantities needed for the type of wood you have. After you brush the stain on the surface, allow it to penetrate into the wood for about fifteen minutes, then wipe the excess from the surface with soft, clean cheesecloth, stroking the cloth with the grain of the wood. Stain takes about twenty-four hours to dry; keep surface intact until it is completely dry.

Water stains are made by dissolving special powdered dye in water. These dyes come in various types and colors and are water-soluble; the directions on the package labels should be followed. Usually 1 ounce of dye powder is added to 1 quart boiled water; the mixture is placed in a metal container, then allowed to cool. The advantage of water stain is that it produces a much finer finish than oil, but it is not as simple to handle, and the amateur handyman may not be able to achieve as fine a result with this; the work requires experience and skill. One disadvantage of water stain is that it must only be used on wood that never has had a finish on it before; it does not penetrate wood that has had a previous finish coat, even if the old surface is completely removed.

Spirit stain, sometimes called alcohol stain, is used to touch up small defects as well as to finish large surfaces. The stain is made by dissolving powdered dye in alcohol, using ½ ounce powder to 1 quart spirits. The dyes come in various colors. Spirit stain is not especially recommended to anyone but an experienced workman, because the alcohol has a tendency to evaporate too rapidly, and if a large surface is to be stained there may be difficulty in achieving a good result.

Chemical stains are not commonly used by the inexperienced workman; however, they are mentioned because of their use in obtaining special wood effects. Chemical stains are either acid or alkaline, and they come in powder or crystals (sometimes in liquid form). The usual formula is to dissolve about 6 ounces powder or crystals in 1 gallon warm water. If the stain is too light, add more chemical; but if it is too dark, add more water. Store the liquid solution in glass jars; never put it in metal containers. Sometimes household chemicals such as lye, ammonia, sal soda, potash and even vinegar are used to dissolve in water to form various colors of stain. Chemical stains give permanent color to the wood, and when applying them you must wear gloves and goggles to protect your skin and eyes. Consult with your paint dealer before mixing or using chemical stains; it may be advisable to forego them because of the care needed in handling them.

Varnish stains are sometimes used because of the

misconception that they are accomplishing the double job of staining and coating the wood with one operation, and that there is a cost saving. The basic purpose of a stain is good penetration and clarity, neither of which is found in the varnish stain. However, if you are not concerned with giving work a professional appearance, you may find it practical to use varnish stain on interior floors in closets, cabinets or other inconspicuous places; in this case you will achieve the staining and protective coating in one operation.

Varnish and shellac

There are many grades and types of these two most commonly used wood finishes, both for interior and exterior uses. They cannot all be listed here, because each kind of wood and each purpose for which the finish is needed calls for a specific type of varnish or shellac. Before buying and using these materials, your local dealer will recommend what is best for you, and the manufacturers' directions should be followed.

For suggestions, refer to "Finishing Floor Surfaces" and "Causes of Failure in Finishing" in Chapter 10, also to "Varnishing and Shellacking" in Chapter 13.

Plastic finish

This finish is a fairly new product, which gives a long-lasting, glossy finish to floors and walls. Instead of using the conventional brush method, the plastic finish is applied on a clean surface with a cloth in long, even strokes, or it is sprayed on. This is a quick and easy task; follow the directions on the container.

Chapter Seven

DOORS, WINDOWS AND SCREENS

SOMETIMES MERELY a loose hinge on a door or a stuck window or door may cause more serious damage later on if not repaired immediately. These parts of the house require constant maintenance to keep them in sound working order.

Door repairs

If the door does not swing easily when being opened or shut, it may be that the floor is not level or has rough spots; if that is so, it should be planed to smoothness. But if the floor is level, look for other causes.

LOOSE HINGES

To determine whether the fault lies with the hinges, first examine the margin or crack between the door and frame when the door is closed (Fig. 7.1a). Loose hinges, whether at top or bottom, usually allow the door to sag, causing the upper outside corner to strike against the side of the jamb and the lower outside corner to drag on the threshold, making an uneven margin around the door. As a further test, try to shake the hinges by taking hold of the knob at each side, when the door is open, and

pulling and pushing the door away from and toward the hinges.

If the hinges move, try tightening the screws. It may be necessary to insert wooden plugs in the screw holes or to substitute longer screws, to make them hold properly.

If hinges are not loose, or if upon tightening the screws the margins or cracks are not made uniform, it might be well to try the effect of cardboard shims under the hinge leaves. To do this, loosen the screws of the top hinge in the leaf, which is fastened to the jamb (b), and insert a strip of cardboard under the inner edge. Then tighten the screws and try closing the door. This will usually correct the trouble, since it will tend to pull the upper part of the door closer to the jamb.

If this corrects the trouble as far as the striking is concerned, but leaves considerable space above the door and along the outside edge (lock edge), loosen the screws in the leaf of the bottom hinge, which is attached to the jamb (c), and insert cardboard under the outer edge.

If, after tightening the screws and again trying the door, it is found that there is an even crack or margin on

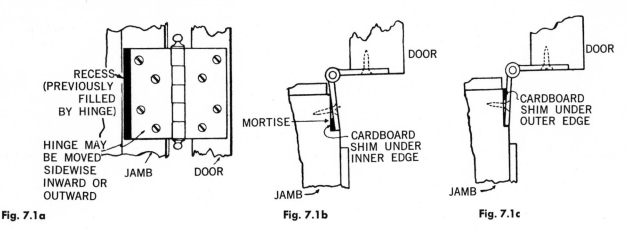

Fig. 7.1a   **Fig. 7.1b**   **Fig. 7.1c**

43

all sides, and that the hinge pins do not move when the door is closed, the repair is permanent. If, however, the hinge pins move when the door is being closed, it will probably be necessary to use thinner shims under the hinge leaves.

On the other hand, if the door strikes all along the outer edge, remove the pins, take down the door and remove the hinge leaves from the jamb. Then, with a sharp chisel cut away some wood from the outer edge of the mortises in the jamb, being careful to taper the cut so that no wood is removed from the back edge. When the hinges are replaced, this beveled deepening of the mortise will tend to pull the door away from the lock jamb and toward the hinge jamb. If, upon closing the door, the hinge pins move, it is a sign of binding against the hinge jamb as a result of excessive beveling of the mortises. This binding can be remedied by slight shimming under the outer edge of the jamb leaves.

PLANING DOOR

It will seldom be necessary to plane the door if the trouble has been caused by loose or improperly mortised hinges. However, if planing is necessary, as in the case where the side margins are uneven and the door strikes at top or bottom because of settlement of the frame or similar causes, points of contact can generally be located by noting where paint is worn. If this is not possible, open and close the door several times and mark with chalk those places where the door seems to stick.

Then plane the edges of the door slightly where marked. Do not plane too much off the door, for when dry weather comes the wood may shrink, and if an outside door has been planed too much, it may require weather-stripping or filling in. After planing a little, try the door by opening and closing it, to see whether additional planing is needed.

If planing is required on the top or front edge, it can usually be done without removing the door. If bottom or back edges need planing, the door will, of course, have to be taken down.

If the door is of the type that has removable hinge pins, it is a simple matter to remove them and lift the door off. If not, the screws holding one leaf of the hinges will have to be removed to release the door.

After planing, touch up the bare spots to match the finish on the door.

SWELLING

Damp weather is often the cause of a door sticking. The absorption of moisture results in swelling of the framework and door and causes the paint or varnish to soften and become sticky.

If the door has an even margin along the top and bottom edges, and if the hinges are firm, it will be necessary to plane either the hinge or lock edge. Usually it is best to plane the hinge edge, since the hinges are more easily removed and remortised than the lock. However, care should be taken not to plane off too much wood.

Replacing window panes

A window on an upper floor may not be easy to fit with a new glass; if possible, remove the sash that has the broken pane and lay it on a flat surface to do the replacement job. A window on the ground floor may be reached by a ladder and the pane replaced; however, even in this case, remove the sash if at all possible and put it on a table or workbench.

TOOLS AND MATERIALS NEEDED

You will need a glass cutter (unless you buy glass cut to measure), ruler or steel square, small knife or chisel to remove old putty, putty knife, small flat paintbrush, glazier's points, new glass of same thickness as the broken one, putty, raw linseed oil to be used as a filler and to soften putty and matching paint for the putty after it hardens. It is easiest to buy putty ready-made. However, if you prefer to mix your own, combine whiting of the best grade with enough pure raw linseed oil until it reaches the proper consistency.

REMOVING A BROKEN PANE

Carefully take glass out of the pane. With a knife or chisel chip off the old putty. Pull out the glazier's points. With the point of a small knife scrape clean the wood where you will insert the new glass. With a small brush apply a coat of linseed oil or thin paint on the wood; this acts as a filler and prevents the oil in the putty from becoming absorbed by the wood and causing subsequent drying and crumbling of the putty.

SETTING THE NEW PANE

Knead putty on a surface that is not absorptive (such as a piece of glass or a glass plate) until you have a pliable working mass. It the putty is not sufficiently fresh, you may need to make it more pliable by mixing in a small amount of linseed oil until you can knead it to the proper consistency.

Into the groove in the sash put a thin coat of putty (about $\frac{1}{16}$ inch). Carefully set the glass into the puttied grooves. Gently press the glass so the edges of the pane are embedded in the putty. Now lay three or four glazier's points on the glass on each of the long sides of the window, and two or three points on each narrow side. With the flat edge of the chisel, force the points into the sash so that the glass will rest more firmly in the bed of putty.

Then roll a small piece of putty between the palms of your hands until it is a pencil-shaped roll. Make as many rolls as you will need. On one side of the pane, lay the rolls end to end where the glass meets the sash. With a putty knife press rolls down tightly but gently, drawing the knife along the sash from one end to the other. Hold the putty knife at an angle to form a smooth bevel, as shown in Fig. 7.2. You will have excess putty on the sides of the bevel; cut this off and use it to fill any depressions that may occur. Then repeat this procedure on the other side of the new pane.

Remove any putty spots from the pane with a cloth dipped in gasoline or turpentine. When putty is hardened, paint it to match the window sash.

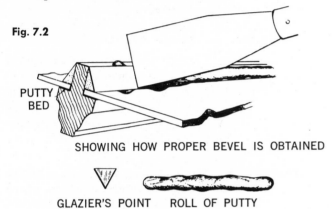

Fig. 7.2

PUTTY BED

SHOWING HOW PROPER BEVEL IS OBTAINED

GLAZIER'S POINT   ROLL OF PUTTY

REPLACING PANE IN A METAL SASH

Generally the manufacturer of metal window sashes has printed directions for replacing a broken pane. But even if you have no directions to follow, you can proceed on your own. You will need a putty knife, screw driver, small flat paintbrush and plate glass or double-strength glass. You will also need putty made of whiting and white lead, and paint of the same color as the sash to finish the top of the putty.

Your window may be glazed either on the inside or the outside. Remove broken glass and old putty, and scrape the sash clean where the new glass is to be set in. Some metal sashes have wire spring clips to hold the glass; these must be removed before broken glass can be taken out.

Spread putty over the metal where the glass is to rest. Push the glass into place tightly but gently, and see that the putty fills every crevice. If wire clips are used, reinsert them into their holes in the sash and fasten them securely. When the new pane is firm, apply putty in the same way as directed for wooden sashes and paint the putty after it has hardened.

In other types of metal windows, you may need to unscrew and remove the metal heading or glazing strips to take out the broken glass. Then scrape the old putty from the sash and embed the new pane in the putty as

directed in the foregoing. When the new glass is securely in place, put back the metal beading or glazing strips and fasten them tightly against glass. These strips are generally held in place by brass screws, and they make a neat frame around the pane.

Window repairs

A window that doesn't move easily may have been affected either by damp weather that caused swelling in the sash or frame, by paint that has hardened or by paint that has become soft and sticky. You will need the following tools and materials to correct the condition: screw driver, small knife, claw hammer, flat wood chisel, nail set, plane, medium sandpaper, small paintbrush, pieces of felt or cloth to be used as pads to protect woodwork from tool marks, paraffin, linseed oil and varnish or paint in matching color.

Figure 7.3 shows a double-hung window with its various parts and its frame.

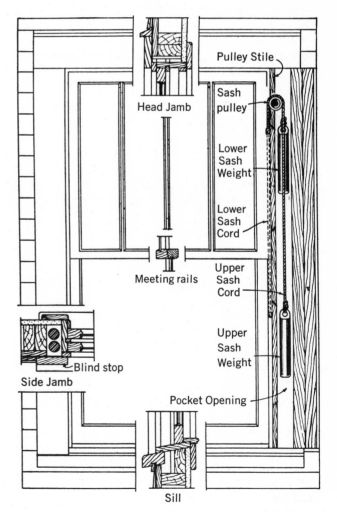

Head Jamb

Pulley Stile

Sash pulley

Lower Sash Weight

Lower Sash Cord

Meeting rails

Upper Sash Cord

Blind stop

Side Jamb

Upper Sash Weight

Pocket Opening

Sill

Fig. 7.3

STICKING SASH

Examine pulley stiles and stops. A paraffin waxing of the parts in contact may be all that is needed to eliminate excessive friction.

If the inside stops press too tightly against the sash, either move them away from the sash or plane down the edge adjacent to the sash. If the stops are secured by nails, it may be a good idea to renail them in a new position. If the stops are secured by screws, it may be easier to plane them off.

If a wood window sash swells so that its vertical edges stick against the pulley stile or the running face of the window frame, remove the sash and plane a little off its vertical edges. Then coat it with linseed oil, and after the oil is dry give it a paraffin waxing.

Ordinary soap is a substitute for paraffin; it won't be as lasting a lubricant as paraffin, but it serves the purpose. You can also use petroleum jelly or even a stiff cup grease; but these need to be used very sparingly to avoid soiling the paint.

Damaged weight cords

If a window falls abruptly when raised, the cause is undoubtedly a defective weight cord. It may have become stretched or broken, and should be replaced. You will need a wood chisel; claw hammer; screw driver; nail set; small weight or nail; new sash cord, chain or stranded wire cable; and pieces of felt or cloth to be used as pads to protect woodwork from tool marks.

If the cord in the lower sash is damaged, remove only that sash. Take off casing stop on the side of the window where the defective cord is. If it is fastened by screws it may be removed with the help of a screw driver; if it is nailed, use the chisel to remove the nails. In either case, take care not to damage the woodwork; you can help prevent damage by wrapping cloth or felt around the blade of the tool and placing of a piece as a pad under the blade.

The brads should come out with the stop. Do not knock them through and pull them out in the usual way; instead, bend brads slightly and with the claw hammer pull them through the stop from the back.

If the defective cord is in the upper sash, it will be necessary to remove both the upper and lower sashes. In removing the upper sash, first lower it to the sill, then pull out the parting stop on one side of the window frame. Generally the stop is not nailed down and ought to be easy to remove; however, if it is painted or held fast in some other way, you may need to pry it loose with a flat chisel, starting at the middle of the stop.

Either beneath the casing stop or adjacent to it, there is a small oblong cover that conceals a pocket in the sash.

This cover is nailed or screwed down; remove the cover to get access to the cords and weights that are suspended in the long narrow slot at the side of the sash. There are four weights in a double-hung window, two on each side of the frame; the two nearest the outside of the house balance the upper sash, and the two nearest the inside of the house balance the lower sash.

One end of the cord is knotted and anchored in a hole bored in the side of the window sash near the top; it passes over the pulley near the top of window frame and is then tied to the weight. To make it easy to work the new cord over the pulley and down through the slot to the bottom, attach a small metal weight of some sort (like a heavy key or a fishline sinker) to a piece of string, then pass it over the pulley and lower it through the inside of the slot until you can reach it through the pocket. Now attach the string to the cord, pull it down within reach of your hand and fasten it to the weight before cutting it to the proper length. Pull the cord over the pulley until the top of the weight is up against the pulley; the cord should drop about three inches below the knot-retaining hole in the sash when the sash is in the extreme low position. The extra length of cord is provided to form the retaining knot. Tie the knot and pull the sash out far enough so you may insert the knot in the mortise.

Then replace the window and raise and lower it several times to be sure it is in proper working condition, or else you may need to adjust the new cord. Replace the pocket cover and stop.

Screens for doors and windows

Damages to screens should be fixed as soon as they are noticed, to avoid later larger repairs or replacements. It is advisable to inspect them before you take them down to store away for cold weather months, and before you put them on again in the spring.

PATCHING SCREEN WIRE

It is easier to mend a window or door screen before putting it up. If a hole appears, it should be patched so that the tear does not become larger (Fig. 7.4).

1. Cut out a screen wire patch that measures one-half inch larger (all around) than the hole. You can also buy a ready-cut wire patch at the hardware or variety store; they come in many sizes.

2. Ravel out two wires on each of the four sides of the patch.

3. Bend the exposed ends of the wires until they are at right angles to the main part of the patch. The bent wires will form prongs on all four sides. An easy way to make these prongs is to lay the patch on a flat surface,

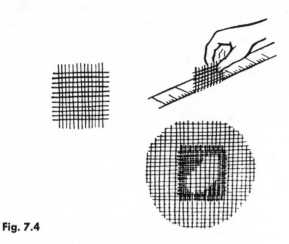

Fig. 7.4

then hold the edge of a ruler over the raveled wires and pull the patch upward to form a right angle.

4. Place the patch over the hole and push the prongs through the screen from the inside. Press the prongs flat against the screen's surface, turning them so they extend toward the center of the patch.

It helps to have someone on the other side of the screen to fasten the prongs while you hold the patch in place.

REPLACING SCREEN WIRE

To replace screen wire you need a pair of old scissors or tinners' snips, screw driver, pliers or tack puller, light claw hammer, tacks, nail set or screen stapler and staples, small tacks, small brads or nails and screen wire.

Prepare the frame for the new screening by first removing the molding that holds the screen, taking out all screws or nails or tacks. Remove the old screen. Measure the new wire, allowing about an extra inch all around to tack onto the frame. Cut the screen wire with the scissors or tinners' snips.

Lay the frame across two sawhorses and prop boards, as shown in Fig. 7.5, or whatever similar means you can provide. To the supporting boards clamp the side rails on both sides of the frame, at the center, and make the clamps tight so the rails will be pulled down.

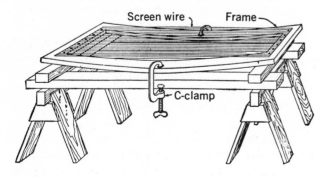

Fig. 7.5

Place the new screening over the frame and tack down wire at both narrow ends of the frame. When you remove the clamps, the two side rails of the frame will go back into position, causing the screen wire to become taut and allowing you to tack along the two side rails of frame without stretching the screen wire to fit. If you have a screen stapler, you can attach the wire with staples, which takes less time than tacking. Replace the molding on top of the tacked wire edges. Trim off any excess wire that may protrude from the molding.

SAGGING SCREEN DOOR

If the door frame joints become loose the bottom of the door may start to drag on the threshold. In such a case a diagonally placed turnbuckle, as shown in Fig. 7.6, will tighten the frame. One end of it should be screwed to the top rail in a corner of the frame, the other end to the bottom rail. Turn the turnbuckle in the center of the rod until the door frame is properly adjusted.

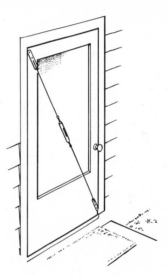

Fig. 7.6

PAINTING SCREEN WIRE

Place door or window screen on a flat surface. With a stiff brush clean the wire of all dust and rust. If you desire, you may wash the screen with a brush dipped in lukewarm water and soap suds, rinsing it with clear water and drying it with a cloth.

After the screen is thoroughly clean and dry, apply special screen paint with a brush on which you have a moderate amount of paint. Better still, use a screen paint applicator, which you may get at the paint dealer with instructions for its use. You can also make one yourself, using a block of wood measuring 1 by 3 by 8 inches and covering it with a piece of carpet or thick felt glued down to the side of the wood that will be used as the paint applicator. On the opposite side of the block nail down a wood cleat to act as a handle.

Galvanized wire screen may not need frequent repainting. Low-quality wire may need to be painted every year. Bronze or copper screen wire does not need to be painted if you desire to leave it in natural state, although it is a good idea to use a good grade of spar varnish on both sides of the screen. Since varnish doesn't last as long as paint, the screen should be revarnished annually.

If the paint you use clogs the tiny holes in the screen, it may be too thick. Thin it with turpentine or boiled linseed oil.

The door or window frame around the screen usually does not need to be painted as often as the screen wire.

STORAGE SCREEN HANGER

When you remove door and window screens before the winter sets in, record on the frame of each with chalk, where it goes, or hang a tag on it with this information, so that when you want to replace them in the spring you will be able to put them in the right place at once.

A suspended hanger under the basement ceiling is an ideal place for storage, as shown in Fig. 7.7. Build a framework of wood strips. Nail flat boards, about two feet apart, to the floor joists (that is, the floor above, which connects to the basement ceiling), and on these boards nail the framework.

First lay the larger and heavier pieces, such as screen doors and storm doors, then, on top, put the smaller screens. Cover with canvas or paper to protect them from dust. The reason for putting them high up is so that air can reach them freely and to provide freedom from dampness and possible damage from jarring.

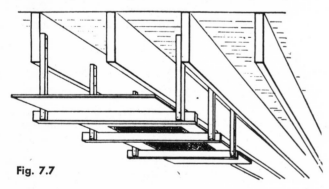

Fig. 7.7

Care of awnings

Inspect the awnings when you take them down, after the summer, to see if there are any damages. Make all repairs before you store awnings away, so that when you are ready to hang them on the windows the following spring you will be sure they are in good shape.

REPAIRING DAMAGES

To match material to an awning, choose a fabric of the same heavy texture as the awning. Cut a patch one inch larger (all around) than the hole. Use a rubber cement or other special cloth-patching adhesive recommended by your hardware dealer. Apply the cement on the extra material (which you allowed for around the hole); then press down the patch over the hole on the outside of the awning. If you put the patch on the inside of awning, it may become loosened by rain.

If there are any seam rips, all you need do is sew them together with matching heavy thread.

Replace worn cords if they are in bad shape.

If framework is rusted, sandpaper off the rust and then cover the metal with paint. Apply lubricating oil to the pulleys.

WASHING BEFORE STORAGE

Never store an awning that has not been thoroughly cleaned. Use a stiff brush dipped in lukewarm water and mild soap suds to rub over the surface of the awning; then go over it with a clean cloth dipped in clear lukewarm water to remove the suds. Let the awning dry thoroughly before putting it away.

Fold the awning and wrap it in a paper or cloth covering. Never store an awning that is damp, or put it in a damp place, since mildew is likely to occur.

REPAINTING AWNING

If when you take the awning out of storage in the spring you think the color looks faded or perhaps want to change the color, buy special canvas paint in a color slightly darker than the original awning.

The most convenient way to apply the paint is to hang the awning on a window on the ground floor, so you may reach it by ladder. Let the awning hang fully open. Dip the brush lightly into the can of paint. Start at the top of the awning and paint with long, even strokes of the brush. Finish the job in one painting, because if you do part of it and come back the next day to finish it, the finished awning may show streaks where the paint was applied at two different times.

Generally one coat of paint is sufficient; but if you want to apply a second coat, make sure the first one is completely dry.

DAMAGE PREVENTION

When awnings are raised, tie the cord firmly, especially if there is a strong wind.

When rain starts, lower awning in order to prevent any dirty water from accumulating in the folds and staining the fabric.

Keep the awnings lowered after a rain until completely dry. Mildew may occur if they are raised while still damp.

Pulleys must be kept properly adjusted and oiled, so the awning won't be ripped when you lower or raise it.

Chapter Eight

WEATHERPROOFING AND INSULATION

Weather-stripping doors and windows

ALL HOUSES SHOULD BE well ventilated, but this does not mean that unregulated drafts of cold air should sweep through the house at all times. In cold weather the warm air escapes through loose windows and doors and is at once replaced by the cold out-of-doors air. The result is that the heating plant must be pushed to capacity to maintain an even temperature and on windy days, where such conditions prevail, it will be difficult to keep the house warm.

It is to improve these conditions that the weather-stripping of doors and windows is recommended.

There are many kinds and grades of weather stripping on the market, at various prices. Most metal weather strips must be installed by an expert, since they usually involve removal of the sash and cutting of grooves, but some of the simpler forms can be applied by the average householder. However, since complete instructions are furnished by all manufacturers, you may not require the services of an expert.

There are many kinds of strips that are easy to apply, and inasmuch as these types are similar and are attached in about the same manner, their installation will be discussed as a group. This group might be divided into three types: the rigid type, which includes narrow wooden strips with rubber or felt edges made in standard-length pieces; the flexible type, which includes the patent cloth variety with a padded contact edge; and, cheapest and simplest of all, the ordinary felt strip. The flexible-type strips are put up in rolls of various lengths.

TAKING MEASUREMENTS

Measure the four sides of the window frame where the face of the sash adjoins the casing, and also the distance across the meeting rail. Measure around the four sides of door on the outside where they abut the door stops and threshold.

TOOLS AND MATERIALS

You will need a rule or steel tape, marking pencil and light hammer. If the strips are of wood, a small saw and miter box are also needed, but if the strips are of cloth a pair of scissors may be used for cutting them. Also get a number of linear feet of stripping, some three-quarter inch wire brads if wooden strips are used, four-ounce tinned trunk tacks (rustless) for padded cloth stripping and smaller trunk tacks or common carpet tacks for felt stripping. It is advisable to use tacks that will be least noticeable and that will not rust.

WEATHER-STRIPPING A WINDOW

The window should be locked when weather stripping is attached to insure best results. See that the contact edge presses snugly at all points against the sash or casing, as the case may be, before the tacks or brads are driven.

Upper sash. The weather stripping should be tacked to the frame adjoining the sash on the outside of the window. If the flexible type is used, one piece can be cut to extend around the two sides and top. If, however, the rigid kind is used, three separate pieces will have to be cut, with the two corners mitered, to make a neat fit.

Lower sash. The weather stripping is attached on the inside, and four separate pieces are required, regardless of the type used. The two side pieces are tacked to the face of the inside stop bead adjoining the sash, with the contact edge pressed against the face of the sash, and should extend from the top face of the stool, or inside

49

sill, to the top of the meeting rail. The piece across the width of the meeting rail is tacked to the top of the lower sash, so that the contact edge will cover the crack where the upper and lower sash rails meet. This piece will probably have to be cut in two parts to provide space for the window lock. The piece across the bottom is tacked to the face of the sash with the contact edge down to butt against the top of the stool or inside window sill.

WEATHER-STRIPPING A DOOR

The door should be closed while weather stripping is being applied. If flexible-type stripping is used, two pieces will do: one the width of the bottom of door, and the other one long enough to extend around the two sides and top. If rigid strips are used, four pieces will be required, with the two top corners mitered, to make a neat joint. The bottom piece should be tacked to the inside face of the door with the contact edge down and pressed snugly against the top of the threshold. If the threshold is so badly worn that it is impossible to obtain a tight contact at all points, it should be replaced with a new one. The side and top pieces are tacked to door stops on the outside, with the contact edges pressed evenly, but not too tightly, against the face of the door.

CASEMENT WINDOWS

Casement windows are weather-stripped in the same manner as doors, with the stripping tacked to the window stop and the contact edge pressed against the face of the sash when the window is closed. A strip of felt tacked to the inside face of the meeting strip will seal the vertical crack where the two windows meet.

Weatherproofing the outside of window frames

For various reasons damp spots may appear on the interior surfaces of walls, but only in relatively few cases are they caused by leakages through the walls proper.

Most of the trouble is usually found around window frames that are poorly built or improperly weatherproofed. Such frames admit air and moisture, and the adjoining interior walls soon become unsightly with dirt and water stains. Water may work its way along inside the wall and make a spot on the plaster surface several feet distant.

CORRECT WINDOW FRAME CONSTRUCTION

In extra-good frame construction the blind casing (behind the outside casing) extends back to the window studs, and the building paper (between the sheathing and the siding) extends over the crack between the blind casing and the sheathing. In addition, the outside casing is nailed directly to the blind casing and the siding or shingles butted up against it.

If there is no blind casing, waterproof paper is used under the joint between the outside casing and the siding to prevent the entry of wind and rain.

The cap over the window should be constructed to turn water away from the joint between the frame and siding. In some types of frames the siding or shingles extend over the cap, and a drip groove is provided along the underside of the cap, or, in case the cap does not have these features, the joint may be covered with metal flashing, as shown in Fig. 8.1.

The connection between the upper sill and subsill should also be tight. In some types of frame, the bottom of the lower sill is plowed to allow the siding or shingles to extend into the sill a short distance, and an offset (or rabbet) is cut near the back edge to make a tight joint with the top sill.

REPAIRS IN FRAME CONSTRUCTION

If there are leakages around the lower part of the window, look particularly for holes or large cracks at the top of the window sill. There may be a crack under the inside stool or window ledge, if it is not nailed down securely; and if the stool has been cut too short there may be cracks at either or both ends. Also, where parting strips and pulley stiles meet the top sill, there may

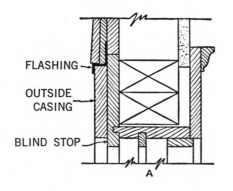

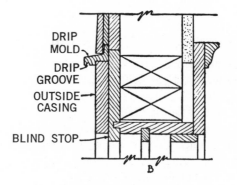

Fig. 8.1

be holes left as a result of careless fitting. Such cracks and openings may be closed satisfactorily by driving the stool down firmly and filling the spaces with white-lead putty or calking compound, as previously described.

Sometimes driving rain or water from melting ice on the sill outside the window may be forced in under the window and run down the wall. This seepage may usually be prevented by removing the lower sash and plowing a furrow or groove along the bottom of the lower rail from one side to the other with a plow plane having a blade of one-half to three-quarters of an inch long. A cavity is thus formed that will check blowing rain before it can get inside the window.

Where the top sill joins the subsill, there may be a crack that will admit air and moisture unless it is calked with white-lead putty or calking compound, or covered with metal flashing. Examine the drip mold and flashing at the top of the frame to see whether they are in good condition. Put on new flashing if necessary, preferably made of copper, with the upper edge bent up under the siding or shingles and the lower edge extending over the outer edge of the window cap about one-half inch and bent down to form an apron.

Before putting on the flashing, seal the cracks around the frame with white-lead putty or calking compound (a putty-like substance made for calking purposes).

If the outside casing or adjoining molding becomes loose it may require renailing. In some instances the outside casing may be nailed over the siding or shingles instead of being fastened directly to the blind casing. This method leaves triangular openings between the back of the casing and each shingle or siding board, and air will enter if the joints under the outside covering are not properly protected.

In such cases the outside casing may be removed and the cracks underneath filled with white-lead putty or calking compound, or the triangular openings may be closed without removing the casing; that is, they may either be calked with oakum (hemp fiber from tarred hemp rope) to within one-half inch of the surface and then filled with calking compound, or covered by means of a strip of wood (about two inches wide and as thick as the casing) notched out to fit the irregularities in the surface and nailed to the siding or shingles adjoining the outside casing.

FRAME REPAIR IN STUCCO CONSTRUCTION

Window frames in stucco are usually of the same type as those used in frame houses, and the same instructions for weatherproofing may be followed. To apply flashing over the cap mold at the top of the frame, however, it may be necessary to cut away a few inches of stucco along the top of the frame. When the flashing has been applied, it should be sealed along the top edge against the backing with elastic cement of good quality.

FRAME REPAIR IN BRICK CONSTRUCTION

Window frames in brick are usually set in a thin bed of mortar and the spaces between the brickwork and frame filled solid with mortar to seal the joints.

There is seldom any trouble at the tops of the windows, since the frames are generally set back under the brickwork in such a way that water cannot enter under ordinary conditions. If there are leaks around the window, they are usually found along the sides or around the top or bottom of the sill.

In making repairs, remove the molding adjoining the brickwork, calk with oakum all cracks that appear to need attention and finish off the job with calking compound or good Portland cement mortar. Before replacing the molding, paint the back with white lead as a further precaution against leaks and decay.

If it is not desirable to remove the molding, cracks between the brickwork and molding can be sealed with a plastic calking compound. This can be applied with a putty knife, a calking knife or a calking gun; this last may possibly be borrowed from a dealer in such material. If this method is used, care should be taken to obtain a high-grade compound that will not shrink, crack, run or dry out under the action of the weather.

DORMER WINDOWS

If the sill of the window rests on the roof, and no flashing has been provided, metal flashing should be worked into the underside of the sill and run down over the roofing material so that water will not get into the crevices between the sill and the roofing. As an added precaution, it may be advisable to calk the crack with roofing cement before applying the flashing.

Preventing frosted window panes

In the wintertime, in certain localities, frost may form on the inner surface of window panes—often to such an extent that it is impossible to see through the glass. If obstruction of vision were the only result of such a condition, it might not be seriously considered, but often, when the frost melts, water runs down over the woodwork and plaster, ruining both the finish on the woodwork and the wall decorations.

Frost is formed by the condensation and freezing of moisture from the air upon the cold surfaces of window panes. It would seem, therefore, that the logical solution would be to protect the window panes as much as possible against extreme cold and to reduce the amount of evaporation in the rooms.

PROTECTION AROUND WINDOWS

The windows may be protected by installing storm sash tight enough to prevent cold air striking the inner windows. It might also be well to tighten the stops around the windows and to install weather stripping.

Humidity and health

It is claimed by physicians and others familiar with the subject that a certain amount of humidity is necessary to preserve good health in the household. It is held that colds, which are prevalent during the heating season, often result from overheated rooms, particularly where the percentage of moisture in the air is not sufficient. According to the "comfort chart" prepared by the American Society of Heating and Ventilating Engineers, a humidity of 45 per cent (saturation of the air) at 70°F. room temperature is considered good from a comfort standpoint.

In addition to health requirements a certain amount of moisture is necessary in a house to prevent the drying out and opening of joints in furniture and woodwork. Too much moisture, however, may result in condensation, and, because of these possibilities, it is essential that a proper average be maintained.

The room temperature is easily determined by means of a thermometer, but measurement of humidity is not familiar to the average householder. There are two instruments, the psychrometer and the hygrometer, which are used for measuring humidity and which are sold at reasonable prices by dealers in scientific instruments. Instructions for their use are usually furnished by the manufacturer.

SOURCES OF MOISTURE

Moisture in the air is traceable to numerous sources. House plants throw off moisture; steam from cooking and evaporation from the laundry and bathroom also contribute to the supply.

In localities where a considerable amount of gas is burned, a large portion of the moisture in the air often comes from that source. Gas is composed chiefly of compounds of carbon and hydrogen, and, in burning, the hydrogen unites with the oxygen in the air to form water vapor.

If the humidity is too great, it can be reduced by eliminating, insofar as possible, the sources of the moisture, and by frequent changing of air in the rooms by ventilation.

Much of the difficulty arising from the burning of gas may be overcome by providing an adequate vent or hood over the gas stove to carry the fumes to the outside.

During the heating season, the amount of moisture in the air of a house is often less than required, rather than more. In such cases, moisture may be supplied by means of various appliances used in connection with the heating system. There are also a number of humidifying devices on the market.

Installing storm doors and windows

Providing storm doors and windows is a more expensive method of keeping out the cold and retaining warmth in a house than some of those already mentioned, but storm doors and windows often pay for themselves within a reasonable period in reduced fuel bills.

STORM WINDOWS

When properly installed, storm windows provide a dead-air space, reducing heat conduction to the outside and preventing infiltration of cold air. They are particularly helpful in preventing frosting of windows, because they protect the surface of inner panes from chilling winds that cause condensation and subsequent freezing. If you cannot afford storm windows for all window openings, they may be provided for those on the side of the house facing prevailing winter winds.

To insure good protection, storm sashes should fit tightly. They may be fastened with ordinary wood screws, hooks and eyes or other devices. They may also be provided with a sliding opening in the bottom rail to admit air when it is desired; an even better way may be to hang them from the top on hinges or other hangers, so that they may be swung outward, when necessary, for ventilation or other purposes. If storm windows are hung, rather than fastened permanently in place, special care must be taken to obtain a good fit all around the sash. They may be held open when necessary by means of long hooks inserted in screw eyes or by special devices made for the purpose.

If the storm sash is placed flush with the facing board of the window casing, loose-pin butt hinges may be used to support them. This will allow the sash to be removed by simply pulling the pin of the hinge. In case ordinary hinges cannot be used, there are special storm-window hinges designed to fit any type of frame. A local hardware dealer may be consulted regarding the type of fastenings best fitted for use on a particular house.

STORM DOORS

Storm doors also involve extra cost, but in many cases it is profitable to install one on the windward side of the house. If made in the form of a vestibule it will prevent the inrush of cold air when the outside door is opened and provide a place to remove rubbers and shake off snow.

To save time in removing and replacing storm doors and screen doors, and to avoid the necessity of removing screws and plugging up screw holes, interchangeable loose-pin butt hinges may be used. Four hinges are required. Two hinge leaves are attached to the door jamb to serve both the storm and the screen door, and the two corresponding ones may be discarded. The remaining halves of the hinges should be attached to the doors, so as to fit into the two parts attached to the jamb.

Storm doors and windows should last a long time if they are kept well painted and are stored in a dry place during the summer (see "Storage Screen Hanger" in Chapter 8).

Treatment of walls to prevent sweating

Dampness may appear on the inside surfaces of exterior walls as a result of conditions other than leakage through mortar joints or around window frames. In some cases, such dampness is so pronounced that the frost can be swept off the walls during prolonged cold spells. It causes wallpaper to become loosened and stained and has similar damaging effects on other wall decorations. It also creates a damp, musty atmosphere in the rooms affected, which is unhealthful and generally unpleasant.

This dampness may come not from the outside as is often suspected, but be the result of condensation of moisture from the air in the room upon the cold surfaces of the plaster. It develops by the same process as that which causes beads of moisture to form on the outside surface of a pitcher of ice water on a warm day.

FURRING AND WATERPROOFING MASONRY DURING CONSTRUCTION

Whether or not insulating material is used, it is advisable to use furring strips (strips of wood to form an air space) on exterior walls, especially in regions subject to low temperature, high winds, heavy rains or extreme humidity of considerable duration. Where plaster is applied to a masonry wall without furring or other form of insulation, condensation may occur, and, in addition, any moisture which penetrates the joints will probably appear as wet spots on the plaster surface.

Furring is always advantageous, but it adds to the cost to such an extent that, in some cases, recourse is had to waterproofing applied to the inside surface of the masonry wall before plaster is put on. This waterproofing may be of bituminous material that is swabbed on with a roofer's mop, or may consist of a scratch coat of Portland cement mortar containing waterproofing compound. A recent development in bituminous waterproofing demands that the material be applied through a gun; this method is considered more efficient than swabbing. If bituminous or other plaster material is used, plaster should be applied while the bitumen is still sticky, to insure proper adhesion. Waterproofing of any kind when used by itself will tend to stop leakage only through the joints and will provide no insulation against condensation.

INSULATING OLD WALLS

The simplest way to treat old walls to make them warmer and prevent sweating is to nail furring strips over the old plaster upon which to apply new lath and plaster, insulating board or insulating material and wallboard.

Before the new surface is applied, it will probably be necessary to remove the trim and, when the wall is finished, to insert pieces of wood behind the trim before it is replaced, to bring it forward to form a suitable offset. Another method is to leave the old trim in place and to apply new trim on top of this after plastering.

Replastering, especially in a furnished house, can be rather objectionable because of dampness resulting from the large quantity of water required and because of the splashing and spattering in applying the materials. There are several good wallboards and insulating boards on the market, however, which can be applied upon the stripping in place of lath and plaster, and with less difficulty. A specially prepared joint-treating system is used with these boards, and when completed the wall has the appearance of a plastered surface and may be decorated if desired. Directions covering the application and decoration of these boards can be obtained from the manufacturers.

Insulating the attic

Heat passes through a wall or roof if there is a difference in temperature between the two sides. The direction of flow is from the warmer to the cooler side, and heat seeks the lowest temperature level just as water seeks the lowest level.

It is therefore apparent that to heat a house economically, it is necessary to prevent, as far as possible, this flow of heat. In the wintertime, for economy, the heat must be kept within the house; and in the summertime, for comfort, the out-of-doors heat must be kept out.

INSULATING MATERIALS

There is no material that will entirely stop the passage of heat through a wall or roof, but marked progress has been made in the manufacture of efficient insulating materials and there are many good brands on the market. Some are made in blanket form of soft, flexible materials such as felt, wood, hair and fiber, to be stretched and tucked between the studs, floor joists and rafters; others come in loose form and can be packed into hollow spaces; and others are in stiff board form to be used as sheathing, plaster base or merely as insulation.

The manufacturers of these materials will usually furnish literature describing their products and giving full instructions for applying them, as well as special advice when necessary.

WHERE INSULATION IS NEEDED

The roof is the most exposed part of the house, since it is subject to the direct rays of the sun in summer and to strong cold winds in winter. In an unfinished attic a great amount of heat is lost through the roof during the winter months. The rapid melting of snow on the roof is evidence of this. In the summertime the heat passes through into the attic, making the temperature in the upper part of the house almost unbearable. It is therefore important that the roof or the upper story of the house be insulated.

HOW TO IMPROVE CONDITIONS

If the attic is being used and there is necessity for keeping it at a comfortable temperature throughout the year, application of at least one-half inch—and preferably more—of good insulation to the underside of the roof rafters or against the roof boards between the rafters is advisable.

If there is no necessity for keeping the attic space at a comfortable temperature, insulation is best applied under the attic floor on top of or between the joists. If there is no floor, a few boards may be laid down to walk upon.

Spaces between the studs at the floor line should be boarded over. This boarding not only blocks the free passage of air from within the walls but also provides a fire stop, which is recommended for good construction.

Attic windows should be weather-tight and, if there are louvers or vents to admit air, they should be made to close like shutters or be provided with doors on the inside that can be closed during severe weather. The louvers should also be screened to keep out insects, especially those that injure woodwork.

Chapter Nine

FLOORS, STAIRS AND FLOOR COVERING

THE FLOORS in your house are made of wood. In certain places, however, such as the basement, they may be made of concrete. A floor is in constant use; it has to be kept in good condition by proper maintenance as well as by instant repairs should they become necessary.

Wood floors

Wood floors generally are constructed with a subfloor, building paper and a hard- or soft-wood flooring as a finish, as shown in Fig. 9.1. However, in construction that is not as meticulous, the subflooring is omitted and the finish flooring is placed directly over the joists. In such cases, the floorboards may loosen and produce a squeaky noise when you walk on them, cracks may occur in the wood, boards may become worn and the floor may even sag. To correct these conditions, the following methods should be used:

CREAKING FLOORS

When floors creak the trouble may lie in either layer of the floor. The joist nailing may be loose. If the subflooring boards are exposed on the underside of the floor, merely nail a cleat along the joists as added support to the board that creaks. Or you may insert a thin wooden wedge between the subfloor board and the joists, as shown in Fig. 9.2.

If the ceiling in the room below the subfloor is finished, you may not find the cause of the creak too easily. Tap the floor with a hammer until you locate the nearest joist, then drive in two or three long floor-finishing nails, at an angle, going through the floor and into the joists. Beware of cracking the floorboards while doing this; use a nail set to drive the nail below the wood surface, then fill the hole above the nail with plastic wood filler.

A board may be loose in the floor; this should be nailed into place and nail set at an angle as described in foregoing paragraph.

A simple solution to creaking may be to apply hot glue between the loose boards, very carefully, warming the floor boards first to get good adherence.

CRACKS IN BOARDS

Clean the crack thoroughly with a wire brush. Fill it with putty or plastic wood filler, packed down tightly. These materials are available at your hardware dealer; but, if you want to mix your own filler, you may do so by combining sawdust and glue to the proper thick consistency.

Should the crack be large, it may be best to cut a strip of matching wood, force it into the opening and glue it securely (Fig. 9.3).

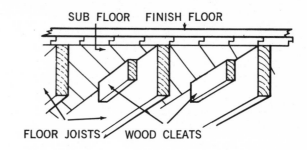

Fig. 9.1

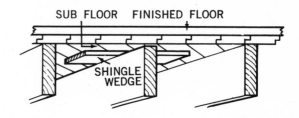

Fig. 9.2

Fig. 9.3

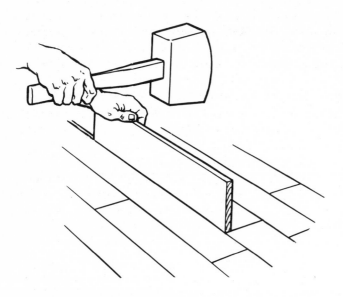

PLANING WORN BOARDS

A board may be worn from too much walking over it. To smooth it, first make sure the floor is meticulously clean and dry. If there are any cracks, clean them thoroughly with a wire brush. All nails should be driven below the floor surface to avoid their damaging the plane's sharp edge.

Set your smoothing plane to a medium cut and go over the high places in the floor, working in the direction of the grain of the wood. Then set the plane to make a finer cut, and go over the irregular spots to even them. The last step is to go over the smoothed spots with sandpaper.

REPLACING WORN BOARDS

See where the floor boards have been joined originally, and you will find that the line of nails indicates the position of the joist. Bore a hole in the board, near the side of the joist, big enough for a keyhole saw to go through. Saw the board at the point where it is closest to the joist. Now work back along the board until you reach the other end (where it is nailed to the next joist). You may need to remove the whole board; but, if only part of it is damaged, you can saw it through near a joist and leave the other part of the board intact. Pry up the damaged board (or part of it) from the joist, then remove the nails with a claw hammer.

Extra Precautions: Be careful not to damage any water or gas pipes or electrical connections that might be in the vicinity of the floor you are repairing.

If you need to remove a few boards because of damage, cut the replacement boards in uneven lengths so you will not join them all over the same joist, since that might put a strain on the joist. For additional support, before nailing the floor board to joist, first nail a cleat (three inches wide by two inches thick) to the side of the joist under the spot where new board will be applied.

If your floor is made of tongued-and-grooved boards, you will need to saw across the tongue before you pry up the board. With a chisel remove the pieces of tongue left in the remaining floor board. You will need to use great care when positioning the new board to make sure the tongued edge matches the grooved edge on the board left in the floor.

SAGGING FLOORS

To measure the sag, stretch a string taut across the floor, at right angles to the joists. Tack each end of the string to the floor, at opposite sides of the room. If at any point between the string and the floor board you find space, you know you have a sag and where it is located.

A special screw jack, with adjustable steep posts, is available at hardware dealers, for the purpose of lifting the sag in the floor. You may need to use more than one jack, and you must have accessible space underneath the room (such as a cellar) to accommodate the jack post.

As shown in Fig. 9.4, set the bottom of the post on a firm foundation, such as a concrete floor in a basement, or a masonry base built on the ground if there is no rigid flooring.

On top of the post set a very strong beam, and then place the jack so that the beam is at right angles to the floor joists. You may need to use the jack post only temporarily to correct the sag, while you erect a wood post and beam to go under the sag in the floor; in this case put the jack post off-center under the sag, so you will have room to install the wood post centrally under the sag. However, you may find it desirable to leave the

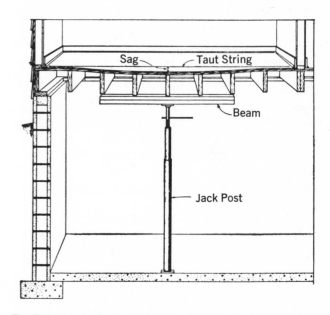

Fig. 9.4

jack post as a permanent fixture; in this case there is no need to build a wood post.

Wood stairways

Repairs to stairs follow the same general procedure as a wood floor when it comes to cracks, creaks or worn surfaces.

If a board on one of the steps becomes loosened, it may be because either the tread or the riser is worn. Examine the step to see which board is at fault. It may be necessary to remove it and replace it with a new one. Use the old board as a pattern to cut the new board to size. Place the new tread on top of the stringers, which are the side pieces supporting the stairway. Then nail the tread into the stringers, using finishing nails. Complete the job by nailing the top of the tread to the riser below it.

Finishing floor surfaces

For a transparent finish that will remain as near the color of the wood floor as possible, you may choose either varnish, shellac or a clear, penetrating floor sealer.

1. Varnish produces a deeper luster and is more glossy than other finishes. It is not slippery if left unwaxed and does not discolor if washed with water and soap.

2. Shellac is a quick-drying finish. It does not make the color of the wood any deeper. It dries quickly, but cannot be washed with water and soap. Therefore it may be best to use it as a first coat under another finish.

3. Penetrating floor sealers penetrate the wood surface, seal the wood fibers in a solid mass and give a velvety sheen to the floor. The floor must be thoroughly clean before the sealer is applied to the wood. This finish is resistant to stains and to water and soap, and does not chip or show scratches. If worn spots occur when the floor is finished with a sealer, they may be refinished without refinishing the whole floor.

For a finish that will change the color of the floor boards, you can use a varnish stain or a colored wood sealer. Or you can use a coat of oil stain and over this apply a coat of varnish, shellac or sealer.

If you don't want the floor boards to show through at all, paint the surface with a coating of enamel made especially for floors (see "Painting Floor Surfaces" later in this section).

When you want to achieve a perfectly smooth finish on open-grain wood, use paste wood filler or filler-sealer. First thin the filler to a heavy consistency, and apply it to the wood with the grain. Then, after it loses its wet gloss, use a cloth to rub it across the grain. Work in small areas, applying only as much filler as may be wiped off before it has a chance to harden.

REFINISHING FLOOR SURFACES

Before applying a new finish, you must remove all the old finish. An electric sanding machine, which may be rented from a hardware dealer, is the best way to do this. If no sander is available, you may need to remove the old finish manually with coarse sandpaper. Sanding must be done with the grain of the wood, not across it.

Fill holes or cracks with plastic wood filler or any other filler recommended by your hardware dealer for your special purpose. Any spots of wax, grease or oil should be removed with turpentine, naptha or whatever other cleaning agent you prefer to use.

You may want to bleach the floor; for this purpose add ¾ pound oxalic acid to 1 gallon hot water. When the floor is dry, rinse with denatured alcohol.

CAUSES OF FAILURE IN FINISHING

You may have difficulty in getting the floor finish to dry properly. If so, one of the following may be the cause:

Are you applying the coating too heavily? Try applying the finish in a thin film, according to manufacturer's directions.

Does the surface have grease or wax spots, or is it damp? Remove all grease and wax, and make sure the floor is completely dry.

Are you doing the job in cold, damp weather? Wait until the indoor temperature is between $60°F.$ and $90°F.$ Also provide for cross ventilation in the room.

Do you have difficulty with the second coat? Perhaps the first coat isn't completely dry before you apply the second one. Test the first coat for thorough dryness by pressing your thumb down on it; if you leave a thumbprint, the base coat isn't ready for the second one.

Painting floor surfaces

If a floor is discolored and in poor condition, it may be more practical to cover the imperfections with two or three coats of porch and deck enamel than to refinish by other methods. First remove all dirt, grease and wax from the floor, to produce an attractive, abrasive-resistant finish.

Enamels are obtainable in many colors, and they may be applied as a solid color or to give a splatter-dash effect by using several colors.

Follow the manufacturer's directions for thinning and time allowed for drying between coats. After the last coat is thoroughly dry, apply two coats of solvent-thinned wax and then buff to achieve the desired gloss.

To keep the floor clean, use a dry mop on the surface. When wax coating becomes worn in traffic areas, renew it with new wax application.

Concrete floors

Usually concrete floors are finished with a smooth surface, are strong and don't need much maintenance. However, you may need to make some repairs, and the way to handle them is given in the following sections.

REPAIRS TO SURFACE

Once the surface cracks it needs to be refinished with new material. The new finish should be of concrete reinforced with wire mesh and at least two inches thick.

Sometimes the concrete, if not of finest workmanship and quality, may produce "powder" on the surface of the floor. To reduce this powdering apply two coats of a solution made of 2 pounds magnesium fluosilicate dissolved in 1 gallon cold water. Paint on one coat and let it dry for twenty-four hours, then apply the second coat. This should harden the surface; if it doesn't you may need to paint the floor.

VARNISHING AND PAINTING

Often a colored pigment is mixed with the concrete when laying the floor. In such cases the surface may be treated with a seal of penetrating varnish. Floor stains and dyes that penetrate the surface may also be used. These should be scrubbed onto the floor surface with a bristle brush.

On a colored or varnished concrete floor, a bright luster may be achieved by a periodical waxing of the surface. Use a floor polishing machine to buff on the wax.

PAINTING FLOOR

You may obtain paint for concrete floor surfaces in a selection of colors, in the two following categories:

Use floor and deck enamel of varnish type on a floor in a room that is thoroughly dry and where no moisture from condensation or seepage may affect the floor.

Rubber-base paint may be used in a room where there may be occasional dampness.

A concrete floor in the basement should not be painted until it is about a year old and has had time to age properly. Before painting, the floor must be thoroughly dry. If you have heat in the basement, the best time to paint the floor is early spring or winter, when humidity is low. If this is the first time the floor is to be painted, you will need to apply three coats. The first coat should be thin, for penetration; the second and third coats should be of the usual thicker consistency. Apply a coat of floor wax when the paint surface is dry.

REPAINTING FLOOR

If some worn spots appear in a painted and waxed floor, scrub the surface with a cloth dipped in turpentine or petroleum spirits; then while still wet rub the spots with steel wool to remove the wax. Then apply new paint and finish.

If the old floor paint shows considerable wear, remove paint by mopping the surface with a mixture of 2 pounds caustic soda (usual household lye) dissolved in 1 gallon hot water. This wet solution should remain on the floor for half an hour; then wash the floor with clear hot water and at the same time scrape it with a wide steel scraper. Rinse the surface with clean water.

An alternate way of removing badly worn paint is by soaking some sawdust in the caustic solution, then spreading a thin layer of the sawdust over the floor. Let it remain overnight, and the next morning wash the floor with hot water and use the wide steel scraper to take off the old paint. Rinse the surface with clear water.

If your floor has a rubber-base paint surface, you may not find the caustic soda an effective treatment. If it is not effective, you may need to use a remover of an organic solvent type, which your paint dealer can supply.

Extra Precautions: Be extremely careful not to get any of the caustic soda on your skin, into your eyes or on your clothes. Work slowly and avoid splashing.

Types of floor covering

The choice of materials to use over the surface of the floor is large and varied; coverings are made of linoleum, vinyl plastics, cork tile, asphalt tile and many other types that are available in the shops. A floor must be covered in a professional manner, since it needs to last a long time and is a focal point of your decorating scheme. If you feel that you cannot produce the best result, even when following the manufacturer's directions, it may be best to call in a skilled person for the task.

Before installing any floor covering, the surface of the floor must be thoroughly smooth and clean. Any rough spots should be removed by sandpaper or other abrasive. If your dealer feels a lining is needed between the floor and the covering to be laid upon it, he will suggest the one that is most practical.

The covering you choose will depend on the room into which it is to go, your decorating scheme and of course your budget. Following are the types and characteristics of the coverings from which you may choose; the instructions to maintain them will be available at the dealer where you make the purchase:

Inlaid linoleum (sheet or tile) is durable; the pattern goes through the entire thickness and is suitable for the decorating scheme of every room in the house. Although it is a very strong covering, it is not recommended for the basement or any floors that have contact with the ground.

Printed linoleum is not as expensive as inlaid linoleum, nor is it as durable, and the pattern is printed only on top. It is not recommended for basements or floors that have contact with the ground.

Asphalt (sheet or tile) may be used almost anywhere in the house. Its colors and design go through the entire thickness and therefore cannot wear off. It may be used over a basement concrete floor, or on a concrete slab laid directly on the ground. While it is resistant to water, stains, abrasion and fire, it is not recommended on floors where there is a likelihood of spilled oil or grease.

Vinyl plastic (sheet or tile) is a sturdy and resilient covering, is easy to maintain and lasts a long time. It is sound-absorbent and is resistant to grease, acid, alkalis and solvents.

Rubber (sheet or tile) is sound-absorbent and therefore quiet to walk on. It may be used in any room. It prevents skidding and does not need as much waxing as do other types of floor covering. Dirt does not penetrate it, and it is resistant to fire and to insects.

Cork (sheet or tile) is suitable in the living room, bedroom, nursery and playroom. It is comfortable to walk on and is sound-absorbent.

Concrete, marble and *terrazzo* make very strong floors and are usually easy to maintain. Concrete is an economical material, but marble is fairly expensive.

Clay tile, stone and slate make very durable floors, are easy to keep clean, heat-resistant and may be used both indoors and outdoors. Clay tile is good for kitchen and bathroom floors.

Carpeting and *rugs* are usually used directly on the wood floor or laid over linoleum or other covering. Before laying a carpet or a large rug on a wood floor, make sure to correct any protruding nailheads or other defects in the flooring that might cause tearing of the carpet threads. Usually a pad is placed on the floor, under the carpet or rug; the pad may be bought in felt, foam rubber or other such material. If small scatter rugs are used, you cannot keep a pad under them; but you may make them skidproof by painting the underside of the rug with a thick rubbery liquid made especially to prevent sliding; directions are given on the container in which you buy it. Some scatter rugs may be bought with foam-rubber backing, which adds safety to their use.

Chapter Ten

INTERIOR WALLS AND CEILINGS

Repairing cracks

ALTHOUGH WALLS AND CEILINGS are covered with various materials such as wood paneling, wallboard and wall tile, which are discussed later in this chapter, the most common covering is plaster as the base for a finish, for paint or for wallpaper. There are many reasons for cracks and other defects in plastered walls and ceilings, but the most common are the following:

Structural cracks are caused by structural weaknesses in a building, chief among which are either settlement resulting from inadequate or improperly located footings, the use of undersized or improperly spaced members, omission of bracing or shrinkage of lumber. These cracks are usually large and well defined, extending across the surface and through the plaster. They may start near the corner of a door or window, or run up and down the corner where two walls join, or along the joints between walls and ceiling.

Map cracks are caused by inferior workmanship and the use of poor-quality plastering materials. They are usually caused by improper bonding between the plaster and the base. They are less noticeable than structural cracks and go through the plaster, but do not extend entirely across the surface, as do the latter. They are made up of a series of cracks running at various angles and embracing areas usually six or more inches across.

Shrinkage cracks have causes similar to those of map cracks. They resemble map cracks, except that the cracks themselves and the areas they enclose are much smaller. They differ from the map cracks inasmuch as they do not go entirely through the plaster and are usually confined to the finish coat. Careless workmanship is usually the cause of these cracks. In a sanded finish they are caused by plaster that has been allowed to dry too rapidly or has

not been sufficiently troweled. Troweling at the wrong time in a white finish will often produce equally unsatisfactory results.

Loose plaster is sometimes caused by the fact that the keys or clinches that hold the plaster to the base break off or become loosened and cause the plaster to bulge and crack. On ceilings especially, it will often hang in this condition for a long time before falling off, being held together by the hair or fiber in the plaster. Occasionally the nails or fastenings used to hold laths in place may corrode and break, allowing that part of the plaster covering the loosened lath, or laths, to sag and crack.

Plaster repairs

To remedy small holes and cracks you will need a small diamond-shaped mason's trowel or a broad-bladed putty knife. For larger areas you will also need a plasterer's trowel. Plaster may be mixed with plaster of Paris, ordinary glue and clean water, but if you want to save yourself this task, you can purchase a commercial patching plaster.

MIXING PLASTER

Plaster should be mixed in a clean box or pan, and the water must also be clean. Do not mix a new batch of patching plaster in a container that was previously used for the purpose unless it is absolutely free of all particles of old plaster.

First place the water in the mixing box, then sift the dry plaster into the water. Start with a small amount of water, adding more as needed. Stir thoroughly to dissolve

60

all lumps. The mixture should be of a putty consistency so that it may be picked up on a trowel or knife and forced into the crack or the hole in the wall.

PLASTER OF PARIS

If you use only a small amount of fresh plaster, you may use plaster of Paris alone. Bear in mind that it sets very quickly and if the plaster is to be used without a retarder, mix at one time only as much as can be applied in ten minutes or less.

RETARDER FOR SETTING PLASTER

If you find the plaster sets too quickly for the repair job you are doing and that you have difficulty in getting it into place, you may retard the hardening by the addition of small amounts of ordinary glue dissolved in the mixing water. Commercial patching plasters generally contain retarding material, so they may usually be worked for a longer period than ordinary plaster of Paris. They may also contain other ingredients to improve the working qualities of the plaster; this information is on the label of the container or can be obtained from your dealer.

REPAIRING STRUCTURAL CRACKS

If a crack is deep, it is necessary that it be wide enough so that the fresh plaster may be forced in to form a good bond with the old plaster. If the crack is not sufficiently

Fig. 10.1

wide, it should be scraped with a knife blade until the opening is at least one-quarter inch across. Loose sand and plaster should be brushed out and the surface thoroughly wetted with water before fresh plaster is applied. The plaster should then be pressed well into place and struck off flush with the surface of the main body of plaster (Fig. 10.1). If the old plaster has not been thoroughly wetted, it may draw the water out of the fresh plaster, which may in turn dry out and remain in a chalky condition. You may prevent this by spraying water onto the surface after the plaster has set and keeping the surface damp for about twenty-four hours.

MAP AND SHRINKAGE CRACKS

These cracks usually occur only in the finish coat, and are generally so numerous that if the job has not been well done it will be necessary to refinish the whole surface; this work requires the services of an experienced plasterer.

LOOSE PLASTER

The loose plaster around each hole should be removed, the remaining sound plaster wetted thoroughly and the plaster applied in the same manner as prescribed for structural cracks. Because larger amounts of plaster are usually required for holes than for cracks, it is advisable to retard the setting of the plaster so that it may be worked for a longer period.

BULGED OR HANGING PLASTER

If the plaster is bulged or hanging it is best to remove all the loose plaster around the break and apply new material. In case the lath, or backing, has drawn away from the joists, it will have to be refastened before new plaster is applied. If the patch is an unusually large one, it is generally best to call in a plasterer, since this work requires so much skill that it is difficult for an amateur to perform a neat-looking job.

DEFECTIVE LATHS

Laths are nailed to the studs of the building, to create an air space and protect the plaster from penetration of moisture. Sometimes the laths may rot, break or become loose. When you buy replacement wood strips at the lumberyard, take along a piece of the old lath to be able to match it in thickness and type of wood.

To remove the damaged laths, first pry off the old plaster with hammer and chisel, allowing sufficient space to nail in the new laths. Take out the old lath, as shown in Fig. 10.2.

If the damage is not too big, you may not need to remove the lath, but simply to nail a piece of wallboard right over the defective part and cover it with plaster.

Before you put in new wood laths, soak them in a container of warm water for at least twenty-four hours

Fig. 10.2

before nailing them to the studs. In that way both the lath and the plaster over it will dry at the same time, which is preferable to applying damp plaster over dry wood. When putting in the new strips, start nailing them to the stud in the center of the lath, then nail at each end.

DRYING PLASTER

It is essential to have the plaster dry quickly. Keep windows open to get air circulation in rooms. Don't let the room reach the freezing point, however, since this might cause the plaster to set before the water has evaporated; this condition is usually called a sweat-out.

Nor should you do any plastering in very hot and dry weather, because the plaster may dry out before it is fully set, leaving soft spots that are usually called dry-outs. Should you have to work in hot, dry weather, however, spray the plaster with water to keep the wall or ceiling damp until the plaster has set. The ideal situation is to have fresh air circulation and the heat turned on for at least the first twenty-four hours if there is danger of freezing weather.

PAINTING PLASTER PATCHES

You run the risk of having a different shade over the patch, even if you use the same paint and same color as on the old wall. If the patch is done in a conspicuous part of the wall and you want to repaint the entire wall yet avoid any risk of the patch showing up lighter than the rest of the wall, first cover the wall with a sizing. You can buy a commercial sizing ready to be mixed with

water; the paint dealer will furnish you with specific instructions on how to mix and use it. After it has been sized you may paint over the entire wall.

Wall and ceiling paneling

An old wall or ceiling may be covered with a paneling of plywood; a composition wallboard such as gypsum board, fiberboard or asbestos-cement board; or with wood paneling. In some cases, wall tiles may be used. Paneling is not only functional in concealing old cracks or faded spots, but it is also helpful in giving a "new look" if you are modernizing the room decoration. Paneling may be used throughout the house, in any room you desire, as well as in the basement and attic.

Generally paneling comes in large sheets and is sold by the square foot. First measure the surface you want to cover, allowing margin of about ten per cent for waste when having to cut around odd dimensions in your room.

Some types of panels come in various colors and finishes so that they may not need any extra painting, varnishing, staining or papering after they are put up. However, since some panels may need a special finish, it is advisable to procure specific information and instructions from the dealer when you make your purchase.

Paneling a ceiling calls for professional skill; but if you want to attempt it, get a handy helper and follow the general directions given in the following for covering walls.

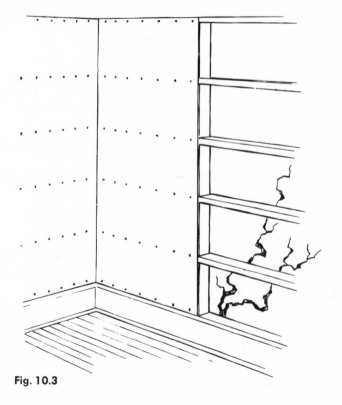

Fig. 10.3

APPLYING PANELS

Panels are not put directly onto the plaster. First nail furring strips (horizontal and vertical strips of wood) over the studs in the wall. The furring strips may be made of plywood, and should be at least two inches wide and one-quarter inch thick. The paneling should be cut to fit tightly at the floor or baseboard as well as at the ceiling. Nail the paneling to the furring strips with large-headed nails (Fig. 10.3).

Some types of wallboard may be applied with a resin glue coated to the furring strips and to the inside of the board. Press the board down. Then nail in place to the furring strip.

To cover the seams of wallboard panels before finishing them with paint or wallpaper, put a cloth tape with adhesive backing over the seams or fill in the spaces with plaster. On wood panels you may want to use molding at the seams.

At the ceiling and at the floor or baseboard, a quarter-round molding is a good finish. This type of molding is also recommended for doors and windows.

Wall tiling

Tiles may be bought in sheet form or single, but the former may be easier to handle. Tiles are available in metal or plastic, as well as in the usual ceramic materials. They come in many colors and designs, and have a smooth, waterproof finish. The method of installing them on your wall varies with the type of tile you buy. Your dealer will furnish you with specific directions.

CERAMIC TILE REPAIRS

The moment a tile becomes loose it must be secured in place to prevent its edges from crumbling or else replaced with a new tile.

Thoroughly clean out the space from which you remove the old tile. On the back of the new tile spread a thin coating of plastic cement (made especially for tiles, and available at a hardware or paint dealer). Set the tile into the space and press down until it starts to harden into place. If you use too much plastic cement, the excess will squeeze out under the tile. (If this occurs scrape it off while the cement is still damp.) Now fill the cracks, between the new tile and the tiles surrounding it, with the cement or with plaster of Paris. Do not touch the tile until it is completely dry.

Keeping walls and woodwork clean

Dirt and stains on papered or painted walls, as well as on the woodwork, may be removed if proper care is taken.

PAINTED WALLS AND WOODWORK

The quality and condition of the paint should be considered before you decide to wash it. Any paint can be destroyed by improper rubbing, by strong cleaning agents or by abrasive powders. Poor-quality paint and soft or flaky paint will sometimes wash away. To wash painted surfaces that are in good condition proceed as follows:

1. Use a mild soap or detergent solution, or one of the soap jelly preparations described at the end of this section.

2. Have on hand two containers, one for soapy water and one for rinse water.

3. Start at the bottom of the wall and work upward.

4. With a soft cloth or cellulose sponge apply the wash water or jelly to a small area at a time.

5. Rinse this area carefully. Be sure to squeeze the excess water from the cloth or sponge each time.

6. Change the rinse water frequently.

7. Avoid unnecessary rubbing that may soften the paint.

8. Dry with a soft clean cloth.

Many commercial paint cleaners are excellent if you follow directions carefully. Some cleaners do not need to be rinsed off.

Soap jellies are easy to apply and are excellent cleaning agents. Other products are sometimes added to improve the cleaning action. Whiting can be mixed with a little jelly to remove stubborn spots, and glue is often added to speed the cleaning action of the soap.

Soap Jelly. Dissolve 1 cup soap flakes in 4 cups boiling water. Pour into wide-mouthed glass jars. Use when cool and jelled.

Whiting and Soap Jelly Paste. Mix well 4 parts fine whiting and 1 part soap jelly. Apply with a soft cloth and rub lightly.

Glue and Soap Jelly. Dissolve 4 tablespoons (1 ounce) granulated glue in 1 cup cold water, and let stand 1 hour to soften. (Do not use a casein or synthetic glue, since it may not be satisfactory.) Then dissolve 3 cups soap flakes in 2 quarts boiling water. Add the softened glue mixture to the hot soap solution and stir until dissolved. Let the mixture stand until it jells. Apply with a damp cloth or sponge to a small area. Rinse the area and wipe it off before the solution dries.

CAUTION: Soap jelly and glue solution is difficult to remove if it dries on the surface or runs onto a dry soiled surface.

PAPERED WALLS

General cleaning for both washable and nonwashable wallpaper involves frequent light dusting with a vacuum cleaner attachment, a soft brush or a clean cloth over a clean dry mop or broom. It is usually better to start at the top of the room and brush downward. If there are cobwebs, however, remove them with a lifting stroke. They are greasy and may cause streaking if brushed downward.

For heavily soiled surfaces, the method of cleaning depends on the type of paper. Washable paper may be washed gently with cold water and a mild soap. First wet the area to be cleaned, then apply suds gently with a sponge. Rinse off the suds with a sponge wrung out of cold water. Avoid rubbing and unnecessary wetting. Both types of paper may be cleaned by commercial or homemade wallpaper cleaners.

One popular recipe for wallpaper cleaner contains 4 teaspoons baking soda, 2 cups flour, 2½ tablespoons household ammonia and 1¼ cups water. Stir the soda into the flour. Mix the ammonia with the flour and soda, and add the water. Beat the mixture until smooth. Steam it in a double boiler for 1¼ hours, and keep it covered until the cleaner is cool enough to handle. Then knead it in your hands until it is as smooth and soft as art gum. Use it as follows:

1. Test the cleaner on an inconspicuous spot of the wallpaper to see how it works.
2. Start at the top of the room and rub gently with a downward stroke, kneading the cleaner as you work.
3. Overlap the strokes to prevent streaks.
4. Dust with a soft cloth to remove crumbs.

WALLPAPER SPOTS AND STAINS

Spots and stains are not easy to remove from wallpaper. Immediate treatment, however, is usually more successful than cleaning after the stain has been allowed to penetrate. The following are suggestions for possible treatment of this kind of soil:

Grease, on nonwashable paper. If fresh, it may be partly removed by applying a clean blotter to the spot and pressing over the blotter with a warm iron. Then make a paste of fuller's earth (or other absorbent powder) and carbon tetrachloride. Cover the spot with this mixture and let it remain until dry. Remove with a cloth dampened with carbon tetrachloride.

CAUTION: Some pigments "bleed" when carbon tetrachloride is applied. Test on a small inconspicuous area first.

Grease, on washable paper. Use the same method given above. The treatment may be followed by washing the paper.

Crayon, on nonwashable or washable paper. Scrape off as much of the crayon as possible with a table knife. Sponge lightly with a cloth dampened with a fat solvent such as carbon tetrachloride, acetone or denatured alcohol, or apply a blotter to the crayon spots and press with a warm iron.

Ink, on nonwashable paper. Blot up surplus quickly. Apply absorbent powder such as cornstarch or table salt. Brush off as fast as it takes up the ink. Repeat. An ink eradicator may also be used. Several light applications are usually preferable to an extended one.

CAUTION: Ink eradicator may remove color from the paper. First test an inconspicuous area of the wallpaper.

Ink, on washable paper. Use the same method as in (4). Instead of the ink eradicator, if you prefer, it may be possible to apply a chlorine bleach, carefully. Pat the spot gently with a cloth dampened with bleach. Wash the bleach off with water. Avoid rubbing.

Chapter Eleven

PAINTING AND VARNISHING MATERIALS AND METHODS

PAINTING AND VARNISHING is a broad subject, and because it involves so many different kinds of materials and practices it will not be possible to treat it fully here. However, since such work is necessary to a certain extent in the household, and since there are many paint jobs that can be done satisfactorily by a person with little or no experience, some of the fundamental principles of this work will be discussed.

Much useful information will be found in the directions printed on container labels and in booklets distributed by the manufacturers of paint materials. These instructions should be carefully followed, since different materials usually require different handling to produce the best results.

Buying and mixing paint

The quality of paint, varnish and other materials used on surfaces to preserve them or improve their appearance is of great importance. It is also essential to have good brushes with which to apply the materials. Without good materials and tools no amount of care or skill on the part of the worker will produce satisfactory results.

Where a large quantity of paint is required, considerable saving may be effected by purchasing the necessary ingredients and mixing the paint yourself when needed. If, however, only a small amount is needed and you are not willing to risk mixing your own paint, it is better

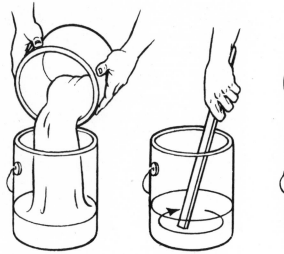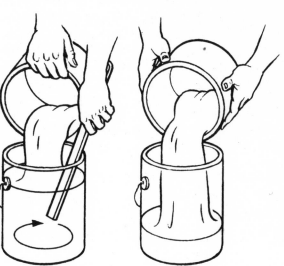

Fig. 11.1

65

to buy it ready-mixed. There are many high-grade paints on the market, and if you buy one of these in the original sealed container of the manufacturer you need have no fear regarding its quality.

MIXING OR BOXING

Since paint is a mixture of solid and liquid components, it is important to mix thoroughly the contents of the container before using any portion thereof. To do this, follow the steps illustrated in Fig. 11.1.

1. Pour the greater portion of the liquid contents of the can into a clean bucket somewhat larger than the paint can.

2. With a stiff paddle loosen the settled pigment in the original container and, with a figure-eight motion, mix thoroughly.

3. Stir the mixture vigorously while slowly adding the liquid that was previously poured off the top.

4. Complete the mixing by pouring the paint back and forth several times from one container to the other.

STRAINING

Paints should be strained after they have been mixed, to remove hard lumps and skin and to mix the ingredients more completely. A piece of wire fly screen may be used for this purpose, or, better still, a suitable strainer may be made by tying a double thickness of cheesecloth over the top of an empty pail. Pour the paint slowly through the cloth, using a small brush to stir the paint in the cloth pocket until it all passes through.

PROTECTION

When not in use the paint container should be covered to prevent evaporation.

Paint removers

You may want to use one of three methods of application: brush, spray or roller. If you are undecided which is best for your purpose, your paint dealer will be able to advise you. These methods will be discussed later in this chapter. However, whichever you use, it is essential that, before you start, the surface on which you will apply the finish be thoroughly clean. Do not put new paint, enamel or varnish on a dirty or cracked surface.

To remove peeling paint or smooth rough spots, you may need to resort to either a scraper or a wire brush, or sandpaper or other abrasive material. To fill nail holes or plaster cracks, you may need to use putty or plaster. Sometimes it may be preferable to remove the paint from the entire surface; for this procedure you may need a chemical paint remover.

CHEMICAL REMOVER

You may buy a commercially prepared paint remover with accompanying directions for use. It may come either in a pressurized aerosol spray can, in prepared liquid form or in powder that you will mix to make a liquid.

Usually a liquid remover is preferred. For this method you require a large paintbrush, a two-inch scraping knife, steel wool, a wire brush, a pail to hold the remover, alcohol to wash the surface after the old paint has been scraped off and cloths.

Apply the remover with the flat side of the paintbrush, going in one direction. Apply a thick coating, so you won't need to add more later. Work quickly for twenty minutes, applying the remover to as much of the area as possible. Then go back to the spot where you began the application and, with the scraping knife, test to see if the old paint or varnish is sufficiently soft to come off. As soon as you find it comes off easily, scrape with the knife. Continue applying remover to the next surface area for twenty minutes more, scraping off paint or varnish when the area is soft enough. Sometimes it may be necessary to apply the remover a second time and go through the scraping a second time. Do not try to hurry the remover; let it stay on longer if you think it necessary.

If you use an aerosol spray remover, follow directions on the container. The general procedure is similar to the liquid remover.

When all the paint is scraped off, soak the cloths in the alcohol and wash over the surface. Although it is not usually the case, there may be some roughness on the surface after the paint is removed. If so, go over it with fine sandpaper to achieve proper smoothness before applying paint or varnish.

Suitable painting conditions

There is often a wrong time to do painting, and if you paint at such times results may not prove as good as you desire. Weather conditions have to be taken into consideration.

EXTERIOR WOOD AND METAL

These surfaces must be painted only in dry, clear weather, when the temperature is not below 50°F. In cold weather stop painting early in the afternoon, so that the paint will have had time to set should the temperature suddenly drop lower.

Wood surfaces must be thoroughly dry and seasoned before you apply paint.

Masonry surfaces must be dry if you use oil-base paints; however, if you use rubber-base, resin-emulsion or cement-water paints they may be applied to damp surfaces.

INTERIOR PAINTING

Interior painting may be done any time of the year provided the house is warm and you have sufficient air circulation to allow the fumes of the paint to be carried off.

DRYING TIME

Do not rush a second coat over the first one until sufficient time has elapsed for the first one to dry to a hard surface. Allow at least eighteen hours for paint to dry on floors, wood trim, metal or plaster before applying a second coat. Allow at least twenty-four hours for oil paint to dry on exterior wood surfaces and, if there is no reason to rush, let it dry for several days before another coat is applied.

PAINTING METHODS

The three general methods of applying paint are by brush, spray or roller. If you are not sure which would be best for your purpose, consult your paint dealer.

Use and care of paint brushes

The importance of a good brush cannot be overestimated. Besides wearing better than a poor one, it holds more paint, does not leak or spatter, leaves a clean-cut edge, produces a more uniform finish and does not shed its bristles.

Though brushes with bristles set in cement or vulcanized in rubber cost somewhat more than other varieties, the investment always proves to be a wise one. The best advice that can be given is to buy good brushes and take proper care of them.

SELECTION OF BRUSHES

The shape and size of the brushes depend both upon the materials used and the types of surfaces to be treated. For painting broad surfaces, flat brushes four inches wide with four-inch bristles are recommended for the unskilled. Such a brush is easy to handle, and surfaces may be covered rapidly with it. With wide, flat brushes, however, the paint cannot be rubbed out as well as with a suitable round brush. For window sashes and other narrow surfaces a one-inch oval brush with a chisel-shaped end is generally used. Varnish brushes are also tapered at the end in order to permit the necessary even flowing-on of the material. A very wide brush is usually employed in applying whitewash or calcimine, since these materials are spread lightly over the surface and are not rubbed in.

CARE OF BRUSHES

When a painting job is carried over from one day to the next, it is generally sufficient to wrap the brushes in several thicknesses of paper to keep them soft and pliable. If, however, a brush is not to be used for several days, it should be well cleaned before putting it away.

One of the most satisfactory materials for washing a brush is turpentine, but kerosene can be used with almost equally good results. After removing as much paint as possible with one of these solvents, wash the brush thoroughly with soap and warm water and shake all excessive moisture out before hanging it up to dry, bristles down. After the brush is thoroughly dry, wrap it in paper to protect it from dust, being careful not to bend the ends of the bristles.

If much painting is being done the brushes may be left suspended in the paint or in linseed oil to keep them in good condition. To keep the oil from getting fatty, a little turpentine may be added from time to time. The brush can be suspended by drilling a small hole through the handle near the top of the ferrule or binding, pushing a straight piece of wire through the hole and resting the ends of the wire on the edges of the pail or container, as shown in Fig. 11.2. Some brushes are made with holes drilled for this purpose. The bristles of the brush should be completely submerged in the liquid, but the ends should not touch the bottom of the container, since pressure tends to bend or curl the ends of the bristles and ruin the brush.

In general, a varnish brush may be suspended in the varnish in which it is used and may be cleaned by washing it first with turpentine and then with warm water and soap.

Brushes used with whitewash and calcimine should simply be washed thoroughly in clean water, then hung up to dry with the bristles pointing down.

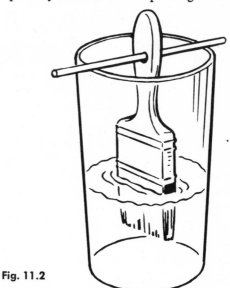

Fig. 11.2

USING THE BRUSH

Dip the brush lightly into the paint, immersing more than half the length of the bristles. Then slap the brush against the side (inside) of the paint can to remove excess paint and avoid dripping from the brush.

Use slightly curved, light strokes to apply the paint, and gradually lift the brush from the spot to avoid leaving a thick edge of paint (Fig. 11.3). Apply the paint only with the end of the bristles, and reverse the brush frequently.

When you apply varnish or enamel, use light, short strokes, and let the finish flow together with as little brushing as possible. Sometimes there may be sags or runs in enamel; check for this condition within thirty minutes so they won't have a chance to dry. If you find any sags or runs, brush them out with very light strokes.

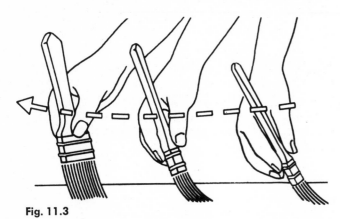

Fig. 11.3

When applying flat wall paint, you can use a heavier brush stroke. Start each brushful of paint on a dry surface, working toward the wet edge of the area you just painted. When painting walls, start at the top and carry the brush down to the baseboard of the floor in narrow strips; this will not give the paint edges a chance to dry out and show marks where the brush stroke overlapped.

When you are painting a narrow strip use the flat side of the brush. If you use the edge the bristles may divide into clumps, and should these clumps remain in the brush for a few hours they may remain that way permanently. For narrow surfaces use a sash brush.

Have an old brush at hand to use when you have to paint into corners. If you use a good brush the bristles may become distorted.

Further discussion of painting the interior and exterior of a house with a brush is taken up in the two following chapters.

Spray painting

While this method is faster than using a brush, the finish may not be as smooth if the spray gun is not properly handled.

TYPES OF SPRAY GUNS

Spray guns come in various sizes and types; but for the householder the motorized spray gun that may be at-

tached to the vacuum cleaner is easy to use; it works well with thin liquids because the air pressure is low.

You may be able to rent a pot-type spray outfit from a paint dealer; this holds about three gallons of paint and may be used for spraying the exterior surfaces of your house because it works without refilling for two hours.

In the pot type used for interior painting, the container holds about a quart of paint and is attached to the spray gun.

You will need three spray tips: one to be flexible and have a wide range, another to produce a flat fan-shaped pattern on flat surfaces and the third tip bent at an angle for work on the ceiling.

BEFORE SPRAYING STARTS

1. Surfaces must be cleaned thoroughly, rough spots smoothed with sandpaper and dust wiped off.

2. Cover all furniture and floors with canvas drop cloths or old sheets or papers to prevent spray from settling on them.

3. Cover wall switches, doorknobs and lighting fixtures with masking tape. You can procure this tape at the hardware store.

4. Also use masking tape along frames of mirrors and windows. Coat the glass with masking compound, available at paint or automobile supply dealers. If you cannot

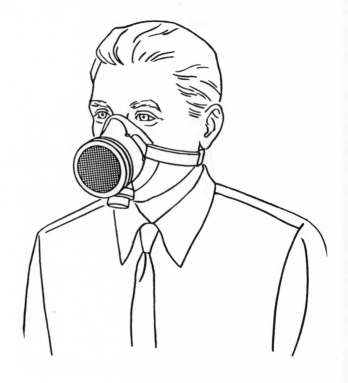

Fig. 11.4

conveniently use masking, make a shield from a piece of stiff cardboard or metal that you will move along as you spray.

5. Strain the paint through a clean, lint-free cloth before you use it in the spray gun.

6. Adjust the gun and do some test spraying on scrap material to get the right flow of paint. Practice handling the spray; hold the gun in one hand and use the other hand to keep the air hose clear of the surface you are spraying. Keep the spray tip six to ten inches from the surface that is being painted. During the trial sprays, adjust the gun for a speed consistent with your ability to handle it and with the desired finish.

AVOID HAZARDS

1. Wear a respirator, as shown in Fig. 11.4, for outdoor as well as indoor painting. This protects you against paint poisoning.

2. Wear a cap to prevent drift spray from going into your hair.

3. Do not smoke while you are spraying!

4. Do not spray near an open flame or any place where there may be flying sparks.

5. Ventilation is necessary when painting indoors. Keep windows wide open. Never spray in a closed room unless you have an exhaust fan going.

HOW TO SPRAY

The dealer from whom you buy or rent the equipment will have directions from the manufacturer, and it is advisable for you to read them. Use the spray as follows:

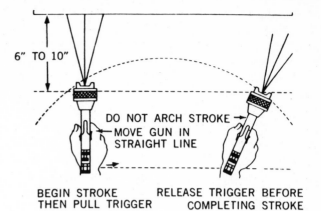

Fig. 11.5b

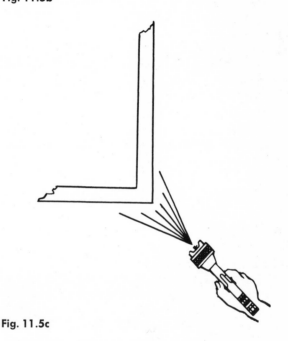

Fig. 11.5c

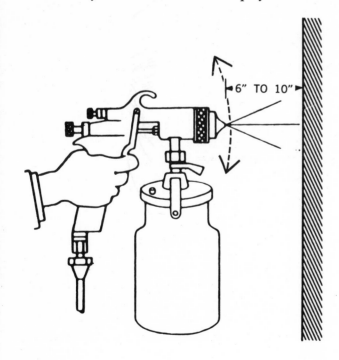

Fig. 11.5a

Keep the spray as nearly perpendicular as possible to the surface being painted. This prevents dusting, a condition in which paint spray evaporates and hits the surface in nearly dry particles. Figure 11.5a shows by dotted lines how to tilt the gun so the surface may be sprayed on one side from a shorter distance, thus applying more paint at this point.

Use a free arm motion and feather-cut the end of each stroke (b). This is done by pulling the gun trigger after beginning the stroke and releasing it before the stroke is completed. Do not arch the gun; this causes an uneven deposit of paint and excessive overspray at the end of the stroke.

When approaching a corner, stop one or two inches short of the corner. Holding the gun in the position shown (c), spray the entire corner in one operation.

If a large area, such as a wall, is being sprayed, start

at the upper corner and work from right to left (or the reverse if you are left-handed). Keep moving down as each swath is laid on the surface. Generally the center half of the last sprayed strip gets the thickest paint coat; lap the upper fourth of each new stroke over the lower fourth of the preceding stroke. On each stroke start swinging the gun from a point to one side of where the spray is to begin. When you reach the starting point, press the trigger and hold it down until you reach the outer edge where spray ends. Keep the tip of the gun always at the same distance from the surface so that the spray will strike at right angles. Don't change the speed of your stroke. If you should stop or slow up without releasing the trigger, you will let too much paint accumulate on the surface at that spot, causing a run or a snag.

Roller painting

When you buy a roller it usually comes with its special slanted metal tray into which you pour the paint. Roller painting has become a popular family project, being much easier in many ways than brush or spray painting. The size and cover of the roller and the paint you need for your purpose will be explained by your paint dealer, and manufacturers' directions accompany the material.

ROLLER COVERS

Dynel is a good all-purpose cover for use with oil- or water-base paint.

Wool is used only for oil flat paint. It is not good for rubber- or water-base paint.

Dacron is used with heavy exterior paint.

Mohair is used with heavy-bodied enamels.

Fleecy type covers are used with oil-base paint and can produce different kinds of finishes.

Carpet cover is used interchangeably with fleecy covers.

Sponge rubber cover is used interchangeably with fleecy covers, but it may also be used with water-base paint.

There may be other natural or synthetic fiber covers available; the paint industry constantly tries to find new materials and methods.

BEFORE PAINTING STARTS

Clean the surface in the same way you would if painting with a brush or spray. On a new surface you may need a primer coat; ask your paint dealer to recommend the type you need and follow manufacturers' directions.

Prepare the roller tray in a convenient place (attached to the top of a ladder, on a table or on the floor). At the bottom of the tray put a lining of foil or heavy-coated paper; this saves much cleaning and permits you

to make quick changes in color in the same tray when different paints are to be used. Pour paint into the tray, filling it halfway.

INTERIOR PAINTING

Before you start roller painting a large surface (such as a wall), use a small trim roller or a brush to apply about 1½ inches of paint along the edges of the floor, ceiling and woodwork. Don't do this all around the room—just on one wall at a time to prevent shading of the paint.

Load the roller with paint by dipping it into the tray, then keep rolling back and forth on the ribbed surface of the tray to remove the excess paint.

Apply paint to the surface by rolling in any direction with an easy back-and-forth motion. Some people find it helps them do a good job to start with a crisscross stroke. With care, slowly progress toward the painted edge you applied at the corners, edges and windows.

CEILING PAINTING

You need a long-handled roller for this. You may be able to buy one for the purpose, to fit a long handle to your regular roller or to buy an extension handle that you can pull out like a telescope to whatever length is desired.

After you dip the roller in the paint, work it easily back and forth across the narrow width of the ceiling. Do not leave the ceiling partially painted, finish the job in one painting; this will prevent any shading of the paint where the edges lap.

FLOOR PAINTING

You will not need to stoop or bend when you use a roller with a long handle. You may use the roller on wood, concrete or linoleum-covered floors.

EXTERIOR PAINTING

Rollers for exterior painting are similar to those used for interior painting, except that they are usually larger and the covering may be of a different fabric in order to apply the heavier paints smoothly. Although the paints and rollers you buy for exterior use bear directions, the following extra hints will help you:

Before applying paint to unpainted wood, the surface must be thoroughly dry. Seal the knots or resin streaks with a knot sealer (which you may buy at paint or hardware shop) or shellac.

Before repainting an old surface, nail down loose boards, tighten any projecting nailheads, fill cracks or pits from nailheads with putty, remove loose paint with a scraper and finish the area by smoothing it with sandpaper or other abrasive.

Before painting a concrete surface, remove all dust and loose, crumbly particles. Fill any cracks and examine the corners to see if they are broken and need repair.

On clapboard walls, paint the under edges, one section at a time, using a small lap roller. Start at top and work downward. Then paint the flat surfaces with a 5½-inch roller.

On stucco or cement block, use a roller with a long-nap cover, especially if the surface is very rough. This type of roller is also good on siding and shingles that have deep crevices. It can also be used to paint wire fences.

CLEANING AND STORING ROLLERS

Remove the cover from the roller. After using oil paint, squeeze the excess paint out of the cover with a squeegee, which you can buy for this purpose. Or you can place the wet cover inside a heavy paper or plastic bag, leaving the top of the bag open, and squeeze by hand; excess paint will flow out of bag. Pour commercially prepared roller cleaner, turpentine or kerosene in a basin. Put the roller cover into the cleaner and move it around quickly. Squeeze the cover dry. Then repeat the process.

After using with water- or rubber-base paint, squeeze out the excess paint in the same way. Then wash the cover in lukewarm water and soap, and rinse in clear water.

Do not store rollers unless they are thoroughly dry. Keep the rollers in plastic containers when not in use.

Chapter Twelve

INTERIOR PAINTING AND WALLPAPERING

IN THE PRECEDING CHAPTER the various methods of painting were discussed; in this chapter, although we tell how to use paints and prepare surfaces for all kinds of painting, we are concerned mainly with the conventional brush method.

When painting walls and ceiling you may save a lot of time by using a large brush; at the same time you will want to be comfortable while working, and should choose a brush with a handle that fits your hand. Before you start to paint, spread newspapers or cloth coverings on the floor and the furniture to avoid spotting them with paint. The brush might drip on the woodwork, and it is well to have a clean cloth handy so you may wipe off the wet spots as you go along.

Do not pick up too much paint on your brush at one time. Paint from the ceiling down, and if you should happen to miss some spots on the wall, go back and repaint them right away, to prevent leaving streaks once the paint has dried.

Painting plaster walls and ceilings

Your walls may be new or unpainted, or they may be already painted and need a new coat.

PREPARING NEW OR UNPAINTED PLASTER

Before you start to paint, prepare the surfaces by filling all cracks and holes with patching plaster. Cut out plaster along the crack or around the hole in an inverted V-shape so that the edges converge toward the surface. Soak the edges with water to bond the patching plaster with existing plaster. Fill the crack to within one-quarter inch of the surface and allow the patching plaster to set partially before leveling the wall surface. After cracks and holes have been repaired, smooth rough places with fine sandpaper. Remove loose dirt, dust or chalky plaster by brushing or by washing with clean water. Wash off grease with warm water and mild soap, and rinse the surface carefully with water. If the grease has penetrated deeply, cut out the plaster and patch the area affected. Wash only small areas at a time and rinse immediately. If an oil paint is to be applied following plaster repairs, allow the wall to dry for at least seventy-two hours.

PAINT SELECTION

Before painting a new or unpainted plaster surface, if possible age the new plaster at least two months before painting, especially if oil paint is to be applied. If painting must be done sooner, use calcimine, cold-water paint or resin-emulsion paint. All of these are flat, lusterless wall paints, ordinarily preferred for interior surfaces because they provide better distribution of illumination. However, flat paints do not withstand as much washing as semigloss and gloss oil paints, and they are not as moistureproof. Calcimine is not washable, but is easily removed by washing and is therefore a good choice for a temporary coating while new plaster is aging. Cold-water, resin-emulsion, eggshell-flat oil, semigloss and gloss paints are each more washable, in that order. When possible, wash surfaces instead of repainting them. Where maximum lighting and best vision are desired, choose paint of the lightest suitable color; to reduce glare from excessive sunlight, use more subdued colors.

PAINTING NEW OR UNPAINTED PLASTER

Depending on the paint you use, the following methods are suggested:

Calcimine. Before using calcimine paint on new plaster, apply a glue-water sizing. Where the plaster is dry, use either glue size or a varnish size. The latter is pre-

72

pared by thinning 1 gallon interior varnish with about 1 quart turpentine. Apply calcimine in one thick coating, using special calcimine brushes. Spread the paint on thickly and evenly with the least possible brushing and without leaving brush marks. Start in a corner, working away from the light in narrow sections, and do not allow the edge of a section to dry and show the point where laps meet. If this happens, apply plain water with a clean brush lightly and carefully before joining the painted areas. In joining, do not apply more pigment to the lap than elsewhere, but gently brush paint from one section into the edge of the preceding one. After painting, ventilate room fully, or heat the room if there is excessive moisture in the air. Slow drying often causes a spotted appearance.

Cold-water Paint. Apply in one coat of substantial thickness on unsized plaster, new or aged, working as with calcimine. If necessary, a second coat may be applied after the first has dried.

Resin-emulsion Paint. Apply in the same way as cold-water paint, but thin the resin-emulsion paint in the proportion of 4 pints water to 1 gallon paint. Two coats may be applied, but one coat is usually sufficient.

Flat-finish Oil Paint and Semigloss Enamel. When applying, spread the paint on the surface with as little brushing as possible. Once it has set, do not touch it with a brush. Work in narrow sections, covering a small area with each brushful of paint. Join sections with light curved or semicircular strokes. If left undisturbed, the paint levels itself and hides the brush marks. For a flat finish on plaster surfaces in temporary and semipermanent structures, apply one or two coats of self-priming flat paint. For flat finish on plaster, use one coat of plaster primer and one of eggshell-flat finish paint.

Gloss Enamel. Use gloss enamel in the same way as flat paint. For finer gloss finishes, apply plaster primer, allow eighteen hours for drying and then apply gloss enamel finish. Gloss coatings may be applied either by brush or spray.

REPAINTING PLASTER SURFACES

The condition of plaster surfaces to be repainted determines the number of coats needed. Repeated painting builds up film thickness and leads to paint failure. With surfaces properly cleaned and prepared, one coat is usually sufficient.

Cleaning the Surface. When the wall surface is in good condition and painted with casein, resin-emulsion or a flat paint, the only preparation necessary is to clean the surface by brushing or wiping with turpentine. For dirty or greasy surfaces such as kitchen walls and ceilings, apply a preparation made by adding to warm water a small amount of washing powder, soap and sufficient flour, glue, or paperhanger's paste to make a slightly sticky mixture. Spread this mixture with a large calcimine brush, allow it to remain on the surface two or three minutes and wash it off with a sponge or cloth and clean water.

Removing Old Paint. Wash off calcimine coating before applying another type of paint. Oil paint may be applied over casein or resin-emulsion paint in sound condition if there are no more than two coats of old paint on the surface. Remove all loose, scaling or flaking paint by scraping or wire-brushing. Sandpaper the edges that have been scraped. Do not remove the entire coat if only a small area has deteriorated.

Removing Resin-emulsion Paint, Flat Wall Paint and Enamels. To remove resin-emulsion paint, flat wall paint and enamels, use paint-and-varnish remover. Brush on remover and scrape or wipe off the softened paint. To remove paraffin before repainting, wash walls with turpentine, or commercial wall cleaner and warm water.

Removing Casein Paints. To remove casein paint, scrub wall with a strong solution of trisodium phosphate and hot water, using a stiff brush. Rinse the surface thoroughly with clean water and allow it to dry before repainting.

Retouching the Surface. After loose paint has been removed or the wall surface has been cleaned, fill all cracks and holes with patching plaster as described earlier in this chapter. To patch areas larger than one square foot, use hydrated lime and gauging plaster. Spot-paint the patched areas before applying a new coat.

Painting wallboard

Wallboard refers to such boards as plywood, plasterboard and cement-asbestos board, which are used in place of plaster or over plaster in interior surfaces.

To prepare the surface, fill all joints and nailheads with a putty preparation made by the manufacturer of the board, plaster of Paris or white-lead whiting putty. Allow putty or plaster to set and sandpaper it to a smooth surface.

Paints for wallboard are the same as those for plaster. Resin-emulsion paint is particularly satisfactory on cement-asbestos board.

Apply paint as described in the section on painting new or unpainted plaster. Certain types of wallboard are more porous than plaster or highly pressed wallboard, so the spreading rate of priming paint is not always the same. Prime the plywood in the way recommended for interior woodwork. Prime plasterboard and cement-asbestos board as recommended for plaster.

Painting masonry walls and ceilings

Before applying paint, the masonry surface must be thoroughly dry. Although the same general method is used as in painting over plaster surfaces, use an alkali-resistant primer such as a rubber-base paint if you are to use oil paint as the final coat on a wall containing Portland cement (for example, in concrete).

In a basement, where the walls are likely to be damp because of condensation or leakage, it is advisable to use cement-water paints. The way to apply these is described in the following chapter in the section on painting exterior masonry walls. In any case, before buying paint for masonry walls or ceilings, consult your paint dealer as to the kind best suited for your needs.

Painting over wallpaper

If the paper on your wall does not contain dyes that will bleed into the paint, you may use water-base paint to cover the wallpaper. If there are several layers of paper on the wall, it may not be advisable to use paint without first stripping the paper off. This is also the case if the wallpaper is torn or bulges in spots. Ask your paint dealer to recommend suitable paint and brush or roller for this job.

Calcimining a ceiling

Refer to the information about calcimining given earlier in this chapter. Before you start to remove the old calcimine from ceiling, remove all the furniture you can from the room, and cover the big pieces you can't remove with heavy cloth or newspapers. Protect your hair by wearing a cap, and wear overalls or old clothes.

Wash off the old calcimine, using a sponge, an old calcimine brush and a pail of cool water. The calcimine coming off looks like milk. You will need to keep changing the water in the pail because it grows cloudy.

When applying new calcimine, keep windows closed to prevent the finished parts from drying out too much ahead of the parts applied later in the process. Open the windows for air circulation when the job is completed.

Painting a window sash

First scrape off old putty, and if there are any small cracks left in the wood coat them with linseed oil before putting in new putty. Paint the mutins or sash bars first, then the stiles and rails of the sash, then the window frames and end with the sill and the apron below it.

Cut a metal or cardboard shield to hold over the glass with one hand while you brush on the paint with the other hand. This shield will protect the glass from dripping paint. But should paint spots drip onto the glass, wipe them off immediately with a cloth that you have handy. Should you overlook some paint spots, and they become dry, you may later wipe them off with turpentine or scrape them off with a razor blade.

Painting a door

Start with the upper panels, then paint the lower panels, spreading the paint evenly and using an up-and-down motion. Then paint the horizontal bars between the panels, going with the grain, next paint the vertical stiles or sides of door and finish with the central vertical stiles.

Before you apply a second coat, the first coat must be completely dry. Painting the door may take longer on a hot or humid day than on a clear, cool day. It may even take a few days for the paint to dry thoroughly. If, after the first coat is dry, you find any uneven or rough spots, smooth them with sandpaper before the second coat is applied.

The first coat must be thin and painted in even up-and-down strokes. However, the second coat of paint may be thicker. You may prefer to use gloss paint on the door to achieve a high glaze on it.

Painting and varnishing woodwork

NEW OR UNPAINTED SURFACES

Prepare the surface by removing with sandpaper such imperfections as planer marks, hammer marks and raised grain. Wipe off dust and dirt with turpentine. If wood frames, trim and wood base have been installed against damp plaster, do no painting until the plaster has dried.

Apply one primer coat and one finish coat. Two coats of finish paint may be applied if the primer and first finish are applied thinly. Allow at least eighteen hours between coats. After priming, fill all nail holes, cracks and other defects with white-lead whiting putty. After the putty has dried, sand the surface. Coat the knots or sappy places with shellac.

REPAINTING OLD SURFACES

Prepare the surface by wiping off painted or varnished woodwork (flat or low gloss) with turpentine. Remove the glaze by sandpapering, then wipe the surface clean with turpentine. Remove cracking, checking or scaling coatings with paint-and-varnish remover. Use turpentine to remove wax deposited by the paint remover, and refinish the surface as new work. If paint has been applied over a stain that bleeds through, coat the affected area with a seal coat of aluminum varnish composed of 2 pounds paste to 1 gallon varnish.

One coat may be sufficient to apply paint on old work, if applied over paint of the same or a similar color. Otherwise, two coats may be necessary.

VARNISHING AND SHELLACKING

It is important that all materials and tools be kept as free from dust as possible, since dust is harmful to good results in varnishing. Keep the rooms in which varnishing is being done free from dust.

Open-grained woods such as oak, chestnut, mahogany and walnut should be treated with a filler before being varnished. There are two classes of fillers on the market—paste and liquid fillers.

The paste fillers that are most commonly used should be thinned with turpentine to brushing consistency before being used. The filler is first brushed across the grain and then with the grain. An old stiff brush may be used for this purpose, and if the filler sets too quickly the surface may be wiped with turpentine. After the filler has set for about half an hour, wipe across the grain with excelsior to remove the excess. Burlap may be used instead of excelsior for this purpose. Some liquid fillers are intended for use on open-grained woods, but most are intended for use on close-grained woods and are applied by simply brushing them on. Some authorities recommend ordinary shellac in alcohol as a liquid filler.

The surface should be allowed to dry for a day or two after a filler has been used before the first coat of varnish is applied. The first coat should be allowed to dry from five to ten days, after which time it should be rubbed with excelsior or burlap to remove the gloss. The second coat is then applied and treated similarly, or rubbed with fine sandpaper or emery cloth. If a first-class job with a gloss finish is desired, the next-to-last coat should be well rubbed with pumice and water before the finishing coat is applied. The final coat (preferably the fourth coat) may be left with the natural gloss, or rubbed with pumice and water if a dull or flat finish is desired. Some manufacturers now make varnishes that dry with a flat finish.

Shellac is often used as an interior finish, especially where it is desired to retain the natural color of the wood. It should not, however, be used where it will become hot —near a fireplace, for example—since it is likely to blister.

Shellac should be applied in thin coats and given ample time to dry. The first two coats may be applied six hours apart, and two days should be allowed between additional coats. It does not require rubbing except, perhaps, after every third or fourth coat.

Stenciling

If you want to add a decorative touch to the walls, especially in a child's room or some other informal room in the house, you may make your own stencils or buy them ready-made at a paint store. When purchasing, you will get directions from the dealer.

Since the stencil design must be held firmly against the wall, more than one person will be needed to do the job. Brush a paint of heavy consistency over the stencil,

then carefully take the stencil away from wall to prevent smudges.

Stippling

For decorative purposes, or to disguise a faulty wall surface, you may stipple the surface while the paint is still wet.

A flat brush with stiff, short bristles is good for this purpose. Using quick movements, plunge the bristle ends into the wet paint on the wall, but do not make any brushing motion. The result is a series of dots. Repeat this over the surface you wish to cover with stipple. Wipe the brush frequently with a clean cloth so there will be no accumulation of paint on the bristle ends.

Painting interior metal

There is a twofold purpose in painting functional metal pieces such as exposed water pipes, radiators, heat registers or grilles: first, to help prevent rust, and second, to make them inconspicuous.

If the metal has not been painted before, wash it with turpentine to remove any grease or dirt. If there is any rust on it, use sandpaper to remove it, then apply a first coat of metal primer. The finish coat may be a semi-gloss enamel or a flat wall paint. Apply paint with a brush or spray.

Before painting the radiators with either a color to match the wall or in gold, aluminum or bronze paint, ask a heating expert if it is advisable to do so, since some paints retard the full entrance of heat into the room.

If there are any pipes that detract from the room's appearance, paint them the same color as the wall. Or you may prefer to use gold or aluminum paint on them, especially if your radiators or grilles are painted that way.

Exposed air ducts of galvanized metal, in the basement or other parts of the house, need a primer coat of zinc dust–zinc oxide paint before applying the second and final coat.

Lighting fixtures and ornamental metalwork may be painted the same color as the room itself if you want them to blend in inconspicuously, or they may be finished with bronze, gold or aluminum paint.

Brass lighting fixtures and other brass objects need no painting; but their brightness may be retained by coating them with metal lacquer. This may be brushed or sprayed onto the brass surface.

Hanging wallpaper

Measure the walls (and the ceiling, if you want to paper it). When you buy the wallpaper the dealer will assist you in purchasing the necessary amount, since the paper comes in rolls. If the design is a definite one that needs to be matched at the seams, you must buy more paper to allow for wastage at each end. If you include a separate border, this may be bought by the foot.

MATERIALS NEEDED

You will need a pair of large shears to cut the wallpaper; a small knife, razor or wheel trimmer to cut selvage edges; smoothing brush; wide paste brush; soft cloths; sponge; seam roller; powdered colored chalk; string for chalk; yardstick; ingredients for paste; large pail for mixing paste (unless you buy paper which has adhesive backing); and a table or other flat surface on which to cut and paste the paper.

It is advisable to buy ready-prepared paste mix at the paint shop, then mix it in the pail with water until it reaches the consistency of very thick cream. Stir to remove all lumps.

If you don't have a long table, make one by using two sawhorses or other supports, laying across them boards about eight feet long by two feet wide. If you want to put paper on the ceiling, you need a scaffold. Use two sturdy stepladders or two heavy chairs or other supports, and place across them two heavy boards on which you will walk while holding up the paper and pasting it onto the ceiling. First test the scaffold by walking on it, to make sure it can properly support you and to adjust it to a comfortable height so you won't need to stretch to reach the ceiling.

PREPARATIONS FOR PAPERING

Remove as much furniture from the room as possible, and cover with canvas or paper whatever cannot be taken out. Also cover the floor.

If the surface is painted or is covered with its original plaster and has not been papered before, repair plaster cracks, fill up nail holes and sandpaper any rough spots.

It is sometimes feasible to apply new wallpaper over old paper. If you want to repaper on the bare surface, strip off the old paper. Pry up the paper with a wide knife (if you don't have one, you may buy it at the wallpaper shop), starting at a loose spot in the paper. You can usually peel off whole strips with ease. But if there is any difficulty in removing the paper, wash the surface with clean, warm water to loosen the paper. It may be necessary to wash it several times with water to make the paper loose enough to be stripped off. If the surface is covered with varnished paper, use paint remover to loosen it instead of water. Then, when the surface is dry, use a soft, clean brush to remove all dust and loose particles of plaster or paste.

If you are going to hang paper over old wallpaper, or on a newly plastered surface, it may be advisable to size

the walls; your paint dealer will suggest what to use for the purpose. With a coarse brush, apply the sizing over the whole surface, and to achieve greater penetration you may add acetic acid or vinegar to the sizing. Give the sizing plenty of time to dry, since wallpaper will not adhere to a damp surface.

PAPERING CEILING

If you are going to paper the ceiling as well as the walls (or for certain decorating purposes you may choose to paper only the ceiling and paint the walls), start first with the ceiling. While it may be easier to apply the paper across the narrow width of the room (if the room is oblong), a better finish is produced if the paper is applied across the length of the ceiling.

Use string dipped into powdered chalk to make guidelines on the ceiling to keep the paper straight. First attach the chalked string at one end of the ceiling with a thumbtack, then hold the string taut at the other end of the ceiling and snap it against ceiling; the colored chalk dust will be left on the surface as a guide. Make this first chalk line about sixteen inches from the wall, then continue making chalk lines across the ceiling about sixteen inches apart. Measure the length of the ceiling, and allow two or more inches at each end for the paper to drop down on the wall.

The following is the procedure for cutting and pasting the wallpaper, as illustrated in Fig. 12.1:

Start at the beginning of the roll, place the paper down on table and let the roll trail over the end (a). Cut off the first strip of paper at the desired length. Then roll the next layer of paper over the first one, face down, and cut off a second length. Repeat this until you have the necessary number of strips to cover the ceiling. If there is a distinct pattern in the paper that needs to be matched at the seams, you will need to exercise great care in doing so, and may need to cut some strips longer than others.

Move the top strip of paper over to the front edge of the table, then pull the strip over to hang down on the

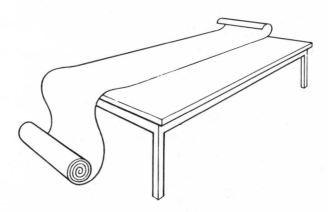

Fig. 12.1a

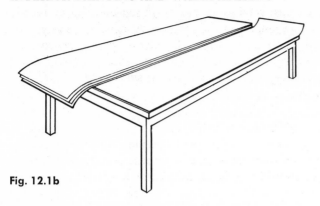

Fig. 12.1b

right side of the table while the left end of the paper is flush with the left edge of the table (b).

Brush paste onto the paper, starting at the left edge and moving toward the right (c). When about two-thirds of the strip is pasted, fold over the pasted end onto the pasted center, to within three inches from where the paste ends. Make sure the lower edges of the paper match evenly. Pull the folded paper to the left, bringing the rest of strip up on the table, and apply paste to the balance of the strip to within two inches from the end of the paper.

Fold the right end of paper over, allowing it to overlap the first end by one inch in order to make it easier to unfold the paper when hanging it (d).

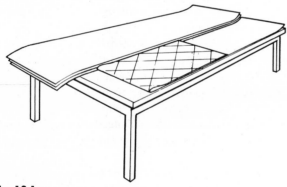

Fig. 12.1c

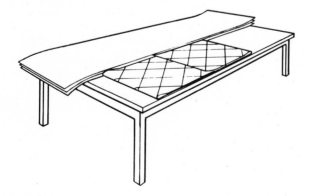

Fig. 12.1d

If there is a selvage edge on the paper, line up the folded strip and cut through the double thickness with quick strokes of a sharp knife or razor, or use a wheel trimmer (e). You do not need to cut off two selvages (one on each side) if you are going to overlap one strip of wallpaper over the other at the seams. Some papers come with no selvages, and some have perforated edges to allow the selvages to be torn off.

Before getting up on the scaffold with the folded, pasted wallpaper, equip yourself with a smoothing brush, an unpasted roll of the paper and a soft clean cloth or sponge. Keep the brush and the cloth in a large pocket

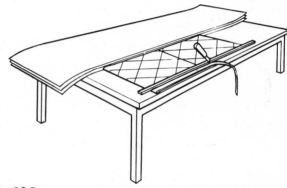

Fig. 12.1e

in your overalls or apron so you can have it constantly at hand, and have a roll of paper handy also for quick use.

Start at the far end of the room. Open the folded, pasted paper, adjust it with one hand to the chalk line to keep the paper straight, and in the other hand hold the roll of paper to prop the rest of the paper against the ceiling (f). When you are sure it is properly placed, start at the center of the paper to press it to the ceiling with long strokes of the smoothing brush. If you feel you cannot do this by yourself, have someone on the scaffold with you so that you can hold up the paper and brush it at one end while the helper holds up the paper and brushes it at the other. If the job is not smooth or straight, you can peel the paper off carefully and do it over again.

To avoid mounting and dismounting the scaffold continually, and to save time, a helper may prepare one strip with paste while you are applying another to the ceiling and be prepared to hand the new one up to you when you are ready.

Each strip is applied in the same way, but you must use care at the seams so they will be flat (and match the design, if that is necessary). You can use a small, inexpensive seam roller to roll over the joining seams and produce a smooth flatness.

If any paste comes into contact with woodwork, clean it off immediately with the cloth or sponge; if some oozes

Fig. 12.1f

WALLPAPER BORDER

Cut the border to the desired length. Then paste and fold in the same way as directed for wallpaper. Adjust the top edge of the border directly under the ceiling, or the bottom edge directly over the floor or baseboard, or right up to the edge if used vertically, and press down smoothly with a brush. Sometimes a border is used in a room that is painted (not wallpapered), purely for an original decorative theme.

PRE-PASTED PAPER

Some wallpapers and borders come with an adhesive material on the underside, so it is not necessary to use paste. Cut the paper into strips of the necessary length. Then, one strip at a time, immerse the paper in a bath-tub, sink or large basin of lukewarm water, and make a very loose roll of the paper while it is in the water in order to wet the underside sufficiently to have it stick to the wall surface. Then proceed to apply the paper to surface by smoothing it with the wide brush.

If you are not sure whether this type of paper will suit your requirements, consult your paint dealer.

onto the paper, blot it off immediately with the cloth or sponge.

PAPERING WALLS

Use the same procedure of measuring, cutting and pasting wallpaper as directed for papering the ceiling. But in this case you must consider the spaces around windows, doors, fireplace, and so forth, especially if you use paper with a definite pattern that must be matched (Fig. 12.2).

When you come to the corner of the room, you may paste the paper either by working it in smoothly into the corner without cutting the strip; or you may prefer to cut and match the paper, especially if there is a distinct design you wish to follow and match.

Mark the walls with guidelines so that you can keep the paper straight; use the chalk-string method, a plumb bob line or a spoon or small screw driver at the end of a string so it will hang down straight.

Start pasting the paper with your brush at the top of the room and work downward. Use a sharp knife, razor blade or wheel trimmer to cut the paper at such places as electric light switches.

Fig. 12.2

Chapter Thirteen

EXTERIOR PAINTING

THE MOST IMPORTANT FACTOR in painting the exterior of the house is that the surface be in the best condition before any paint is applied to it. All defects such as rotted boards, rusted or corroded metal, mildew, mold, cracks in the surface, crumbled putty or exposed nailheads must be corrected.

Do not paint when the house surface is wet or damp, while rain or snow is falling or when there is a threat of rain. Wait for clear, dry weather.

Repairing wood surface defects

Paints with oil base are used, and if they are of good quality they should last long. Sometimes they weather by chalking, and before any repainting is done the powdery substance should be thoroughly brushed away. If the paint has peeled, it should be removed and given a coat of paint over that spot; this means you first have to put a primer coat over it and then finish coats so that it will come up to the same level as the wood surrounding it. Coat the knots with shellac or aluminum paint. Replace split or rotted boards, fill holes with putty and fill with calking compound any cracks around door and window frames.

Preventing wood decay

If there are signs of rot developing in the house structure, porch steps, garage doors, fence posts, and so forth, apply a wood preservative with a spray or brush before you do any repainting. In some cases the wood may be dipped into the liquid, and you may use an oil can to squirt the liquid into tiny crevices or holes. Preservative may be purchased under many brand names at hardware or paint shops; it is usually a light volatile oil solvent that contains either zinc or copper naphthenate, or pentachlorophenol.

Zinc naphthenate solutions are clear and may be used under varnish so the natural grain of the wood may be preserved. The solutions may also be used on bars or unpainted basement walls or on concrete to check any mildew. These solutions are generally more expensive than the two following types.

Copper naphthenate solutions are green, so they may be used without paint if you want the wood a green color. Should you desire the treated surface to be painted in a light color, first seal the surface with shellac or aluminum paint.

Pentachlorophenol solutions may be bought either clear, to be used aboveground, or in crude oil type, for use in belowground protection. These may be harmful to young plants, so they should not be used where they can come into contact with the roots. Also, if you plan to apply a paint finish, do not use these solutions, since it is not advisable to paint over them.

When applying any of the foregoing solutions give the surface two coats. However, even if you apply only one coat it will give some protection. One gallon of solution covers up to four hundred square feet of wood.

CAUTION: To protect your skin and eyes, wear gloves and goggles when handling these preservatives.

Use the preservatives at the point where the wood touches the ground, and on porch steps; window and door frames and sills; where two pieces of wood join; in joints between wood and masonry or metal building materials; at the bottom row of wood siding or shingles; in wood shutters or other outside blinds; wood gutters; garage doors; and any other area where moisture collects and could rot the wood.

Also use preservative on fence posts, soaking the bottom twelve inches of the posts for two or three days in a container of the solution. Thus, if you sink the posts six inches into the ground, you will have another six inches (above the ground) protected. It is good to use the preservative on the rails of the fence and on the spots where they are nailed into the posts. If screws are used on fence and gate, squirt some solution into the drilled screw holes for extra precaution.

The three aforementioned types of preservatives are unpalatable to boring insects such as powder post beetles, wood wasps and ants, and they are offensive to fungi that cause rot.

TERMITES

The solutions mentioned in the foregoing section are not effective in fighting termites, which need more positive control measures such as digging trenches around the house and putting poisonous substances into the ground and on structural house parts. If termites are the cause of wood rot they must be fought at once, and it is advisable for you to consult an expert in the field, since the measures that must be taken often carry with them fire or chemical hazards when handled by an amateur. A good source of aid in battling the termite situation is the U.S. Department of Agriculture, to whom you may write for their latest literature and instructions.

MILDEW

Mildew is another objectionable condition that may contribute to wood decay. Before repainting any area in which mildew is present, scrub the area with a solution of 1 pound sodium carbonate or trisodium phosphate dissolved in 1 gallon water. Or you may purchase a commercial fungicide for the purpose. After washing, rinse with clear water. Wait until the area is dry before applying new paint.

Staining shingles

Stains may be applied to shingles by brushing or spraying, or dipping the shingles into stain. These are pigmented oil stains that are similar to easy-flowing paints. It is best not to use a stain of creosote base; if you want to apply paint over it the creosote may bleed through.

You may want to mix the stain ingredients to whatever color you desire, or buy commercially prepared stain. Ask your paint dealer to recommend what is best for your shingles; it is a good idea to take along a shingle as a sample.

Painting new wood surfaces

On new unpainted wood, at least three coats of paint are necessary to produce good results. The first or priming coat may be mixed rather thin to spread more easily

and to fill the pores in the surface; the second coat should form a solid color base for the third or finish coat, which should be smooth and glossy. It is important that each coat of paint be thoroughly dry before another coat is applied.

PREPARING THE SURFACE

On new buildings little preparation is required before the first or priming coat is put on. Before starting to paint, brush over the surface with a dry brush or duster to remove all dust, and with a putty knife scrape off any particles of plaster or other material that may have been splashed on the surface. Knots and other excessive sappy places in the wood should be brushed over with turpentine, orange shellac, solvent naphtha or aluminum knot primer to prevent the resin in such places from being drawn to the surface by the sun and staining the paint.

PRIMING COAT

Since this coat is the foundation for all future painting, it should be carefully applied with the best of materials. The use of old leftover paint for this purpose is not recommended.

An excellent priming coat for new work can be made by mixing 100 pounds pure white-lead paste with 4 gallons pure raw linseed oil, 2 gallons pure turpentine and 1 pint liquid dryer. These quantities will make about nine gallons of paint. If a smaller amount is desired, the quantity of each ingredient should be reduced proportionately. The priming coat should be brushed out well. If possible, it is best to wait two or three weeks before applying the second coat, in order to allow any moisture in the new wood to come to the surface and evaporate.

When the priming coat is dry, all nail holes and cracks in the wood should be filled with putty so that the finished surface will present a smooth appearance.

OTHER COATS

The second coat should dry with a flat (not glossy) appearance. This effect is obtained by using less linseed oil. For example, to 100 pounds of white-lead paste add 1½ gallons of raw linseed oil, 1½ gallons of turpentine and 1 pint of liquid dryer. This formula will make about six gallons of paint, and the amount may be reduced as previously described. This coat should completely hide the grain of the wood and present a more solid appearance than the priming coat.

If white-lead paint is to be used for the third or finish coat, it should consist of white-lead paste, linseed oil and small quantities of liquid dryer. For example, to 100 pounds white-lead paste, add 3½ to 4½ gallons raw linseed oil, 1 pint turpentine and 1 pint liquid dryer. To achieve a surface to which less dirt will adhere, add 10 to 25 per cent of zinc oxide; that is, 10 to 25 pounds of zinc oxide to 100 pounds of white-lead paste, and 10 to 15 per cent more linseed oil, turpentine and dryer. All coats, especially the finish coat, should be carefully applied to avoid brush marks and marks caused by spattering of paint, which result from using too much paint on the brush.

READY-MIXED PAINTS

When these paints are used, it is well to use a white-lead priming coat first, but the ready-mixed may be used for the first coat as well as for body coats, after they are properly thinned. Ready-mixed paint as purchased is generally intended for finish coats. The manufacturers' labels frequently give directions for reducing the paint to a proper consistency for the undercoats. If no directions are given, however, the paint may be thinned by adding linseed oil and turpentine, mixed in about the same proportions as recommended for white-lead paint. No dryer should be added to ready-mixed paints.

Repainting old wood surfaces

The number of coats to be applied depends on the condition of the old paint. If it is in good condition, one coat applied after a thorough dusting may be sufficient. In many cases, not more than two coats will be required. If the house has not been painted for several years and has a weather-beaten appearance, or if the paint is badly cracked or peeling, it may be necessary to remove most of the old paint and apply three new coats.

PREPARING THE SURFACE

The amount of work necessary to prepare a surface for repainting depends largely upon its condition. If the house has been painted at proper intervals and the surface is in good condition, a simple dusting before painting may be all that is necessary. Nail holes or cracks in the wood should be filled with putty after the first coat is applied, as described for new work.

If the old paint is blistered, cracked or peeling in places, it should be removed, and the surface sandpapered until it is smooth and then dusted before new paint is put on. If there are any bare spots they should be touched up with a priming coat in order to obtain an even appearance.

Paint blisters can be removed with a putty knife or broad knife scraper and wire brush. Some of the cracked and scaling paint may be removed in the same manner, but most of it may require other treatment. Coarse sandpaper is also an efficient remover of old paint. It is most easily handled when tacked to a flat block of wood. Probably the most efficient, though expensive, method of removing oil paint is burning it with a gasoline blowtorch. This burning causes the film to soften so that it can be scraped off easily. This method, however, can be used only on flat surfaces and where slight scorching of the wood is not objectionable. Because of the fire risk, a blowtorch must be used with great care and only by an experienced painter.

Painting masonry surfaces

If you find it desirable to change the color of a stucco or concrete surface, or to bring a repaired area to a uniform color, it may be done by the application of either a cold-water wash or an oil paint. You must bear in mind, however, that once you paint a stucco or concrete surface it becomes a painted surface and, as such, requires the same periodical attention as do painted surfaces of other materials.

Before starting to paint, remove all loose mortar and fix all cracks with fresh mortar, then put a first coat of paint on them to make the repaired portions uniform with the rest of the surface.

Following is a description of the washes and paints that are used for masonry surfaces:

COLD-WATER WASHES

Cement washes of practically any color may be prepared by using the proper portions of gray and white cement, and light or dark sand, with a small amount of mineral pigment. A mixture of 1 part white cement and 1 part yellow sand, all passing the No. 20 sieve, with hydrated lime to the amount of 5 per cent of the weight of the cement will give a good, practically white color.

In preparing the mix, the cement, lime, coloring material and sand should be properly proportioned and thoroughly mixed dry. The dry batch should be large enough to do the entire job or at least one side of the structure, in order to maintain uniformity of color. Pour the dry material into a bucket containing clean water and stir vigorously until it has the consistency of a stiff oil paint. The mixture, while being applied, should be stirred from time to time with a brush. In refilling the container, clean out and discard all of the old wash, and use the same amount of clean dry materials as was used in the previous batch.

The area to be coated should be thoroughly wetted just before applying the wash, but there should be no free water on the surface. Start at the top corner of the wall and brush on the wash to the thinnest possible coat that will cover the surface. A thick coating is liable to crack or peel. The work should be carried on so that jointings come at natural breaks in the surface, and care should be taken to blend the adjoining areas together to prevent lines showing between them.

After the coating has been applied it should be gently sprinkled with water for several days. If it dries out before the cement has attained its set, the wash will eventually dust off. The period of sprinkling may be greatly shortened by dissolving 4 pounds commercial calcium-chloride crystals in each 12 gallons water used in mixing the wash. This chemical assists in securing early set and strength.

OIL PAINTS

The following discussion of painting stucco, concrete and brick with oil paints is based on the assumption that it is desirable to hide completely the texture as well as the color of the material. Although this practice is the more common, a better plan is simply to color the cement or brick by applying a thin paint that will wet and penetrate the surface. Use the minimum number of coats to give the desired color, and do not attempt to build up an impenetrable film on the surface, but try to leave the surface porous so that water entering the structure back of the paint can evaporate without blistering the coating.

Before stucco, concrete or similar materials are painted with oil paints, it is advisable to let them stand at least a year to allow them to dry thoroughly and to give the lime in such materials sufficient time to age, so that it will not mar the painted surface. However, if it is necessary to paint before sufficient time has elapsed, the free lime in the material may be neutralized by washing the surface with a solution composed of 3 to 4 pounds zinc-sulfate crystals dissolved in 1 gallon water. This wash may be applied with a calcimine brush or sprayer, and then should be allowed to dry for about a week before paint is applied. All fresh spots of mortar where repairs have been made must be thoroughly dry and similarly treated with zinc sulfate.

The surface may be painted in the same manner as wood, using either a white-lead mixture, or mixture of white lead and zinc oxide. The priming coat should contain some boiled linseed oil, and special attention should be paid to this coat, since it must bind the loose particles of cement on the surface and form a firm foundation for the other coats. After priming, small defects on the surface may be puttied if a smooth finish is desired.

Before painting stucco or concrete that has been previously painted, scrape off all loose paint, fill all cracks with mortar or white-lead putty and treat all fresh mortar spots with zinc sulfate.

Painting brick or stone surfaces

It is generally better to leave brick or stone surfaces unpainted, but in some cases painting may be advisable. The brick or stone should be dry and clean before paint is applied. If there are white spots, known as efflorescence, on the surface they should be treated as recommended in the next chapter. All loose mortar and crumbling brick must be removed by thorough brushing, and joints and cracks must be repainted. To neutralize the alkali in new mortar, treat with a solution of zinc sulfate, as in cement painting.

Before painting very porous bricks or similar materials for the first time, it is advisable to apply a coat of boiled linseed oil and turpentine (mixed half-and-half) to fill the pores and "kill the suction." These surfaces should not be painted in cold weather, and at least two or three days of dry weather should precede the painting.

Three coats are usually sufficient. The first coat should be brushed in well. When it is dry, the joints should be filled with a putty made of linseed oil and whiting, and colored with the same pigments as those used in the paint. For the second coat, the pigment should be mixed with 2 or 3 parts raw linseed oil, 1 part turpentine and a small amount of dryer. This coat should be brushed out well and uniformly. For a gloss finish, the pigments that give the desired color should be mixed with linseed oil and a little dryer, and the paint should be spread on in such a way that it will not run. If a flat effect is desired, 3 parts oil to 1 part turpentine should be used for the second coat, and for the last coat the pigment, ground to a stiff paste in raw linseed oil, should be thinned with $\frac{1}{3}$ liquid dryer and $\frac{2}{3}$ turpentine.

Painting metal surfaces

It is important that metal surfaces, such as roofs and gutters, be kept well painted to prevent corrosion and to eliminate unnecessary repairs. To obtain long-lasting results on metal that has never been painted before, apply two coats of priming paint, then two coats of finishing paint.

Tin, galvanized iron and other metals used for roofing downspouts, garages and other purposes often present difficulties in painting. The paint may not stick well if there has been a thin film of grease left on the material in the process of manufacture. Oil or grease must be thoroughly removed by scrubbing with soap and water, or by rubbing with a cloth dipped in turpentine or carbon tetrachloride. Also use a wire brush, steel wool or a motor-driven rotary brush to remove rust, scale or old paint from the surface.

Before applying new paint over an old surface where some of the paint has been removed, put a priming coat over that spot, then use one or two finished coats as required.

Do not paint or repaint metal except on a clear, bright day, preferably in warm weather. Avoid painting early in the morning, should the surface be damp from dew. Allow sufficient drying time for each coat of paint before you apply the next one.

The priming coat should have rust-prevention pigments, and it may be applied either with brush or spray.

When you use two priming coats on new surfaces, it is advisable to use the second of a slightly different color so you can be sure that you have covered the whole surface.

A practical primer for steel surfaces is red lead, and iron-oxide paints are good for a finish coating. On terne-plate (tin) roofs and structural metal, dull red and brown iron-oxide paints (sometimes called roof and barn paints) are practical to use because they are economical and long-lasting.

For galvanized iron and sheet zinc, use zinc-dust primer that contains rust-preservative properties. Zinc-dust paints are also practical to use as a finishing coat in addition to the priming coat.

On iron or steel you will find that finish coats of dark color and black paints usually last longer than paints of light colors. A good finish coat for metal is aluminum paint, which you may buy ready-made or can make by mixing 2 pounds aluminum powder or paste with 1 gallon spar varnish.

If your house is painted white or some other light color, the copper gutters or copper or bronze screening may sometimes cause yellowish stains on the walls or roof. Clean the metal by washing it with turpentine or gasoline. Then put on a priming coat made of 1½ to 2 pounds aluminum powder to 1 gallon aluminum mixing varnish. When this is dry put on a finishing coat of the desired color, and ask the paint dealer to recommend the paint best suited to your needs.

To paint screens for windows and doors, see the directions given in Chapter 8.

Painting exterior floors

When your floor is laid on the ground, as for example in a patio, or on the porch, it will need to be given a frequent surface finish to keep the wood or concrete in good condition.

WOOD FLOORS

Make certain that floors are free of either rain water or water used in washing the floor preparatory to painting. Wood floors in contact with the earth are usually damp. Paint applied to such surfaces fails prematurely unless adequate provisions are made for dampproofing.

Paint dries very slowly at low temperatures; do not paint when the temperature is expected to fall below 40°F.

Prepare the surface by cleaning off dust and dirt and smoothing rough or uneven spots. Fill all nail holes, open joints and cracks with putty after the surface has been primed.

For the priming coat add to each gallon of floor paint 1 quart spar varnish and ½ pint mineral thinner. Allow the primer coat to dry for twenty-four hours. Apply the second coat without reduction. Brush the paint along the grain in each application and work it well into the wood.

If you need to repaint when the old paint is worn away in traffic lanes but is generally in good condition, showing no blisters or flaking, spot-prime the worn areas and then apply one coat of paint over the entire floor.

For severe paint failures, such as blistering, flaking and cracking, strip the old coating from the wood surface, using paint-and-varnish remover. Determine whether construction defects are responsible for paint failure. Prepare and paint the surface in the same way as a new surface.

CONCRETE FLOORS

It is not advisable to paint a concrete floor until it has aged at least one year. When earlier painting is required, test the surface for evidence of alkali by applying a few drops of a one per cent solution of phenolphthalein in alcohol to scattered spots on the floor that have first been dampened with water. If the masonry is alkaline, the drops turn red or purple. Another method of detecting alkaline material in the concrete is to dampen several pieces of red litmus paper and apply them at random over the floor area. If the litmus paper turns blue, alkali is present and a neutralizing treatment is essential before painting. To remove alkali, wash the surface with a ten per cent solution of muriatic acid and water. Rinse the floor with clean water to remove the acid and lime and allow one to four days for thorough drying.

Apply two coats of paint as described for wood floors. Spread the paint out well and allow four days for drying before applying the second coat. Allow the second coat to dry at least twenty-four hours before using the floor.

Before repainting, clean off dust and dirt with turpentine or mineral spirits. To remove grease and oil stains, scrub the surface with a stiff brush and a solution of 3 to 4 ounces trisodium phosphate to 1 gallon hot water. Use an abrasive powder with the solution if there is a dark-colored film on the surface. Then mix whiting with some of the hot trisodium phosphate solution to form a thick paste; cover the stained areas with the paste and allow it to dry. Scrape off dried paste and rinse the surface with clear hot water. Repeat this treatment if necessary. Solvents such as carbon tetrachloride or a mixture of 2 parts carbon tetrachloride and 1 part volatile mineral spirits are effective in removing oil or grease, but they are quite expensive.

Blistered and flaked paint must be removed before repainting. If paint has failed in small areas, remove it by wire-brushing or scraping, and prime the bare spots. To remove the old paint, mop the surface with a solution of 2 pounds household lye in 1 gallon hot water.

Allow the solution to remain on the floor for one-half hour and scrape off softened paint with wide steel scrapers.

CAUTION: Wear rubber gloves and goggles to protect your hands and eyes. Rinse with fresh water and allow the surface to dry thoroughly before repainting. Apply two coats of paint as directed for wood floors.

For general cleaning of concrete floors, use a solution made by adding 4 ounces sodium metasilicate to 1 gallon hot water. An abrasive powder may be mixed with this solution. To obtain the best results in using this preparation, make certain that the water is very hot. Scrub the solution on the floor with a wire brush or a mop. Rinse with clear water.

Painting swimming pools

Generally the floor and wall surfaces of the pool are finished with vitreous tile. However, if you wish to paint the pool or to add some decorative finish to it, the following are the paints which you may choose, and they are especially attractive in light green, blue or aquamarine:

Cement-water paints are inexpensive and easy to apply. However, the paint may need to be renewed annually since it is not long-lasting under usual pool conditions.

Enamel paints produce an attractively smooth finish and should be applied to a very clean, dry pool. Allow to dry about a week before filling the pool with water. This paint is not long-lasting and may need repainting each season.

Waterproof enamel paints dry to a smooth, hard, glossy finish. They are chemically resistant to water and to any water-purifying agent you may place in the pool. Therefore such paints may not need to be renewed as often as the first two mentioned.

Chapter Fourteen

MAINTENANCE OF EXTERIOR WALLS

DAMPNESS IS A common enemy of walls and may be caused by climatic conditions, rain penetration, leakage due to faulty drainage from the roof or condensation of moisture within the walls. Dampness from any cause is likely to cause disintegration of the walls if it is not discovered and repaired in time.

Masonry walls

Masonry walls are of stone, brick, concrete block and concrete block that is stuccoed or painted.

LEAKAGE REPAIRS

It isn't easy to locate the source of leakage. Check on the roof flashings and around the chimneys, or any other place you think may cause the leaks. Figure 14.1 shows a wall section with dripping from flashing. Make necessary repairs at the source, and fill any cracks in the masonry with mortar. A building materials dealer will recommend the best filler for your type of wall.

RAIN PENETRATION DAMAGE

If the walls have any joints where rain can enter, especially when the rain is accompanied by high winds, inspect the joints to find which are not absolutely watertight. Those that are not watertight may be made so by grouting. Make the grout of equal parts of Portland cement and fine sand, with just enough water to form the consistency of thick cream. Work on a dry day. Put water on the joints just before applying the grout with a stiff fiber brush. Dampening the joints gives a better hold for the grout.

Grout is good for use on a brick surface; but if leakage occurs in a different type of masonry, ask a building materials dealer to suggest some other joint sealer.

MOISTURE CONDENSATION

Moisture condensation may be due to a minor cause such as vapor rising from cooking, washing and other household sources that forms fine little water drops on the windows or interior walls if their surfaces happen to be colder than the dew point of the air in the room. This vapor may penetrate through the wallpaper, plaster and wood, and form a condensation within the wall.

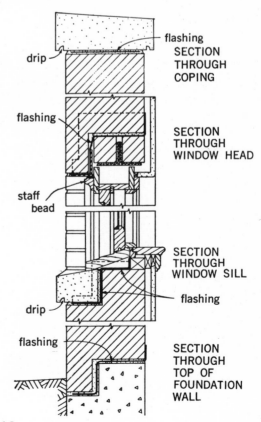

Fig. 14.1

85

One way to correct this situation is by installing a vapor barrier at the inner or warm surface of the wall. This barrier may be made of either asphalt-saturated and coated sheathing paper, smooth-surfaced asphalt roll roofing or special type paper backed with metal foil or whatever other vapor barrier your building materials dealer might recommend. If you use barrier with metal foil, it must not be in direct contact with the masonry or plaster. Your paint dealer may suggest certain paints (lead-in-oil paints, exterior varnish, or paints containing spar varnish or flake-type aluminum) that act as a vapor barrier and are applied to plaster in two or three coats.

GROUND WATER RISING

Moisture rising from ground is not usually the cause of dampness in walls. It can cause dampness, however, if there is inadequate soil drainage and nonwaterproofed foundation walls. The way this situation can be remedied by regrading to divert surface water from the walls is discussed in the following chapter. If your new house is in the process of construction, it would be helpful to install through flashing of an impenetrable material such as slate or sheet metal, inserted through the wall at a height of five to ten inches above the ground; this acts as a barrier against the rise of ground moisture.

EFFLORESCENCE DEPOSITS

Crystallized salts, deposited on the wall surface, are usually white, but they may change in color as they absorb the salts or impurities present in brick, mortar, stucco or other masonry material. The deposits are formed when the salts are dissolved by the moisture in the wall; the solution of salts and water comes to the outer surface, and the water dissolves, leaving the salts. Efflorescence is found more often on new masonry walls than on old ones. It appears more frequently near gutters and downspouts, below copings and window sills and at other spots where there is leakage. A long rainy season can also cause efflorescence in other places on the wall.

To remove these crystallized salts, you may need only to brush them off with a wire or stiff fiber brush. But if this does not accomplish the task, make an acid wash by mixing 1 part muriatic acid and 8 parts of water. Scrub the affected wall parts with a fiber brush dipped into the acid solution, but keep away from the mortar joints while scrubbing. Wash the acid off the wall with clear water. Then wash the wall again with a solution of 1 pint ammonia to 2 gallons water, to be sure all acid is removed.

CAUTION: When washing the wall with the acid solution, protect your skin, eyes, hair and clothes from any spattering. Wear goggles, cap, waterproof gloves and a coverall for your clothes.

Should the deposits reappear on the wall, wash them away as directed. Eventually, when the house gets older

and the salts evaporate in the masonry, this condition may disappear.

Wood-frame wall

Wood frames consisting of studs and other structural members are used as the base for exterior walls of wood siding, shingles, wallboard, brick veneer and stucco.

WOOD SIDING

This siding may be either a drop (or rustic) type or a bevel (or lap) siding, and is generally applied over sneathing paper and sheathing on wood surfaces, as shown in Fig. 14.2. Sometimes the siding is applied directly to the studs without any sheathing, especially in mild climates or to save extra expense. The wall frame should be braced at corners and door frames with let-in or locked-in diagonal bracing when the sheathing is not used or if it is of inadequate strength. Such bracing should extend from plate to sill and be securely nailed at each end and at the intervening studs.

If your house has a soundly constructed wood frame, with siding tight at the joints and with flashing included to prevent water from penetrating the siding, the exterior walls should not need constant attention except for repainting perhaps every five years. But should water penetrate behind the siding it may rot the wood, leaking may occur in siding and the paint coating may blister and scale off. It is essential that immediate repairs be made in such cases by filling in cracks, making the siding watertight, replacing defective siding and trim with new

Fig. 14.2

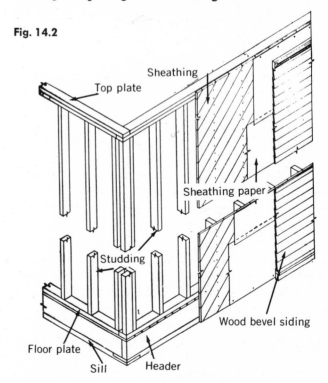

material and installing sheet metal flashings where needed (see the information on flashing in Chapter 18).

Brick veneer wall

This wall is an exterior bricklaying finish applied over the wood frame of a new house or over the walls of an older house in order to create a new look (Fig. 14.3). Sometimes cracks appear because of the brickwork settling or for some other reason. Cracks must be repaired instantly to prevent water penetration.

Fig. 14.3

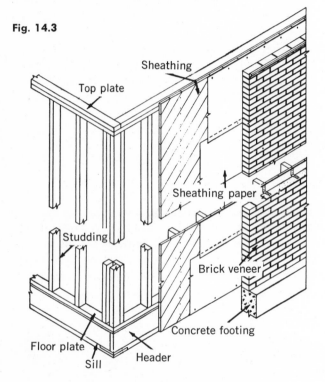

Stucco wall

A stucco wall is applied over the wood frame of a new house or over the walls of an older house (Fig. 14.4). It may also be used over brick, stone or similar materials. The ingredients of stucco are usually Portland cement, aggregate and water. For special color effects a mineral pigment is added to the mixture.

Since the use of stucco has become widespread there have been many unsatisfactory results due principally to faulty construction and lack of knowledge as to proper methods of mixing and applying the material. Cracks are the most common defects found. They may be merely hair cracks or may be large enough to admit moisture, which in turn may result in damage to the underlying structure and interior walls.

Hair cracks may be caused by using too rich a mixture or by employing inferior stucco material. They may also result from too rapid drying. Larger cracks are generally caused by settlement of the walls of the house or by some movement within them as a result of improper foundations or poorly designed framing in the structure.

Stucco over brick, stone or similar materials is liable to crack, especially around chimneys. The reason for this cracking is that the stucco has a different rate of expansion and contraction than the material that it covers, and a shearing stress or "crawling" effect takes place in the plane of contact between the two materials.

If cracks are unsightly and large enough to admit moisture, it is advisable to repair them. If, however, they are not very noticeable and seem to be doing no damage, it may be possible to postpone repairs, since the plastered cracks may appear worse than the open ones.

Before pointing, clean out the cracks thoroughly and chip them out to the shape of an inverted V so that the mortar may be keyed securely to the old work. The cracks should be brushed to remove all dust and loose particles, and the cleaned surface and adjoining stucco dampened, before new mortar is applied, so that the water in the mixture will not be absorbed.

In pointing, it is desirable to use the same brand of cement and mix in the same proportions as used in the original work. If the previous mixture cannot be determined, it is usually safe to use one containing 1 part cement, 3 parts sand and $\frac{1}{10}$ part finely divided materials, such as hydrated lime. The mortar should contain just enough water to make a fairly dry mixture, about the consistency of putty. It should be applied like a calking material—that is, rammed and tamped in well so it will make complete contact and form a secure bond.

Fig. 14.4

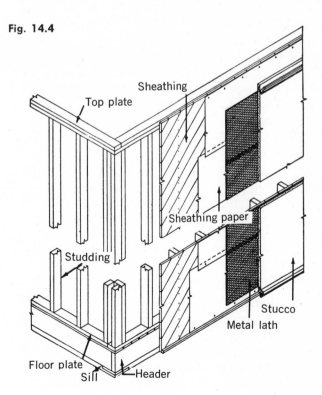

The new work should be wetted down daily for several days after it has hardened to increase the strength of the cement. It is a good plan to hang a tarpaulin or similar covering over the completed work to protect it from direct exposure to the sun and drying winds.

If the cracks show up badly after pointing work is finished, it may be necessary to paint the entire surface with a cold-water wash or oil paint. If the stucco becomes dull or discolored, it may be made more attractive by painting over it with cement-water paint. First clean the surface, following manufacturers' directions. If there are only small cracks in the stucco they will be filled in with the paint. If the stucco already has a finish coat of an oil-base paint, it is inadvisable to use a cement-water paint over it; in this case it should be repainted with either a resin-emulsion or an oil-base paint.

Exterior plywood wall

Boards built up of laminated wood veneers bonded together under heavy pressure with waterproof glue are used for exterior walls (Fig. 14.5). In a house under construction, the plywood is applied over sheathing paper, then nailed to the studs. Plywood boards may be used over the exterior walls of a house already built.

To protect the plywood from weather conditions, paint the surface with exterior house paint or give it a coating of a good-quality spar varnish.

Asbestos-cement board wall

This board is made of Portland cement and asbestos fiber formed under high pressure into a long-lasting, noncombustible material. These boards are applied to exterior walls in same way as plywood (Fig. 14.6).

Since asbestos-cement board is not susceptible to harm from water, it does not need much care while it is new. However, when the board is older, and especially in some localities where there is a likelihood of spotting from dust, soot and rain, it may not be easy to remove these dirt spots. If the wall should become soiled, clean the surface by scrubbing it hard with a stiff brush dipped in clear water, then rinse it with clean water. If you paint the wall, use a resin-emulsion or rubber-solution paint.

Shingled wall

The two types of shingles most commonly used for covering exterior walls are wood shingles and asbestos-cement shingles; they may be applied either directly over the existing surface, or the old wall covering may be removed before shingles are put on.

When you have a shingled wall, you should provide adequate flashing and drips over all the door and win-

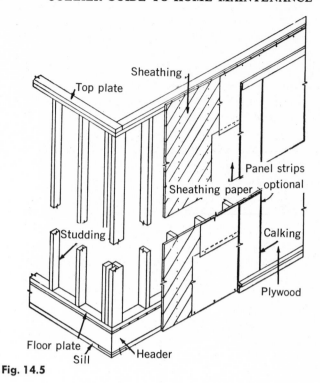

Fig. 14.5

dow openings, and provide drips under the window sills.

Damaged shingles may be removed with a nail nipper, as shown in Fig. 14.7. Slip the blade under the broken shingle and hook the notch around the nail; then strike the offset end until the nail is either drawn out or cut and you can remove the shingle.

WOOD SHINGLES

If best-quality wood is used, the shingles are a good exterior wall covering and have insulating value (Fig. 14.8). For side walls, use western red cedar, California redwood or tidewater red cypress. You may stain the shingles to get good color effects.

ASBESTOS-CEMENT SHINGLES

These shingles are made of Portland cement and asbestos fiber formed under high pressure. They are long-lasting and noncombustible. You may get them in a variety of textures, designs and colors. Usually these shingles don't need much maintenance. However, if they do break or incur other damages, they may need to be replaced. Thus when buying shingles it is a good idea to get extra ones for replacement purposes, since you may not be able to obtain shingles of the same thickness and material at a later time.

Asbestos-cement shingles are not generally finished with a paint coating; but if you desire to change the color, you may use rubber-solution or resin-emulsion paint, meticulously following the manufacturers' directions.

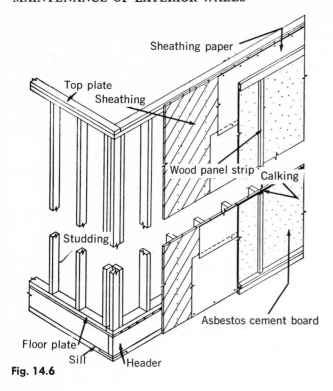

Fig. 14.6

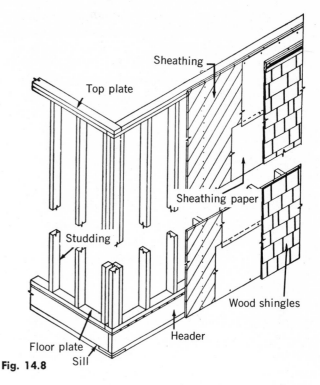

Fig. 14.8

Gutters, downspouts, fastenings, electrical conduits, flashings, screens on doors and windows and other metal on the house exterior are often the cause of stains on asbestos-cement shingles. These metal surfaces should be painted (and repainted when necessary) to prevent such wall staining.

The shingles may accumulate soot and dust deposits; these should be scrubbed with a stiff brush dipped in soap and water, or a solution of trisodium phosphate. Then rinse the wall with clear water.

Fig. 14.7

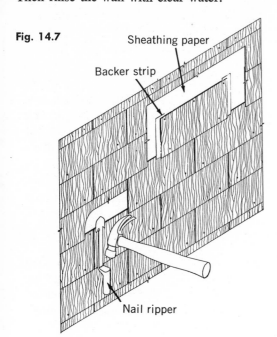

Copper stains on asbestos-cement shingles may be removed by stiff brushing with white vinegar or a five per cent solution of acetic acid, then rinsed with clear, cold water.

Rust stains may be removed by a two per cent solution of oxalic acid or a five per cent solution of phosphoric acid, then rinsed with clear, cold water.

Sometimes brown stains appear because of contact with unpainted wood during construction; these stains may be removed by an oxalic acid solution or a commercial abrasive cleaner, then rinsed with clear, cold water.

CAUTION: When using any acid solution protect your hair, eyes, skin and clothes from any splashing. Wear a cap, goggles, gloves and protective covering over clothes.

If there are fresh paint spots on these shingles, wipe them off with a cloth soaked in turpentine or other paint thinner. If the paint spots are dried, scrape them off with a razor blade or knife, and wipe the surface with paint remover.

Oil stains on the shingles cannot always be completely removed, but you may be able to make the stain less noticeable by several applications (made a day apart) of carbon tetrachloride or a similar volatile solvent.

Tar or asphalt stains on shingles cannot be removed, but you may be able to lessen them by wiping the stains with turpentine or other paint thinner.

Chapter Fifteen

CONDENSATION IN BASEMENT AND FOUNDATION WALLS

Reasons for damage

IN GENERAL, there are two classes of basements where wetness prevails all or part of the time.

There are damp basements where the walls and floors seem to sweat and where moisture runs down the walls. This condition is more pronounced during long wet periods. The difficulty is sometimes caused by penetration of moisture through the walls and floor because of improper subdrainage. More often, however, the damp condition is due to condensation of moisture on chilled wall surfaces.

The second type of damp basement is that in which water flows freely during heavy rainfall or when the snow is melting away, resulting in a flooded condition. Flooding in most cases is caused by defective walls, careless backfilling or improper grading around the walls, which allows the surface water to pass into the basement.

In both types of basement the condition of the walls themselves should be examined in order to detect cracks or loose mortar, and repairs should be made in accordance with directions given later in this chapter.

Good ventilation is essential to a dry basement. As much window space as possible should be provided. When the outdoor air is cool and dry, keep the windows open. If the weather is damp, keep the windows closed, because warm, moist air may result in mildew or condensation of moisture upon the colder surfaces within the basement.

Surface water diversion

Since a wet basement often results from water penetrating the walls or floors, provision must be made to have this water carried off before it comes into contact with the foundation.

Provide adequate gutters, conductors and downspouts to carry the water away from the roof. Connect the downspouts to a drain emptying into a storm sewer, dry well, open water course or whatever suitable outlet you can use. (Find out if in your locality it is prohibited to drain surface water into the sanitary sewers.) If your downspout is not so connected, place a spatter board or a splash block of adequate size at the outlet to throw the water away from the wall.

It is essential that the water be shed as quickly as possible. This may be accomplished in some cases by proper grading. A good method is to place additional filling against the basement wall, then grade it down to a sharp, smooth slope that extends about ten feet from the wall. Sow the slope with good lawn grass seed or sod and roll it down evenly and firmly. If you find it necessary to grade above the basement window sills, build around them a rectangular or curved area wall of brick, concrete or metal. Put on hinged covers for closing the openings when it rains or snows.

An alternate method to divert surface water from basement walls is to lay a paved concrete walk or gutter, about three feet wide, all around the house, providing a gradual slope away from the walls. Before applying concrete for the paved walk, prepare the wall surface by roughening, cleaning and moistening it. When you pave the walk, round the concrete to meet the wall. This makes a good bond and turns the water away from the joints.

If you make a gutter you must construct it so that it will conduct surface water along the wall and lead it to

90

some low spot. Make the gutter about two feet wide, with an outer edge (or lip) five inches wide. The outer edge of the gutter depression should be about four inches deep and should slope up gradually to meet the wall. Treat the joint at the wall in the same way as directed for the walk in preceding paragraph.

Ground water drains

If your house is in a low, damp location, or some place where the subsoil contains a large amount of water, install drain tile around the footings to lower the water level and to carry the water away before it penetrates into your basement. But if conditions are unusually bad, waterproofing may be necessary in addition to the drain.

As shown in Fig. 15.1, dig a trench adjoining the bottom of the basement floor to a depth of a few inches below the floor but not below the footing level. It should be about three to four inches in diameter. Lay the tile so that the grade or fall will be smooth, to avoid any settlement of mud within the pipe. Tile should also be connected to an outlet similar to that recommended for the downspouts. Cover the cracks between the joints with strips of roofing paper or pieces of tin to prevent sediment from running into the pipe. Lay the pipe carefully and surround it with fine broken stone or gravel tamped firmly around the pipe. Then cover the pipe with coarser broken stone (up to one inch in diameter); this covering may be from one to two feet deep. Before backfilling to grade with the earth, spread burlap or grass sods (with grass side down) over the stone to prevent any fine material from falling or washing down into the stone.

Waterproofing and dampproofing exterior surfaces

If waterproofing is to be applied, it should be done before backfilling. There are various methods used, depending largely upon local conditions. In many cities there are representatives of waterproofing companies

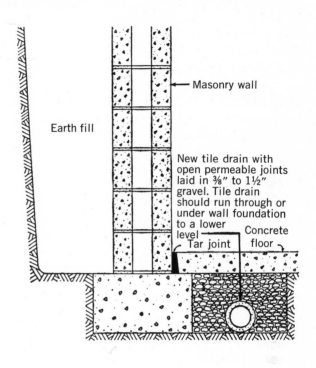

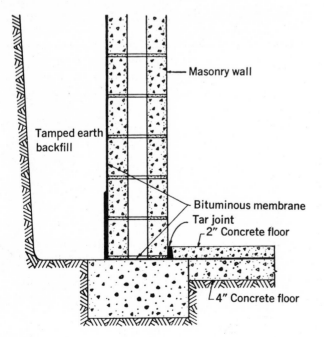

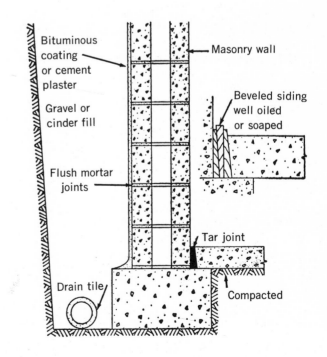

Fig. 15.1

who may be called in to inspect the damp basement and make recommendations for waterproofing. You may also ask your paint dealer to recommend materials to use. When you apply a waterproofing coating to a wall, it should be done on the exterior of the wall. Thus water is prevented from entering into the wall, and the water pressure tends to force the coating into tighter contact. If the waterproofing coating is placed on the interior wall, the pressure through the wall may force it away.

CEMENT PLASTER COATS

Where ground water conditions are not especially bad and dampness only is to be guarded against, a cement-mortar coating is easiest to apply and is perhaps in most common use. This may consist of a one-half inch coating of Portland cement mortar (mixed in the proportion of 1 sack Portland cement to 2 cubic feet clean, well-graded sand, plus finely divided materials, such as hydrated lime or diatomaceous silica) or a plastic cement applied to the exterior surface of the wall with a trowel. To insure a good bond, the wall surface should be thoroughly scraped and cleaned with sharp-edged instruments and a wire brush, then dampened before the mortar is applied.

BITUMINOUS COATINGS

It is best to cover the surface with a bituminous coating if conditions worse than mere dampness exist. This coating may be a simple one of coal-tar pitch or asphalt, or may be a built-up covering of alternate layers of bituminous material and tar paper. These coatings are often used alone on new walls or in cases where walls are in such good condition that they do not require the plaster coat. If walls are rough, however, like brick, stone or concrete block, they usually require a plaster coat before being waterproofed.

In applying cold bituminous coatings, first apply a priming coat of the same bitumen thinned with gasoline or with kerosene to the consistency of paint. This mixture is applied cold, with a mop or large brush, and is intended to soak into the pores and provide a good bond for the top coating.

The ordinary bituminous coatings are usually applied hot and swabbed on with a roofing mop to a thickness of at least one-eighth inch. Several coats may be applied if necessary. Dull spots, which indicate absorption, should be touched up until a uniform shiny appearance is produced.

There have been recent developments in the application of such materials, one of which is the use of compressed air to "shoot" the material upon the surface in much the same manner as that employed in paint spraying.

Bituminous layers, or membranes, are similar to ordinary bituminous coatings, except that they are much thicker and consist of alternate layers of bituminous material and tar paper. The membranes should be used in extremely wet conditions or where there is water pressure against the walls from a spring or other source. The number of layers to be applied depends on the conditions to be overcome.

For dampproofing a brick foundation wall, heavy penetrating bituminous dampproofing paint may be used, after which a cement mortar coat may be troweled directly onto the painted surface to prevent the paint from flaking and peeling.

The application of any coating upon the inner surfaces of walls that are penetrable to water is generally ineffective. If such a method is used, however, a thick layer of mortar is suggested. This should be made of 1 part Portland cement and 3 parts well-graded sand mixed with as little water as practicable. The mortar should be applied to the dampened wall after leakage through the wall has stopped. The finished coat should be kept damp for a week after it has set to increase its watertightness.

Concrete floor repairs

If the floor is cracked and seepage has penetrated through it, apply either a bituminous coating or a membrane waterproofing treatment to the surface before putting a new concrete topping over it.

If the floor is very badly cracked, you may need to put a two-inch layer of new concrete mix over the old surface. In the middle of the new concrete place No. 14 gauge lightweight steel-wire mesh as a reinforcement.

After the new concrete is smoothed down to the desired surface, keep it moist for three days to prevent it from drying out too rapidly.

Foundation wall repairs

Falling mortar between joints and cracks in the walls may be caused by shrinkage of the mortar originally used in building the wall through drying out, or by the expansion of saturated mortar.

Sometimes the walls are built on uneven ground incapable of supporting equal weight at all points, and when the wall settles unevenly it may crack.

Flowing water or an underground natural spring under one part of the foundation can bring about such defects in the wall.

Once a small crack is started, weather conditions may cause larger defects to ensue; for example, extreme cold and heat may result in contraction or expansion. Frost may often cause cracks. Water seeping through these cracks may eventually cause the material to crumble, and rapid disintegration may occur in the mortar joints.

It may be more advisable to call in a skilled workman if the damage is of large proportions; but if there are only minor repairs to be made, start by chipping and picking out any loose mortar, then brush the joints carefully to remove all loose particles and dust. Before you apply new mortar, dampen the cleaned surface so that it will not absorb the water from the mixture.

In the case of cracks in the walls, especially in concrete walls, chip out the crack to a V-shape, leaving the surface of the crack irregular and rough so that the new material may obtain a good grip and be held firmly in place. As explained in the foregoing paragraph, brush the crack clean and dampen it before new material is inserted.

Mortar repairs

The same proportions of material may be used to repair concrete floors and foundation walls. A mixture of 1 part Portland cement to 2½ parts sand, or 1 part Portland cement to 3 parts sand, is recommended; however, for a damp basement or one which is exposed to very moist conditions, a mixture of 1 part Portland cement to 2 parts sand may be better. You need to use your own judgment in making these mixtures, which are dependent on the condition of your basement. Use sufficient water to make a fairly dry mortar the consistency of putty.

In filling cracks the mortar should be rammed and tamped in well (like a calking material) so that it forms secure contact with all the corners and depressions in the wall. After the crack is packed in tightly, use a trowel to smooth the surface.

In pointing the joints in the masonry, apply the mortar with a trowel and finish the surface to conform with the old mortar.

When the new mortar has hardened, wet down the repaired spots each day for about a week, to increase the strength of the cement. If the repair work was done on an exterior wall, a tarpaulin or similar covering should be suspended over it as protection from too rapid drying by the wind and sun.

Chapter Sixteen

BASEMENT IMPROVEMENTS

ASIDE FROM THE utilitarian function of the basement, you may desire to use part of it for family recreational purposes, to pursue hobbies or to have extra space for informal social life. Improvements may be made in lighting, painting, partitioning or any other aspect that would enhance the basement.

Better lighting

Of course nature's own way of lighting is best if it is possible to add new windows or enlarge the existing windows. The exterior of the house, at the windows, should be cleared of any shrubs or weeds that are too close, in order to insure sufficient entry of light.

In addition, have enough electric outlets and extension wires to permit the use of portable or additional lamps in any part of the basement. Frosted bulbs are best for basement lighting, since they give a more uniformly diffused light. Insofar as distribution of light is concerned, two or three twenty-five watt frosted bulbs are better than one fifty- or one hundred-watt plain bulb.

In case a lamp is placed where the bulb is liable to be broken, it is advisable to protect it with a wire basket-like covering or guard. Porcelain fittings are recommended for basement fixtures because of the danger of shock.

Whitewashing walls

A coat of whitewash will generally do much to brighten a dark basement. It is the cheapest of all coverings and provides a sanitary coating. Clean the surface of all dirt, scales or other loose material by brushing well with a clean, stiff brush or by first scraping and then brushing. If the walls have been previously whitewashed,

wash off all of the old material with a cloth or sponge and hot water. Fill nail holes and cracks with a mixture of 4 parts hydrated lime or lime putty and 1 part plaster of Paris, mixed with enough water to make a thick paste. Force the paste into the holes and carefully smooth off flush with the surface by means of a putty knife.

Whitewashes and lime paints must be applied thin. In fact, best results will be achieved if the application is so thin that the surface to which it is applied may easily be seen through the film while it is wet. The coating will dry opaque, however, and the thin coat will give better results than a thick one.

If a brush is used, a large high-grade brush is preferable. Do not attempt to brush out the coating, as in applying oil paint; simply spread the whitewash on as evenly and quickly as possible.

Much time and labor can be saved, and a job as good if not better than that performed with a brush can be done, by using a pressure spray pump or a paint gun. In using either of these appliances, however, the whitewash should be strained through cheesecloth to free the mixture from any lumps that might clog the working parts of the sprayer. An advantage in using a sprayer is that corners and crevices are more readily covered than with a brush.

WHITEWASH FORMULAS

1. In basements where there is a tendency toward dampness and where a durable wash (which will not rub off) is desired, the following formula should be satisfactory and easy to prepare:

Soak 5 pounds casein (glue substitute) in about 2 gallons water (preferably hot) until thoroughly softened (about 2 hours). Dilute 3 pints ammonia with about 1

94

gallon water. Add the ammonia to the casein and allow the mixture to dissolve thoroughly. Make a thick cream by thoroughly mixing 50 pounds (1 sack) hydrated lime and 6 gallons water, or by carefully slaking and screening 38 pounds (½ bushel) quicklime. When both the lime and the casein mixtures are cold, slowly add the casein-ammonia solution to the lime, stirring constantly. Just before use, dilute 5 pints formaldehyde with about 3 gallons cold water and slowly add this solution to the lime mixture, stirring constantly and vigorously. Be careful not to add the formaldehyde too rapidly. Thin to desired consistency.

2. If the basement is dry, the following formula should be satisfactory:

Dissolve 3 pounds glue in about 2 gallons water. Make a thick cream of 50 pounds (1 sack) hydrated lime and about 7 gallons water, or carefully slake 38 pounds (½ bushel) quicklime, straining the soft paste through a fine screen. Add the glue solution to the lime, stirring constantly. Thin to desired consistency.

The area covered by a gallon of either of the foregoing mixtures depends on the nature of the surface. A gallon will cover about 225 square feet on wood, about 180 square feet on brick and about 270 square feet on plaster. The first formula given will make about sixteen gallons of whitewash, and the second about eleven gallons. If a smaller quantity is desired, the amount of each ingredient may be reduced accordingly. For instance, for four gallons of whitewash, according to the first formula, take one-quarter the amounts of liquids and solids given and mix as specified.

OTHER BASEMENT FINISHES

If the walls are damp, they should first be treated as outlined in the preceding chapter. Cleaning and brushing, as previously recommended, are also necessary. After the walls have thoroughly dried, they may be treated and painted with a cold-water wash or oil paint.

If the basement floor is below grade, it is not advisable to use oil paint, even though the floor appears to be dry. Refer to Chapter 10 for directions for painting a concrete floor.

Installing a new ceiling

A finished look is given to the basement when you add a ceiling. Most commonly used for this purpose is asbestos or gypsum board, gypsum plaster board or plaster on metal lath; you may even make a furred metal ceiling. The type of material you use depends on your taste and your budget. Whatever you use, make sure the material is fire-resistant and that it fits tightly.

First inspect the ceiling for any openings through which fire could penetrate to the floor above; you may find such gaps between joists or studs where they join the foundation, or around registers or pipes. Fill the openings with a noncombustible material such as concrete, hollow tile, gypsum block, crushed refuse mortar, plaster, broken brick or whatever your hardware dealer recommends as a firestop. You may use wire mesh to hold the material in place over the opening.

Also add fire protection within one or two feet of the top of a furnace, boiler or smoke pipe by using a loose-fitting metal shield so placed that it gives an air space of one to two inches between the metal and the surface of the wall. Into this air space between the metal and the joists put small blocks of noncombustible material. You may choose an easier way by suspending the metal shields on hooks or wires fastened to the joists. Do not use any tin shield that has soldered joints.

Installing partitions

First make a floor plan of how you want to divide the basement, allowing the necessary space for storage, laundry, gameroom, workshop or whatever space your family's needs require. Then decide on the material you will use for the partitions; to make for an orderly and attractive appearance all partitions in the basement should be similarly made. The first partition, of course, is the one to be built around the furnace, coalbin and woodpile (if you use wood for fuel).

If the partition is to be of wood or wallboard, you will need to construct a framework on which to nail the sheathing. Use 2 by 4 lumber for the studs and plates. If wallboard is used, space the studs sixteen or twenty-four inches apart, depending upon the width of the board. A neatly finished, tight wood wall may be achieved by using three-quarter inch tongued-and-grooved boards.

If you use hollow tile, brick or concrete blocks you won't need to construct a framework. The partition does not have to be very thick, since it does not bear the heavy load that a foundation wall must carry; however, it should be of sufficient thickness to last well.

Partitions may reach to the ceiling or may reach only to three-quarters of the height of the basement; the height depends on the purpose it is to serve (see also "Room Divider Closet" at the end of Chapter 22).

Chapter Seventeen

ROOFS, GUTTERS AND DOWNSPOUTS

Roof damage

THE ROOF IS the part of the house that usually gets the hardest wear, since it is subjected to hot sun rays, strong winds, snow, rain, sleet, ice, freezing and thawing. A roof needs constant vigilance, and repairs should be made as soon as you find the slightest defect so that you will avoid the expense of reroofing.

Repairing a roof or adding a new one is not to be undertaken in an amateurish way; there is too much at stake here to do anything less than a perfect job in a professional manner. If you are to tackle these tasks yourself, make sure to get the best material and the soundest instruction from the dealer who sells it to you. Usually a roof repair is not a one-man job, and it may be best to enlist a handy helper before you start.

It is not always easy to find the hole in a roof that causes leaks through your ceiling. Of course if your house has an attic you can wait for a sunny day and see the light shine through the roof hole. But if you cannot see it and have to go up on the roof to find the hole, be most cautious about how you get onto the roof, especially if it's a slanted one.

Wear rubber-soled shoes when working on the roof in order to be more sure-footed. Avoid doing any more walking on the roof than is necessary, because by such action you may unwittingly cause damage.

Except in case of emergency, plan to repair the roof in clear mild weather when the outside temperature is not below 50°F.

Ladder and nails for roofing

A ladder must be hooked over the roof at an angle that is the same as the slope of the roof. In Fig. 17.1 you will see two different ladders and the way in which the "hook" is made by nailing a strong piece of wood to each ladder leg, at the upper end of the ladder. Brace these pieces of wood with short boards nailed between the hook pieces and the ladder legs.

You may use an ordinary ladder on which to add this hook, or make a special "chicken ladder" by using a long board, one inch thick by ten inches wide. Then, about twelve inches apart, nail one by two inch cleats to the board. At the top of this ladder, add the hook described in the preceding paragraph.

Use only rust-resistant nails, because inferior nails often cause damage to the roof. Select the length of the nails according to the thickness of the roofing material.

For asphalt-prepared shingles and roll roofing, use large-headed zinc-coated nails.

For built-up roofing you may not need many nails, but those you use should be zinc-coated.

For slate and tile roofs, use copper or copper-clad nails.

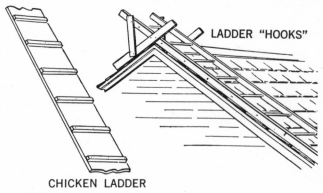

CHICKEN LADDER

LADDER "HOOKS"

Fig. 17.1

96

For asbestos-cement shingles, use galvanized five-penny or six-penny nails.

For a metal roof, the nails should be of the same material as the roofing material. For copper roofing use copper nails. For galvanized and terne-plate (tin) roofing use hot-dipped zinc-coated nails.

Reroofing

A roof may be so damaged that it is more advisable to remove it and replace it with a new one. Or you may select a new roofing that does not necessitate removal of the old material, but can be placed on top of it. The latter method is more desirable because your house is protected from rain while reroofing goes on.

ASPHALT-PREPARED ROOFINGS

These roofings are made in three types: smooth-surfaced rolls, mineral-surfaced rolls and mineral-surfaced shingles.

The smooth-surfaced rolls are less expensive than mineral-surfaced roll roofings, and they do not withstand weather conditions as well, because the asphalt coating is not as well protected from the strong sunlight as is the mineral-granule surface.

Mineral-surfaced rolls are made in a variety of colors, in solid or blended tints. The mineral granules protect the surface of the asphalt coating from bad weather and also increase the fire resistance of the roofing.

When using asphalt shingles, care must be taken not to nail the shingle too close to its upper edge; if you do so, the shingle may be damaged when there are strong winds.

MINERAL-SURFACED ROLL ROOFING

Minor damages. Small breaks or nail holes may be repaired simply by applying flashing cement to the damaged part.

Large breaks. Open the horizontal seam below the break. Under this slip a strip of new roofing, and allow the strip to extend about six inches beyond the edges of the break. The lower edge of the strip must be flush with the horizontal exposed edge. Apply lap cement liberally on the upper surface of the new repair strip before you insert it. After you put in this new strip, very firmly press down the edges of the roof, then nail the strip securely. Nails should be spaced two inches apart and about three-quarters of an inch from the edge of the break. Then apply lap cement to the horizontal seam and renail it in place.

Large area damaged. Remove the damaged roofing. Replace it with new roofing of the same type, and use full-width sheets that you apply by lapping, cementing and nailing down.

Leaks at seams. Sweep out seams to remove dirt and dust. Cut all buckles that terminate at the seams. Insert a strip of new roofing as explained for large breaks.

SMOOTH-SURFACED ROLL ROOFING

This roofing is repaired in the same manner as described for mineral-surfaced rolls (Fig. 17.2). You may apply smooth-surfaced roll roofing over the existing roofing material, provided the old material is in fairly good condition. If it is not, then remove the worn part of the existing roofing before applying any new material.

To get the best service from the smooth-surfaced material, recoat it periodically with a bituminous roof coating.

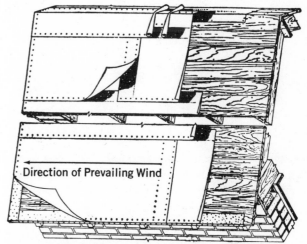

Direction of Prevailing Wind

SMOOTH or MINERAL SURFACED ROLL ROOFING
HORIZONTAL APPLICATION OVER ROOF BOARDS
HORIZONTAL SEAMS LAPPED 4"
VERTICAL SEAMS LAPPED 6"

Fig. 17.2

ASPHALT SHINGLES

The principal damage to asphalt-shingle roofs is caused by the action of strong winds on shingles nailed too high.

To repair shingles that have been nailed too high, place a small quantity of plastic cement under the center and about one inch above the lower edge of each shingle tab; then press the tab down firmly (Fig. 17.3). The spot of plastic cement, which can be applied with a putty knife, trowel, calking gun or other convenient means, should be approximately $1\frac{1}{2}$ inches in diameter when pressed down. Do not use too much plastic cement, since it may prevent the shingle tabs from lying flat, and do not seal the lower edges of the tabs completely.

Usually the shingles most affected by winds are those in the four or five courses nearest the ridge and in the area extending about five feet from the edge or rake of the roof. Sealing down the butts of the shingles in these areas is usually sufficient.

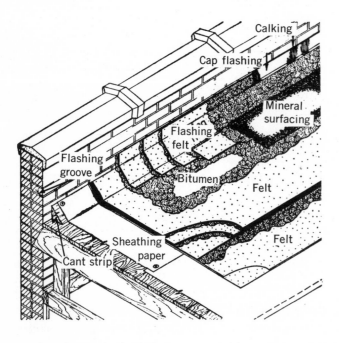

SQUARE TAB
STRIP SHINGLES   Exposure c d = 4"
12½" x 36"
Headlap a b = 4½"

Fig. 17.3

Built-up roofing

This type of roofing is used for a roof that has a low pitch, in order to provide enough pitch for water to drain off the roof readily. The roofing is constructed as shown in Fig. 17.4.

There are unsurfaced asphalt roofs in which the surface coating of bitumen is exposed directly to the weather. There are also surfaced roofs which have gravel or slag embedded in the bituminous coating in the pro-

portion of 400 pounds of gravel or 300 pounds of slag per 100 square feet of roof surface. Last, there are coal-tar roofs that must be surfaced with gravel or slag in the same amounts prescribed.

Repairing built-up roofs

It is important that the same type of bitumen and bituminous-saturated felt used in the original roof be used in all maintenance and repair work.

INSPECTION AND MAINTENANCE

Built-up roofs should be inspected on completion, six months later and then at least once a year thereafter, preferably in the early fall. It is important that the top coating of bitumen be continuous at all times. Whenever inspection discloses that this coating has been damaged or has weathered badly, it should be renewed. When the top coating of bitumen is no longer heavy enough to embed the mineral surfacing properly, sweep or scrape the inadequate areas clean and apply a heavy coating of hot bitumen and fresh slag or gravel.

REPAIRING SMALL AREAS

There may be spots in old neglected roofs where the surface felt has disintegrated. To repair such places, remove the disintegrated felt layers, replace them with new felt mopped in place and complete the repair with at least one additional layer of felt extending at least six inches beyond the other layers.

If there are wood decks and the section cut out extends to the deck, place a piece of sheathing paper under the felt. This piece of sheathing paper should extend six inches beyond the cut edges. Cut any large blisters, making two cuts at right angles to each other and pulling back the cut sections of the membrane to permit the moisture to dry. When dry, cement the cut sections in place with hot bitumen and mop on at least one additional ply of felt as described in preceding paragraph.

REPAIRS INVOLVING THE ENTIRE ROOF

When the old roof is allowed to remain in place, scrape off the slag or gravel surfacing (or, if the roof is unsurfaced, any weathered bitumen or felt) and sweep the entire surface free of dirt. Lay at least one ply of dry felt over the old roof before mopping on the additional plies of felt.

Inadequately nailed smooth-surfaced built-up roofs that have been damaged by strong winds are reinforced by driving double staggered rows of nails. Drive nails preferably through steel or hard fiber discs, starting the double rows of nails at the edge of the roof and keeping them four feet apart. Cover each row with twelve-inch strips of saturated felt cemented to the roof and surface-

Fig. 17.4

mopped with hot asphalt. Use special staples instead of nails for roofings applied over gypsum decks.

Inspect badly wrinkled or buckled smooth-surfaced built-up roofs frequently and make minor repairs to keep them waterproof, using either hot or cold asphalt cement. Complete resurfacing with hot asphalt and the addition of slag or gravel surfacing, or the application of additional plies or felt to such roofs, is not practicable because of the wrinkles. Replace roofs of this type that cannot be made waterproof by surface repairs.

Rigid roofing materials

Slate, tile and cement-asbestos roofings are the rigid roofing materials generally used on permanent buildings with pitched roofs. These materials normally render long service with little or no repair.

SLATE ROOFS

The most common repair on slate roofs is the replacement of broken slates (Fig. 17.5). Remove the broken slate and cut the nails with a ripper. Insert a new plate of the same color and size as the broken one and nail it through the vertical joint of the next course above. Force a 3 by 6 inch (or larger) strip of copper, galvanized iron or painted tin (terne) under the course above the nail and bend the strip slightly concave to hold it in place. The strip usually will extend about two inches under this course and will cover the nail and extend two inches below it. Also replace broken slates on hips and ridges.

Fig. 17.5

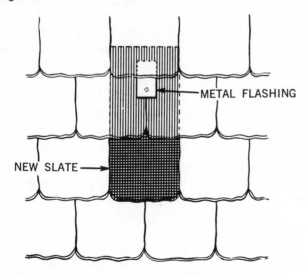

TILE ROOFS

Replace broken shingle tiles in the same way as broken slates. Replace broken Spanish tiles by troweling Portland cement mortar on the new tile surface that will be

lapped by the course above and on the surface that will lap the course below, and by pressing the new tile firmly into position. Fasten the new tile in place with copper wire. Interlocking tiles use special fastenings and are easily replaced.

CEMENT-ASBESTOS SHINGLES

Three types of shingle roofs are shown in Fig. 17.6. To replace broken shingles laid by the *American* (rectangular) method, follow the procedure outlined for replacing broken slates.

To replace shingles of the *Dutch-lap* (square or side-lap) method, or the *French* (hexagonal) method, remove the metal fastener or anchor and nails, then remove the broken pieces and insert a new shingle with a new fastener. If the nails cannot be withdrawn, notch the new shingle to avoid them.

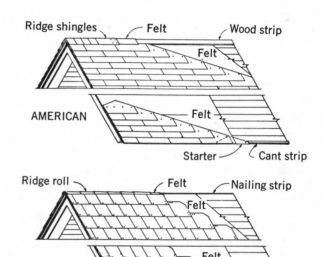

Fig. 17.6

Metal roofings

Roof covering of sheet metal may be of copper, monel metal, zinc, terne (tin), aluminum or galvanized iron. Metal roofs are strong and long-wearing.

COPPER ROOFS

When properly applied to the roof, copper roofs require practically no maintenance or repair. Soldered seams that are broken, or breaks in the metal at points other than at the seams, indicate that provision for expansion and contraction is not adequate. In such cases the only permanent repair that can be made to the roof is the installation of expansion joints.

Small holes in copper roofing can be repaired with a drop of solder. Larger holes can be repaired by soldering a piece of copper over the hole. In soldering copper, scrape clean the surfaces to be joined with a sharp instrument or rub them with emery cloth until the metal is bright; apply zinc chloride or rosin as a flux, and then tin the surfaces with a thin coating of solder. The solder should contain equal parts of tin and lead. Avoid using too much solder.

GALVANIZED IRON ROOFS

This type of roof is maintained principally by keeping it painted. The frequency of painting will vary, but painting should never be put off until rust appears. Should rust be present, clean the metal thoroughly with a wire brush before painting.

Small holes in roofing can be repaired by replacing the smallest unit of the roofing material.

Seams in galvanized iron roofs are, in general, of the following types: V crimp, side and end overlap of corrugated sheets, ordinary shingle lap and pressed standing-seam These seams are not soldered and depend on the pitch of the roof and their overlap to keep out water.

Leaky seams may result from improper application of the roofing, from corrosion between the overlap of the sheets, and in the case of V crimp and corrugated sheets from failure of the exposed nailing. These leaks are corrected by renailing, calking or replacing all or part of the sheet or sheets in question.

TERNE (TIN) ROOFINGS

These roofings are maintained largely by keeping them properly painted. Roofing ternes are normally supplied with the surface that is intended for the underside of the roof painted. They also may be furnished with a priming coat on both surfaces. Paint the exposed surface of terne roofing immediately after the roof is installed. If rust is present, clean the surface of the metal thoroughly with a wire brush before painting.

Many leaks in terne roofings are caused by faulty seams. Leaky soldered seams can be resoldered. Formed seams can be opened and reformed, or, where this is not practicable, they can be calked with plastic calking materials.

Wood shingle roofing

The more important factors that influence the length of service of this type of roofing are the pitch and the exposure of the roof, the character of the wood, the kind of nails used and the preservative treatment given to the shingles.

CREOSOTE TREATING AND STAINING

The life of wood shingles is greatly prolonged by treating them with creosote oil by the full-cell process. Staining is, however, more commonly used to maintain shingles. Creosote and coal-tar preservative for brush and spray treatment is satisfactory for both treated and untreated shingles. It is applied after the shingles are on the roof. If colored stains are desired, use pigmented stains containing creosote oil or its derivatives, since they are superior to stains without creosote. The frequency of staining varies with the climate, the kind of wood, the pitch of the roof and the treatment given the shingles before their application.

OIL PAINT

Do not use heavy oil paints, because they may cause the shingles to warp and curl.

CRACKED AND BROKEN SHINGLES

Cracked wood shingles do not ordinarily cause immediate leaks unless the shingle courses are not properly aligned. However, cracks may allow water to reach nails in the shingles in the next course below, and so contribute to early failure of the nails. For this reason, cracked shingles should be removed. To remove them use the same method as described earlier in this chapter for slate roofs. Replace the broken shingle with a new one of the same size, and nail it through the exposed butt, preferably using thin copper nails. Also nail the shingle immediately above, through the exposed butt.

FACE-NAILING

Do not face-nail shingles except where broken shingles are replaced. Do not try to nail down the butts of warped or curled shingles, because the nails will invariably work loose, and the nail holes will be sources of potential leaks.

Flashing

Flashing is used to make watertight the angle where the roof meets an intersecting surface, such as the junction of the roof and the chimney, skylight and walls, and in depressions or valleys where two planes of the roof join. The purpose of flashing around a chimney, walls or other vertical surfaces is to keep water from accumulating at that joint by having it flow to a lower level. Flashing in depressions or valleys is a way to conduct the water to the gutters or downspouts. Use flashing material that is resistant to corrosion.

REPAIR OF LEAKS

If a leak is below the junction of the roof and the wall, or near the chimney, inspect the flashing to determine the extent of damage. Flashing may have become loosened, and it may be necessary to repair it with mortar or to replace it. You can obtain flashing cement to seal any cracks around the flashing.

If flashing that extends over the top of the roof onto a vertical wall becomes loosened, coat the underside of the extending lap with flashing cement, then nail the lap down securely. Use short nails so you won't penetrate the roof boards.

If you find signs of rust on metal flashing, clean it thoroughly with a wire brush, then paint it with a metal paint to keep it from corroding.

Valley flashing should be made watertight by covering the portion to be overlapped with flashing cement immediately before applying it to the roof covering.

You may need to replace with new pieces of metal any corroded or broken portion of flashing, if the valley is very narrow. In a wide, open valley this is a simple operation; but in a closed valley it may become an intricate chore.

When the closed valley is covered with shingles, leaks may be hard to repair unless you fold into a wedge-shape point the metal that you insert under the shingle. Following the steps shown in Fig. 17.7, insert piece A under the top layer of the first course of shingles at the eaves, and over the top of the old flashing. Slide it upwards until the upper point of the inserted sheet is about two inches above the butts of the second course of shingles (shown with dotted lines at C). Now insert another sheet under the second course of shingles, pushing it upwards on top of the old flashing until the point

Fig. 17.7

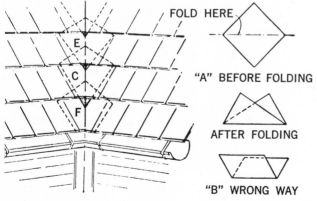

of the inserted sheet is at E. The lower point of this piece will show below the butts of the shingles in the second course, as shown at F. Continue until the top of the valley has been reached, or until you have covered all broken flashings.

Gutters, downspouts and leaders

Of prime importance in their proper maintenance is keeping the gutters clean. Do not permit an accumulation of birds' nests, leaves or any rubbish; they can cause water from rain and snow to back up and result in damage to the roof and house. Buy a strainer from your hardware dealer and put it over the gutter outlet, so the debris won't enter the gutter.

REPAIRING A WOOD GUTTER

If the gutter has sagged, force it back into place with a hammer and a block of wood, then renail it in its original position. Nails should be driven in deeply and all holes be filled with putty. If paint is chipped, touch up chipped spots with fresh paint. After repair, coat the surface with linseed oil or with asphalt paint.

A split in the wood should be repaired by a sheet metal patch. This patch may be either aluminum, copper or coated iron. For aluminum use aluminum nails; for copper use copper nails and for coated iron use galvanized iron nails. First clean the damaged area, then cover it with asphalt paint; over this apply a layer of flashing cement with a putty knife. Now cut the metal patch the desired size and shape it to fit the gutter; the patch should be of sufficient width to cover the inside surface of gutter and the tops of both edges. Press the patch into the cement, nail it down along all edges and cover the nail holes; this will also protect the metal. If the patch is longer than ten inches, add another row of nails about six or seven inches below the first row.

Only rustproof metal should be used to line a wood gutter, but if other metal is used the inside of the gutter should be painted with a metal paint or swabbed with a bituminous material.

REPAIRING A METAL GUTTER

If the metal buckles or folds, you may need to remove the gutter and then use a soft-faced hammer and a block of wood (shaped like the gutter) to hammer out the creases. To avoid marring the gutter surface, use a hammer that has a head made of wood, plastic or fiber.

A small hole may be mended by putting a drop of solder in it. If the hole is large it should be patched with a piece of sheet metal (of the same metal as is now in the gutter). Be sure that the patch and the area where it is to be placed are very clean, and then solder the patch over the damaged part.

You can make a temporary patch, if necessary, with a piece of sturdy cotton duck cloth or a piece of roofing felt. The patch should be clean and dry. On both sides of the cloth put a generous, even coating of flashing cement. Place the patch over the hole, and press down until it adheres. As soon as you can, replace this with a permanent metal patch.

REPAIRING GUTTER HANGERS

A metal gutter is attached to the eaves either by a twisted wire rope, metal brackets that may be adjustable or rigid, straps of sheet metal or long spikes. Whichever type is used on your house, the hangers may become loosened or broken, and this might cause the gutter to sag and impede proper drainage. If such damage occurs, the broken hanger should be either adjusted and repaired or replaced, in order that the gutter slope to its outlet end be uniform in downward grade.

Sometimes the supporting hangers may be placed too far apart; in that case, you may need to add more hangers to make sure that the gutter's downward slope is uniform.

REPAIRING LEADERS AND DOWNSPOUTS

A leak in the leader must be given immediate attention to prevent the damage from going further and perhaps breaking the whole elbow. The size of the hole will determine how it should be repaired, and you may follow the same directions as given for repairing a metal gutter. If there is a bulge in the metal, it may be pressed back into shape. If a small split occurs, it may be repaired by soldering.

A downspout that is rusted or has much breakage in it may be beyond repair, and a wiser procedure would be to replace the whole damaged section. The way to remove a section depends on the kind of fastener that is used to hold the pipe in place. These pipes come in sections that fit into each other. When inserting a new length of pipe, slip the upper section into the lower section (in the old pipe above the new section) and then insert the lower edge of the new section over the upper section of the old pipe. This is done so that water flows on the inside and does not leak out. Solder the sections together where they join in order to make the installation secure.

Skylight

A skylight on your roof must be kept in repair, to avoid leaks.

The base of the skylight must be cleaned periodically to get rid of any leaves or other material that might accumulate there, because if debris becomes soaked with rain or snow it may cause a wood frame to deteriorate.

A rust-resistant watertight flashing must be provided where the skylight rests on the roof. All metal on the skylight must be painted to avoid rust.

If the frame of the skylight is wood, it needs periodical painting to keep it from drying or rotting. Should paint peel or crack, it must be scraped off, then repainted with three coats of exterior house paint.

The glass panes must be repaired or replaced at once if cracks appear. If the putty becomes loose, remove it and replace it with fresh putty.

Chapter Eighteen

PLUMBING AND THE WATER SYSTEM

YOU MAY BE LIVING in a community where you are not permitted by local regulations to handle installations or repairs in connection with the plumbing systems of your house. But it is good for every household to be informed about the workings of the water system and to know how to meet emergencies that may have to be dealt with before a licensed plumber arrives.

How to shut off water

In an emergency, or if you are closing the house for some length of time, you may need to shut off the main water supply. In the basement the wall cock or valve will usually be in the main pipe, and Fig. 18.1 shows you what it looks like. The way to shut it is simply to reverse the present position of the wheel (which is allowing the water to flow through).

Sometimes you may not need to shut off the complete supply of water to the house, but only to shut off the flow

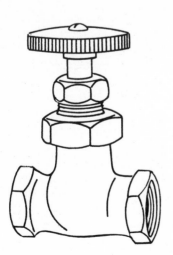

Fig. 18.1

below the water closet or the sink. You will find separate shutoff cocks in the pipes under or adjacent to such fixtures, and all you need to do is turn the wheel completely around.

Draining pipes

For special repairs it may be necessary to drain the water out of the pipes after shutting off the supply. Open all faucets, starting at the top of the house. Then open all faucets on the lower floors. After there is no more water flow from the faucets, the small cap or cock in the pipe's main valve should be opened (or the plug removed) and the remainder of the water drained into a pail placed under the valve for that purpose.

Some water may be left in the traps under water closets, bathtubs, sinks and so forth; if you need complete drainage, open the traps underneath the fixtures and use a suction hose or a force pump to siphon out the water.

Empty the water closet tank by flushing, after the water supply has been shut off. Tie a sponge to a long wire or stick, then put it into the bowl to suck up any water remaining in the trap.

WHEN THE HOUSE IS UNOCCUPIED

To prevent pipes from freezing after you drain the water system, if you are going away in cold weather, you may fill the traps with a mixture of alcohol and kerosene, or plain kerosene, crude glycerine or any other antifreeze liquid that your plumber will recommend for the purpose. Also, protect the hot-water supply tank by opening the faucet at the bottom of the tank and draining it. At the same time open every hot water faucet in the house; this will facilitate drainage.

If you use a hot water or steam heating system in your

house and plan to be away in the winter, another cold-weather precaution is to see that the fire is out before you drain the water system. Then shut off the main water supply and drain the pipes as described in the previous paragraphs. While the water is draining, open the air valves in the radiators, starting at the top of the house, then work your way down and keep on opening all such air valves. If you have a one-pipe system, open up every radiator valve to release any water or condensation. When you want to start the fire in the boiler upon your return, first open the water system and make sure that each pipe leading to faucets and bathroom fixtures is filled.

If your house is to be unoccupied during the summer months, you do not need to drain the water supply system. All that is necessary is to shut off the water at the basement wall to prevent water from dripping from a faucet, or any leak that may occur in the piping.

Care of pipes

Weather conditions have their effect upon water pipes; in winter months they may freeze; in hot weather they may become covered with condensation. The following are ways in which you may protect pipes:

INSULATING AGAINST FREEZING

To protect pipes against freezing, especially the smaller ones that are laid outdoors or in an unheated garage, attic or basement, they should be covered with insulating material (see Chapter 20 for instructions on insulating pipes). In very cold areas it may be necessary to apply two thicknesses of the insulation, as well as to stagger the joints to provide for tighter insulation. If the pipe is outdoors, the insulation should be further protected by a spiral wrapping of strips of tape or felt, covered by two coats of asphalt-varnish. Another way to protect the insulation is to build a watertight box around the pipe.

LAYING UNDERGROUND PIPES

These pipes should be placed as deep in the earth as possible to prevent freezing in cold weather and to protect them from any heavy vehicles that might pass over them. The local soil and climate conditions are factors in determining how deep to lay the pipes; for instance, in southern states enough protection may be secured when pipe is laid 1½ to 2 feet underground, and in northern and central states protection from frost generally calls for pipes to be laid at a depth of 2½ to 3 feet.

THAWING FROZEN PIPES AND DRAINS

To locate a frozen area in a lead or soft copper pipe, look for a bulge in the pipe. In other metals, however, there will not be a bulge to help you.

Before you start the thawing-out process, open a faucet so you will be able to hear the water as soon as it starts to flow. Heat must be applied to pipes to melt the ice in them. Start heat applications at the lower end of the pipe and work upwards in order to start the flow of water through the pipes as soon as the ice is melted.

The methods of heat which may be used are (1) direct flame from a gasoline torch, (2) electric resistance from a welding generator clamped on the pipes, (3) steam through a steamer heated by a plumber's furnace or (4) applications of hot water. The first three methods may prove hazardous unless applied by a licensed plumber. The way to apply heat is either by pouring boiling water directly onto the pipe, or by wrapping the pipe with cloths saturated with boiling water. Provide a pail or basin below the pipe on which you are working, to catch the dripping water. This hot application method is slower, but you can handle it with safety and with less danger of the pipe bursting.

Frozen drains, traps and waste pipes may be opened by pouring boiling water into them. If this doesn't thaw them, make a solution of 1 can drainpipe cleaner or lye and 2 gallons cold water (mixing them in a porcelain container), and pour this solution slowly into the trap or drain opening.

CAUTION: Don't splash the solution on hands, face or clothes, and do not use hot water!

CONDENSATION ON PIPES

In hot, humid climate it is sometimes desirable to cover the cold water pipes with insulation (as explained in Chapter 20). You can buy such pipe covering in cylindrical shape, covered with canvas and made with a slit so you may put the insulation on the pipe easily. The covering may be bought in three-foot lengths and in whatever thickness you prefer.

If pipes are in the attic or basement, and you are not concerned with their appearance, wrap aluminum foil over the canvas jacket and seal it. You may also cover the canvas with asphalt-impregnated paper or paint over it with a coating of asphalt.

If you want the pipes to look well, apply two coats of spar-varnish aluminum paint over the canvas jacket, then over that apply one or two coats of paint to match the walls or in whatever color you prefer. Instead of using aluminum paint, you may want to cover the canvas with large sheets of aluminum foil and then paint over the foil. If you want to paint a canvas-covered pipe located in a basement where dampness exists, use a paint that contains a mildew-preventing fungicide. There is also an insulating tape made for this purpose, which you may wrap around the pipe in spiral form to a thickness of about one-quarter inch. Also available are thick paints that are mixed with insulating materials, and they may be coated on the pipe to a thickness of about one-quarter inch.

Faucets

The three types of faucets generally used are shown in Fig. 18.2.

Compression Type (a). If there is no tight contact at all points of the disk washer and ground seat, water leaks through and causes faucet dripping. A worn-out or inferior grade of washer is usually responsible for this, and a new good-quality washer should be installed. The first step is to shut off the water either directly below the fixture or at the main water supply pipe. With a monkey wrench unscrew the cap nut of the faucet (placing a cloth between wrench and faucet to protect the surface of the faucet). With a screw driver remove the brass screw that holds the washer to the bottom of the spindle. Sometimes this brass screw is worn and may be difficult to twist off and remove. To help you in such a case, put two or three drops of kerosene on the screw and tap it lightly until you loosen it. Remove the old washer and replace it with a new one. Before you put back the screw, check to see if it is worn; if it is, discard it and use a new screw. Then put back the cap nut, using the wrench to secure it.

The water leak may occur at the stem when you open

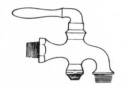

Fig. 18.2a

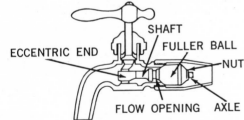

Fig. 18.2b

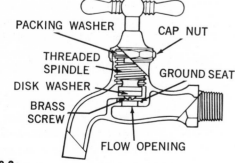

Fig. 18.2c

the faucet. Tightening of the cap nut with a wrench may be all that is necessary. However, do not make it so tight that there is binding in the faucet.

If the leak around the stem is not halted by tightening, the fault may be in the packing washer under the cap nut. Remove the handle and cap nut, take out the worn packing washer and put in a new one.

For temporary stoppage of this leak, wrap a soft string or a small piece of candle wick that has been soaked in oil around the stem under the nut cap (where the stem enters the body of the faucet).

Fuller Ball Type (b). If repairs must be made, first shut off the water supply. If the Fuller ball is damaged and needs to be replaced, unscrew the entire faucet (see Fig. 18.2b) and separate it from the water supply pipe. With pliers or a screw driver take off the nut, then remove the ball and set in the new one.

If the axle or eccentric end is worn, these parts should be removed and new ones put in their place.

If there is water leakage around the stem when the faucet is open, follow directions given for the compression type faucet.

Ground-key Type (c). This type has a tapered cylindrical brass plunger (or plug) fitted tightly into a sleeve and bored vertically through the body of the faucet (see Fig. 18.2c). The handle is used to rotate the plunger.

Water leakage may occur when the plunger or its sleeve becomes grooved or worn by sand or other particles rubbing against the metal. This necessitates repolishing the rubbing surfaces. To do this, first shut off the water supply, unfasten the nut or screw at the bottom that holds the plunger in place and pull out the plunger. With a small flat stick, smear a little valve-grinding compound (a compound of emery dust and grease, obtainable from a dealer in plumbing goods) on the sides of the plunger, and after temporarily replacing the plunger in the sleeve rotate it back and forth to wear the two surfaces smooth so they will form a leakproof joint. If the parts are worn badly and refuse to respond to this remedy, it will be necessary to purchase a new faucet.

Leakage might also be due to loosening of the bottom nut or screw, and this can cause the plunger to move out of its proper position. However, if the nut or screw is too tight, this can bind the plunger and make it hard to turn. In either case, all you need to do is to see that the nut or screw is neither too loose nor too tight.

ELIMINATING FAUCET NOISES

The annoying tapping and hammering noises may be due to something inside the faucet. Shut off the water supply, provide yourself with a monkey wrench, pliers and screw driver and proceed to open up the faucet and examine its parts.

Compression Type. Remove the spindle and disk washer and examine them. If the washer is loose, tighten the brass screw. If spindle threads are worn, the spindle may rattle and you may have to buy and install a new faucet. This holds true of any other part of the body of the faucet that is badly worn.

Fuller Ball Type. Tighten the nut that holds the Fuller ball; this may stop the noise. However, if the ball is worn it is best to remove it and replace it with a new one. Parts of the eccentric end may be worn and thus produce a rattling noise; in this case it may be best for you to consult a plumber. If the eccentric end is beyond repair and if new parts are not obtainable, you may need to install a new faucet.

Drainage traps

Traps are the part of the plumbing fixtures that carries away waste water from sinks, bathtubs and water closets. They are so designed that they form a seal and prevent bad odors and gases from entering the house through the drain. Some traps are part of the drainpipe itself and are formed in a single or double U bend. Other fixtures have a separate trap, of the S or P form, that has a screw cleanout plug conveniently placed in the lower part of the bend. Figure 18.3 shows the P-type trap.

Water closets are made so that the suitable bends for the trap are part of the lower bowl and not a separate fixture.

Fig. 18.3

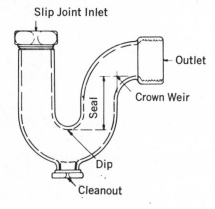

Slip Joint Inlet
Outlet
Seal
Crown Weir
Dip
Cleanout

STOPPAGE IN TRAP

If the water runs out of the sink or bathtub too slowly, if there is a gurgly noise when the water goes down or if the water backs up in the bowl of the water closet, undoubtedly the retarding is caused by some foreign matter (hardened grease, heavy paper, hairpins, cloths or other articles).

Following are some of the methods that you may employ in removing the clogging materials:

The Plumber's Friend. This tool is also called a plunger. It is made of a rubber suction cup at one end of a wood handle, and is usually the first thing to use when you want to get rid of clogging. To use it, the sink or bowl should be partially filled with water and the rubber suction cup placed over the mouth of the drain opening. Then, holding the handle with both hands, work the plunger vigorously up and down for about five minutes. The alternate suction and compression usually loosen the clogging if it has a minor cause.

Chemical Cleaner. Should the plumber's friend be unable to remedy the clogged condition, try a cleaner that is either a mixture of lye and aluminum or zinc-coated aluminum turnings or chips, or a mixture of lye and sodium nitrate and aluminum turnings. Drop the solution into the clogged pipe; this will cause a gas to form when it hits the water, which in turn causes much stirring in the water. It is often a good way of removing the waste matter.

CAUTION: Use extreme care when handling lye or other chemical cleaner; do not let it splash on skin, in eyes or on clothes!

Opening Cleanout Plug. If you have had no success with either the plunger or the chemicals, it may be necessary to remove the clogging material manually. Place a pail underneath the trap to catch the water. With a monkey wrench unscrew the cleanout plug, releasing the water into the pail. When all the water is drained, insert a wire (with a bent hook at one end) into the opening of the trap and pull out any dirt or grease that exists there. Then pour boiling water into the sink or bowl to wash through the open trap, and insert a narrow bottle brush into the open trap to remove small particles of accumulated dirt that may have adhered to the inside of the trap.

Should the trap not have a cleanout plug, there is usually a plug at the slip joint. The slip joint bolt should

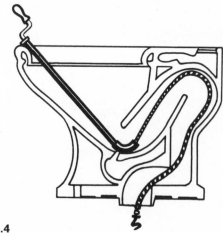

Fig. 18.4

be removed and the trap cleaned out with a wire hook, hot water and bottle brush, as directed in the previous paragraph.

Spring-Steel Auger. If, after the trap is cleaned out, there is still not a free flow of water, it may be necessary to clear out the pipe beyond the trap. A coil spring-steel auger should be inserted through the opening of the trap and the clogging material either pulled out or bored through and forced out. The auger is helpful in opening up clogged drains, long sections of water supply pipes and the trap in the water closet (shown in Fig. 18.4).

Toilet flush tank

The mechanism inside the flush tank is shown in Fig. 18.5, so that you may be able to identify the various parts.

When water continues to run in the water closet bowl after it has been flushed, there is a leakage in the tank that must be located and corrected.

DEFECTIVE BALL

If the flush tank ball is worn, out of shape or has lost its elasticity and does not drop tightly into the hollowed seat beneath it, the ball should be replaced with a new one. To replace the ball, first empty the water tank and shut off the supply pipe. If there is no supply shutoff, put a stick of wood under the lever arm of the float tank ball to hold it up and thus shut off the intake cock and prevent the tank from refilling with water. While the tank is empty, unscrew the flush tank ball from the lower lift wire and attach a new ball of the same size as the one you just removed. Then either open the supply pipe or remove the temporary stick, and water will refill the tank.

Fig. 18.5

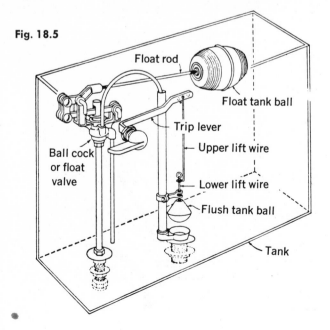

- Float rod
- Float tank ball
- Trip lever
- Ball cock or float valve
- Upper lift wire
- Lower lift wire
- Flush tank ball
- Tank

If the ball is merely covered with a slimy coating, all you need do is wipe it clean.

IRREGULAR STOPPER SEAT

You may find that the top of the outlet pipe, leading to the toilet bowl, is covered with grit or is corroded, and makes an irregular seat for the flush tank ball. Scrape the top of the outlet to clear away any grit or corrosion and rub it with emery paper to get a smooth surface. It will then provide a uniform bearing for the ball.

BENT LIFT WIRES

Sometimes the handle and the lever don't work smoothly, or the lift wires become bent. These latter can cause the flush tank ball to form an incomplete covering over the outlet opening or the ball to remain suspended. Straighten out the lift wires and make them plumb so that the ball will drop centrally into the seat beneath it.

DEFECTIVE FLOAT TANK BALL

If this ball is leaky and becomes waterlogged, it must be examined to find whether or not its condition warrants repairing it. Should there be a small leak in the ball, it may be soldered. However, if the ball is badly worn or corroded it is best to replace it with a new one. If the float rod is bent, remove it and straighten it out, and then set the rod back into place.

The tank may sometimes become filled to overflowing and at other times not be sufficiently filled, because of poor installation. Either condition may be adjusted by bending the float rod either downward to prevent water from rising too high, or upward to get more water flowing into the tank.

WASHER AT INTAKE COCK

Outside the flush tank, located right below it, is a washer that may become worn and need to be replaced. First drain all the water out of the tank. Unscrew the two screws to release the plunger. Take off the washer (held in place by a nut and a ring cap); replace it with a new washer made of leather or rubber. If the ring cap, into which the washer fits, is corroded, it may break when you remove it, and you will need to replace it with a new brass ring cap.

Toilet flush valve

Some water closets have a flush valve instead of a flush tank. There are several kinds of flush valves on the market, but the adjustments and repairs required are usually similar. A common type of flush valve is shown in Fig. 18.6, with the key to the diagram following:

In this type of flush valve the rubber diaphragm separates the valve into an upper and lower chamber, with the pressure, equalized by the by-pass, the same on both sides of the diaphragm. The slightest touch of the handle in any direction pushes in the plunger, which tilts the auxiliary valve, releasing the pressure in the upper chamber. Then the pressure below raises the entire working mechanism (auxiliary valve, diaphragm and guide), allowing the water that flushes the bowl to go down through the barrel of the valve. While this is occurring, a small amount passes up through the by-pass and gradually fills the upper chamber and closes the valve.

The most noticeable difficulty is continuous running of the water into the bowl after the handle has been pressed. In valves similar to the flush tank type, this flow may result from stoppage of the by-pass or from a deposit of grit on the auxiliary valve seat. If the by-pass is clogged water cannot pass into the upper chamber to close the valve. If there is sediment on the auxiliary valve seat or if the seat is badly worn, the valve may not close tightly, allowing water to escape. The diaphragm may also deteriorate in time and need to be replaced. The auxiliary valve seat, or washer, and the diaphragm are made of rubber and are usually purchased together, since it is usually advisable to replace both at one time.

Fig. 18.6

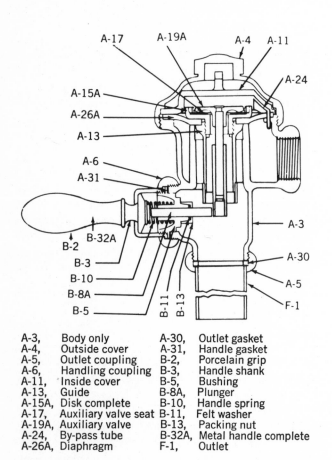

A-3,	Body only	A-30,	Outlet gasket
A-4,	Outside cover	A-31,	Handle gasket
A-5,	Outlet coupling	B-2,	Porcelain grip
A-6,	Handling coupling	B-3,	Handle shank
A-11,	Inside cover	B-5,	Bushing
A-13,	Guide	B-8A,	Plunger
A-15A,	Disk complete	B-10,	Handle spring
A-17,	Auxiliary valve seat	B-11,	Felt washer
A-19A,	Auxiliary valve	B-13,	Packing nut
A-24,	By-pass tube	B-32A,	Metal handle complete
A-26A,	Diaphragm	F-1,	Outlet

It is not often necessary to cut off the entire water supply while repairing a flush valve. The supply to the water closet may be cut off by turning the large screw in the body of the flush valve, or by means of a shutoff valve in the supply pipe.

To obtain access to the parts mentioned, unscrew the outside cover. The inside cover may then be lifted out together with the auxiliary valve complete. The by-pass and the corresponding hole in the cover may be cleaned by running a fine wire through the openings.

In replacing the rubber washer (auxiliary valve seat) insert a screw driver under the washer at the hole in the center and pull it out. Then, with a spanner wrench, unscrew the disk ring that holds the washer in place and clean the surface of the seat on which the washer rests. Insert a new washer and replace the disk ring, screwing it down until it is firm but not too tight.

When the disk is unscrewed, the diaphragm may be lifted out. When the diaphragm is replaced, it should be laid in with the cup down and the copper gasket on the under side. It will be noted that the dowels and tube holding the diaphragm in position are unequally spaced to prevent its being placed in the valve upside down. It may require a few attempts to find the correct position. When this has been done, fasten the diaphragm by screwing the disk into the guide.

If these directions do not apply in your specific case, it may be advisable for you to obtain others from the manufacturer or from a plumber.

Toilet seat repairs

Toilet seats are finished in plastic coverings, paint or enamel. If the plastic seat or its lid is cracked or marred in any way, or if the joints are loose, do not attempt to make repairs; instead replace it with a new seat and cover. A painted or enameled seat and lid, if marred, may be made to look fresh again. Use paint remover to take off the finish. Then use a quick-drying enamel to give a new coat to the seat and cover.

Care of the septic tank

If the house is so located that there is no access to the public sewer system, an effective means of sewage disposal is the septic tank.

A septic tank system is made up of five necessary parts:

The house sewer is the pipe line that carries waste from the house to the septic tank.

The septic tank is the container wherein the sewage disintegrates by bacterial action; this tank must be made watertight.

The outlet sewer line, made of tile, carries liquid waste from the septic tank to to the distribution box.

The distribution box discharges liquid waste (through tile drain lines) into the disposal field.

The disposal field is the last stop from which liquid waste is permitted to seep into the soil.

REPAIRS AND CLEANING

The most common trouble in a septic tank is clogging of the disposal field. This may be due to the tank being too small for the amount of sewage; to the wrong arrangement of the interior so that the tank cannot provide for a slow flow and thus permits the sludge or scum to pass out with the effluent; to the disposal field being too small or incorrectly located; or to irregular cleaning of the tank.

How often you clean the tank depends upon the size of it and the amount of sewage that flows into it. One way to gauge when it is time to clean the tank is to inspect it and see when the sludge and the scum fill one-half of the total depth of the tank. It should be cleaned at this point.

Should the disposal field be clogged, you may need to dig up the tiles, clean them, then lay them back; this time lay them three or four feet to either side of the original position in which they were placed.

You may find it possible to clean a tile line simply by opening the line at each end, then flushing it through thoroughly with a hose. Make some provision at the end of the line, where the water will come through, for disposal of the water that you used in cleaning. Should the flushing not be successful, you may find it necessary to use a flat steel sewer rod to remove solid obstructions or roots.

Roots are a major cause of clogging of the outlet sewer and the house sewer. Sometimes grease causes trouble, especially if there is an inadequate slope of the pipes; use a commercial drain solvent to clear waste material from the pipes.

CAUSES OF ODOR

Should the tile lines be laid with an incorrect slope, there is a likelihood of effluent collecting and then saturating the soil; this may cause unpleasant odors. Bacteria evidently cannot function in such areas, and the lines should be relaid on the correct slope. Odors are sometimes caused by too small a disposal field, or by waterlogged soil.

Chapter Nineteen

HEATING AND VENTILATING SYSTEMS

THE TYPE OF FUEL you use depends on the heating system installed in your house and on what is most conveniently available in your area, and the maintenance of the equipment should be understood by you in order to keep the system in the best working order. It might be well for you to discuss the heating system with the manufacturer or dealer, or with a heating mechanic.

Pressure or gravity hot-water system

The boiler should never be left dry, even in warm months when it is not in use; if you start to build a fire when the cold weather arrives, it must not be built in a dry boiler. Keep the expansion tank filled with water even when the heat is not on. If possible keep the boiler filled during the summer months, to avoid rusting or corrosion.

However, there may be some evaporation while the heat is off, so before starting it again at the beginning of the cold weather season it is essential that the heating system be filled with water; usually this is a two-person job, requiring one person to operate the radiator relief valves and the other person to control the flow of water into the boiler. Use the following procedure:

1. Open all radiator shutoff valves.
2. Close all radiator air valves.
3. Close the drawoff cock at the lowest point in the system.
4. Open the valve in the supply pipe that feeds the boiler.
5. As soon as the water begins to rise in the pipes, open up the air valve on each radiator, starting with the one nearest the boiler in order to release the air and enable the radiators to be filled with water.
6. As soon as water begins to spurt from the air valve,

shut the valve and continue to open and shut the valves until all radiators are free from air and are full of water.

If there is a fire under the boiler when you are adding water to it, keep the fire low and see that the water flows in gradually, because a quick flow of water suddenly injected into the hot boiler could cause it to crack.

FILLING THE EXPANSION TANK

If your heating system includes an expansion tank at the top of it, shut off the water supply valve when the water rises to about one-third full in the tank.

Generally an expansion tank is located on a shelf in an upstairs closet or in the attic, and is usually placed near the chimney in order to protect the tank from freezing. There is usually a water-gauge glass attached to the tank to indicate the height of the water in the tank. Be sure that the water is kept at the level indicated on the gauge, to get the best circulation throughout the heating system.

A pipe for overflow of water should be attached to the tank and should lead to the outside of the house or to a drain to carry off any excess water.

AUTOMATIC REDUCING VALVES

Two valves are generally provided to control water pressure in a heating system. The purpose of a reducing valve is to admit city water when the pressure in the heating system falls below its normal level. The function of a relief valve is to discharge small amounts of water from the heating system periodically, should the pressure become higher than usual because of expansion of the water when it is being heated.

These valves may become corroded and not work properly. Inspect the valves occasionally, and if corrosion exists dismantle the valves and polish moving parts with a fine emery cloth; when the area is cleaned replace the valves.

BOILER MAINTENANCE

Procure an instruction card from the manufacturer, to keep near the water gauge, and follow instructions as to what water level must be maintained and how this is indicated on the gauge.

Inspect boiler parts periodically to see they are in the best condition, and oil the regular parts (following directions that come with the equipment). Both for the sake of the good appearance and durability of the metal, the boiler should be kept clean and the external parts covered with a coat of paint. Use silicone-aluminum or other paint made for this purpose.

BOILER CRACKS AND LEAKS

If a simple crack occurs in a cast-iron boiler, it must be repaired by brazing or welding. Brazing is usually preferable to welding, since the latter is more difficult to perform on cast iron. If you are not sufficiently competent to handle this job yourself, call in an experienced mechanic.

WATER TREATMENT

In some areas there may be very hard water, or there may be a large volume of fresh water introduced into the system. In either case, the boiler water may need chemical treatment.

For hard water, commercially prepared compounds may be added, but care needs to be exercised in adding them to the water. Ask your dealer for instructions.

When fresh water is introduced, sodium carbonate, disodium phosphate or trisodium phosphate may be added to the boiler water; you may buy compounds containing these chemicals; in this case, too, ask your dealer for directions for treating the water.

An accumulation of oil or organic matter in the boiler water may cause it to foam, and small drops of water may be carried out of the boiler with the steam. If you discover this condition, the best thing to do is to let out the water in the boiler and replace it with fresh water. If the foaming situation persists, it may be a good idea to consult a heating expert.

Radiator valve leaks

When a leak occurs around the valve stem, it needs quick action to prevent water from damaging the floor under the radiator and to stop it from going through to the ceiling below.

The leak may be caused by insufficient packing inside the nut at the stem base, by the packing becoming worn or the nut becoming loose (Fig. 19.1). Sometimes tightening the nut stops the leakage. But if it persists, you may need to repack the valve. To do this it is generally advisable to let the fire go out before starting to pack, especially if you are not familiar with such work.

In the case of a hot-water system, lower the level of the water to a point below the radiator being repaired by opening the drawoff cock at the lowest point in the system. To determine if the water is sufficiently low, loosen the packing nut a little. If water spurts out, continue to draw water from the system until flow ceases at that point. The elevation of the water in the system above the gauge on top of the boiler is marked by the black pointer.

In the case of a steam-heating system, it is likewise advisable to let the fire go out, or at least to have a low head of steam, before starting work on the valves.

When these preliminaries have been attended to, close the valve tightly, unscrew the packing nut at the base of the stem and pack the space between the inside of the nut and the stem with plastic, metallic packing compound, using a small screw driver for the purpose. This compound may be purchased in small quantities from a dealer in heating supplies. It may be easier to pack the nut if it is removed from the stem. To do this, remove the handle (held in place by a screw) and lift the nut from the stem. After the nut has been well packed, screw it down tightly and refill the system.

Care of furnace and chimney

The heating surfaces of the furnace must be given a meticulous cleaning at the end of the heating season; clear out all the ash and soot. Clean out the smoke pipe and the chimney. There may be a heating expert in your area who does a professional furnace-cleaning job with a vacuum system; this is an advisable method because it prevents dust from going through the house. There may also be a chimney sweep in your locality who will

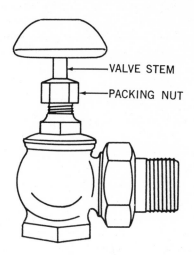

VALVE STEM

PACKING NUT

Fig. 19.1

come periodically to inspect, repair and clean the chimney if you feel you cannot do it yourself.

To clean the inside of the furnace, use a wire brush and scraper inserted through the cleanout door. When the inside and outside of the furnace are cleaned, and the furnace is not to be used during the warm weather months, apply a coat of lubricating oil (either directly on the various parts of the furnace, or sprayed) as a rust-preventative.

Inspect the furnace carefully, and if the door hinges are loose, grates broken or warped, any parts damaged or any joints loose, they should all be repaired or replaced at the end of the heating season so that when you are ready to start the furnace again next season they will be in good working order.

Cleaning a clogged grate

A fire should be shaken down at least twice a day to remove ashes and to provide a better draft through the grates. The ashpit should be cleaned out daily; if it is allowed to fill up to the grate bars there is danger of warping or burning out the grates.

Most stoves and furnaces, just above the grate surface, have cleanout doors through which a poker may be inserted to break up and pull out clinkers. If an unusually large clinker lodges between the plates in such a way that the grate cannot be shaken or turned over, and the obstruction cannot be readily broken up or removed with a poker, it will be necessary to clean out the fire pot to obtain free access to the obstruction. When the fire pot is empty, the poker can again be used to better advantage. Do not try to turn the grate by force to dislodge or break up such an obstruction, since this may break the grate.

Soot removal

To get rid of soot from the heating surfaces of the furnace or boiler, smoke pipe and chimney, you may use either copper, tin, lead or zinc chloride; sodium chloride (table salt); or chloride of lime; these are vaporized by the hot fire and are then deposited on the surface of the soot to lower its ignition temperature. Generally the most effective is copper chloride, and the least effective sodium chloride. You may also buy a commercial soot remover that contains one of these chlorides. When purchasing materials, get directions from the dealer if the manufacturer's instructions are not included with the product.

A rainy day is the best time for soot removal. Be very careful in seeing that the roof shingles or any combustible material in the attic don't catch fire while you are removing soot, since a high temperature usually ensues during this process.

Repairing the furnace water pipe

After a few years of service the water pipe in the combustion chamber of a coal furnace, which is used for heating domestic hot water, may become clogged on the inside with a scaly deposit from the heated water or be burned on the outside from overheating. You may find it more advisable to replace the damaged part with a new one. First drain the water out of the hot-water system. Next, replace the damaged section with a section of pipe that may be bought in standard sizes; then coil or bend it to fit the existing pipe.

Chimney repairs

A common fire hazard is a chimney that shows crumbling of the mortar joints. This damage to mortar generally takes place in very cold weather when the furnace fire is at its maximum and the drafts are strong. Clean away the crumbled mortar thoroughly, then replace it with new mortar. However, if you find the mortar is too deteriorated, it is wise to have the chimney taken apart and a new one built in its place. Such rebuilding should be done in warm weather, when the furnace is not being heated.

Insulating hot-water and steam-heating systems

Insulating, or covering, the boiler and pipes is done to increase the efficiency of the system and to reduce the cost of operation.

It has been found that the heat loss from bare or improperly insulated pipes and boiler may amount to fifteen or twenty-five per cent of the boiler capacity, and that a good covering will save from eighty to ninety-five per cent of bare surface losses. The small percentage of heat that escapes through the insulating material, combined with radiation from the doors and other exposed parts of the boiler, will be sufficient in many cases to warm the cellar, especially if it is soundly constructed and the doors and windows are weatherproofed.

EXTENT OF INSULATION

The extent of covering is governed principally by the type of heating system and existing conditions in individual cases. In any event, it is well to cover at least the boiler and the pipes through which water is distributed to the radiators. Whether or not you cover the return pipes depends on the type of system and the amount of heat desired in the basement.

Covering the return pipes of hot-water heating systems is recommended so that the water may be returned to the boiler with minimum heat loss. In vacuum and vapor steam-heating systems, it is better to leave the return pipes bare, to aid in the condensation of any steam that may escape into the returns through defective thermostatic traps.

INSULATING MATERIALS NEEDED

The covering should be fire-resistant and a poor conductor of heat. These qualities are found in asbestos air cell, asbestos cement, magnesia and mineral (or rock wool) and similar coverings. The application of some of these materials is described in the following paragraphs.

The air-cell covering is made of layers of corrugated asbestos paper wrapped in canvas. It comes in sections three feet long, in the shape of hollow cylinders split lengthwise on one side so that it may be readily placed around the pipe, as shown in Fig. 19.2. The covering is made in several thicknesses and for various pipe sizes. Each section has a canvas lap to be pasted over the longitudinal joint and a canvas flap at one end to be pasted over the joint between sections. To bind the covering with more strength, and to make a neat-looking job, metal bands are furnished, to be placed about eighteen inches apart, over the joints between sections and around the middle of each section.

For insulating boilers and pipe fittings such as valves, ells and tees (L's and T's), where the use of fabricated coverings is not practicable, asbestos cement may be used. This material, because of its natural cell-like structure and fire-resistant qualities, serves the same purpose as the pipe covering.

The tools needed are a steel tape measure, plasterer's trowel, handsaw, sharp knife, pliers, a metal container for mixing cement, a pan for paste and a small, flat paste brush.

Fig. 19.2

A four-ply, or one inch thick, asbestos air-cell covering is frequently used for insulating pipes in home heating plants. To estimate quantity needed, carefully measure between fittings all pipes that are to be covered, and combine measurements for each size of pipe to obtain the total linear feet of each size of covering. Metal band fasteners are furnished with the covering.

To estimate the quantity of asbestos cement needed to cover boiler and pipe fittings, measure the entire surface of the boiler to be covered, together with the surfaces of pipe fittings, and compute the square-foot area of each. A one hundred pound bag of cement will cover from twenty to twenty-five square feet of surface to a thickness of one inch. Some brands are sold also in ten-pound bags.

A sufficient quantity of one-inch mesh wire netting, commonly called chicken wire, is needed to cover the surface of the boiler.

Since it is well to enclose the cement covering around pipe fittings in a canvas jacket, obtain a sufficient quantity of canvas of the same weight as that on the air-cell covering for this purpose.

A suitable paste for pasting the canvas laps on air-cell coverings and for fastening canvas jackets over pipe fittings is sold by manufacturers of the covering material.

A satisfactory paste, similar to that used in paper hanging, may be made of flour and water. Mix 1 part powdered alum with 50 parts sifted white flour and add enough cold water to make a smooth paste. Then add boiling water until the paste begins to thicken, at which point stop pouring and stir the mixture thoroughly.

APPLYING ASBESTOS CEMENT

Mix the asbestos cement in a tub, using only enough water to make the mixture workable. At least two coats should be applied to the boiler and pipe fittings, and they should be put on when the pipes are warm, to insure best results.

Before covering the pipes, see that they are clean and in good condition. Then loosen the canvas lap to open the section of covering and brush the paste along the edge for refastening the lap. Then slip the section around the pipe with the open side up, and with the end that has no canvas joint overlap toward the fittings. Now, press the section tightly together, paste the lap securely over the longitudinal joint and push the section tightly against the fitting. The second section should be applied in the same manner and pushed tightly against the first. The joint between the two should be sealed over by pasting the overlap on the first section over the joint. Continue to cover the pipe in this way until the next fitting is reached. When a short section is needed, cut it with a sharp knife and handsaw.

The first coat on the fittings should be applied roughly with the hands to about one-half inch in thickness. It will have an opportunity to dry while the finishing coat is being placed on the boiler. The second coat on the boiler should be troweled down hard and smooth as it dries (Fig. 19.3).

Finish covering the fittings by applying a half-inch second coat, or enough to provide the same thickness as the pipe covering. This should be troweled hard and smooth and beveled down to meet the surface of the pipe covering.

The cement on the fittings will be protected and will present a neater appearance if it is covered with a canvas jacket. The canvas should be of same weight as that used on the pipe covering and should be pasted down smoothly. For the sake of appearances and to preserve the canvas, all such material may be sized and painted with two coats of lead and oil in a color of your choice.

The metal bands around the pipe covering should be applied after all the work is completed, so that they may be kept clean and give a neat finish to the job. Place the bands about eighteen inches apart, over the joints and midway between the joints. The bands should be pulled up tightly and fastened like a belt. This can be done with pliers.

Fig. 19.3

Insulating a warm-air furnace and ducts

Furnace and ducts may be insulated to prevent the basement from becoming too warm, especially if it is used as a playroom or utility room. If you want a warm basement, however, you may leave the supply ducts bare. Usually the return ducts are not covered.

The tools needed are a steel tape measure, sharp knife or heavy shears; pencil; pliers to cut wire; small trowel; and container for mixing asbestos cement. Materials needed are corrugated asbestos pipe-covering paper, galvanized or black wire and asbestos cement.

Get enough of the corrugated covering so it may be used in three layers to cover all the pipes and the furnace (if the latter is not already insulated). This paper is usually sold in rolls about 36 inches wide and usually contains about 250 square feet of material. Two rolls should be enough for a house of seven or eight rooms; but it is advisable to ask the dealer how much to get when you make your purchase. Black or galvanized wire should be a No. 16 or No. 18 gauge, and you may need one roll.

Asbestos cement comes in one hundred pound bags, and one bag should be enough to cover the furnace's sloping shoulder, allowing a one inch thick coating on about twenty to twenty-five square feet of surface. You might buy the asbestos cement in ten-pound bags if you don't need the larger amount.

METHOD OF INSULATING

The asbestos cement mixture may be used to coat the sloping shoulder of the furnace. The ducts should be covered with a wrapping of corrugated asbestos paper.

Before covering the ducts, you must make sure they are in excellent condition and very clean. You may want to make a pattern first, using heavy paper for marking and cutting it, as suggested in Fig. 19.4. From the pattern (or freehand if you prefer) cut the required strip of the corrugated paper. Wrap it around the duct, and tie it into place with wire or cord at each end and in the middle. Then measure around the outside of the covered duct, adding 1½ extra inches, and cut the second piece of corrugated paper. Tie this piece around the duct (over the first piece), but stagger the ends and the longitudinal joints, and tie this second piece into place in the same manner with wire or cord. Now, for the third and final covering, proceed in the same way to measure and allow 1½ inches, then put the final cover over the second one, staggering the ends and joints. Finish by securely fastening this last cover with bands of wire around the covering, spaced about fifteen inches apart.

BENDS IN DUCTS

It is not absolutely essential to cover the bends with insulating material, since they are but a small part of the system. However, you may choose to do so, for the sake of efficiency and appearance (Fig. 19.5). In that case you will need to cut two or three pieces for special fit, or allow one piece to each separate section in the bend. Cut the pieces diamond-shaped, following the measurements of the narrowest and widest parts of the bend. After the covering is applied, you may paste strips of

Fig. 19.4

asbestos over the joints of the covering to achieve a smooth, finished appearance.

INSULATING A FURNACE

Start with the vertical surface. Cover it with one to three layers of the corrugated asbestos paper, fastening them with bands of wire. On top of the furnace, lay three or four sheets of the corrugated paper, allowing an extra edge of about one inch all around to bend over onto the sloping shoulder into which the ducts are joined.

The shoulder of the furnace should be coated with asbestos cement mixture. You may make this by mixing the powdered cement with just enough water to form a consistency that may be applied to the furnace with a trowel. Make this covering about one inch thick, and with a trowel make a smooth finish (Fig. 19.6).

The asbestos cement will also cover the turned-down edges of the corrugated paper covering the top of furnace and keep these top layers in place.

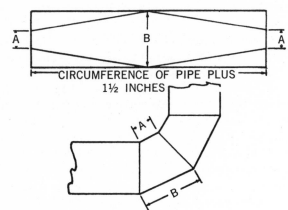

CIRCUMFERENCE OF PIPE PLUS 1½ INCHES

Fig. 19.5

Insulating a hot-water tank

Do not add insulation to a hot-water tank that is heated by pipe coils in a coal furnace or by a water back in a coal cooking range, because there is a greater likelihood of overheating in an insulated tank than in one that is not insulated. However, a domestic hot-water heater benefits by insulation. If it is heated by electricity you will need a thicker insulation than for an oil or gas heater.

Ready-made covers of incombustible materials, to fit tanks of standard sizes, are available at your heating equipment dealer. Some covers have a lengthwise split such as is included in pipe covering; these may be wrapped around the tank and fastened with a special lacing, metal band or any other type of fastener that comes with the covering you buy. Connection pipes may interfere with continuous covering; in that case you will need to cut out openings for the pipes.

Cover the top of the tank with asbestos insulating cement, as described for the sloping shoulders of the warm-air furnace.

Fig. 19.6

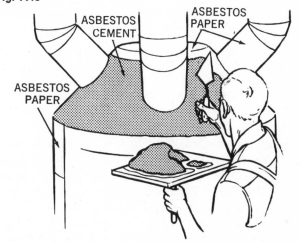

Filters, humidifier pans and grilles

You may have such equipment in your warm-air heating system, and to obtain maximum service from their use you need to inspect them periodically, and keep them scrupulously clean and in suitable repair.

FILTERS

Filters are used to provide cleaner air in the house and to prevent dust and odors. If you have throw-away type filters, they are usually inexpensive, and so it is a simple matter to replace them with new ones. If you have permanent-type filters, accumulated dust may be cleared away by tapping the frame of the filter to shake free the dust; or you may use a cleaning fluid or soap and water.

HUMIDIFIER PANS

The warm-air heating system may contain such pans, either manually or automatically operated. Periodical cleaning of all parts of the pan must be done. If the water-flow regulating mechanism is out of order in the automatic type, it may cause evaporation of water in the pan. Dust may also collect and impede the free movement of levers and pins. The valve that controls the water flow into the pan may become worn and should be replaced. The pan must be thoroughly cleaned because if there is an accumulation of too much dust and dirt, it may cause odors in the house.

GRILLES (OR REGISTERS)

When grilles are placed on the floor they catch dust and small objects. A vacuum cleaner above the grille does a good job of cleaning it. Should there be large objects which cannot be sucked up by the vacuum cleaner, you may need to take the cover off the grille to remove the accumulated material. Wall grilles are not as prone to collect dust and small objects. However, the grille may occasionally become clogged, in which case you may need to use the vacuum cleaner or perhaps dismantle the grille.

Heating equipment maintenance

Heating system equipment includes hot-water heaters, oil burners, coal stokers, gas-fired furnaces and whatever else your house system may include. Some systems are manually fired, and others are automatic.

If your equipment is hand-fired, it is not too difficult to keep it in sound working order and may not need much adjustment. Automatic heating equipment is more complicated, and its mechanisms may often need repairs or adjustments that you may not be able to make. If any difficulty arises that you feel you cannot correct, consult an expert repairman, your dealer or the utility company in your area.

ELECTRIC MOTORS

These motors are used for driving pumps, oil burners and blowers. Before the cold weather season inspect the motor and give the parts proper oiling.

A motor that is not enclosed may accumulate dust inside the casing; this causes faulty operation of the starting mechanism. You may be able to clean it by forcing a jet of air through the casing with a device made for the purpose.

The motor may need to be disassembled and the parts washed with carbon tetrachloride or some other similar solvent, to clear away dust and grease that may have accumulated.

The blower may need a periodical cleaning and oil-ing, especially when filters are not used in the system.

Belts that connect blowers to motors should also be inspected, since they may need to have worn places repaired, or perhaps be replaced.

OIL-BURNING EQUIPMENT

Inspect the equipment periodically, especially before the winter cold months set in. You may need to have the controls adjusted, strainers cleaned, burner lubricated, flue gases analyzed, burner flame adjusted and to look for possible leaks. You may prefer to have this done by the dealer or a skilled heating mechanic on a yearly or other basis.

If you prefer to do it yourself, then fortify yourself with all the printed material from the manufacturer or dealer before you start your inspection, make any repairs or replace any parts. Since each type of equipment has its own special functioning, it is not feasible to give such directions here.

REMOVING SOOT FROM THE OIL BURNER

You may use chemical soot removers as discussed earlier in this chapter to clean out the burner and combustion chamber. However, these removers may not be effective in cleaning out the hard carbon formations on the bottom of the fire pot. If carbon clogs the oil-feed pipe between the float valve and the burner, it can be cleaned by forcing a rod through the pipe.

GAS BURNERS AND GAS FURNACES

If the pilot light goes out, close the main gas valve of the appliance, then allow sufficient time for the combustion chamber to air out before you relight the pilot. Should the pilot light go out too often, and you cannot find the cause, it is best to have it repaired or replaced by an experienced mechanic. The pilot light on the furnace is often left burning during the summer months to prevent condensation and rusting inside the furnace.

If the gas flame burns above the burner parts but is not in contact with them, or if the flame has a yellow color, the primary air shutters need to be adjusted. This should be done by someone from your local utility company.

The plunger of the main gas valve may be stuck, and there may be accumulation of foreign matter in the pressure regulator; these conditions cause malfunctioning of your gas burner. Call in a repairman or someone from the utility company to inspect the burners and to make repairs or replacements if necessary.

PORTABLE GAS HEATERS

A gas heater that is not connected with vents is not recommended because of the danger of carbon monoxide, which can cause asphyxiation, especially in a bedroom where someone is sleeping. The American Gas

Association approves some of these heaters; but it is best to be safe and avoid an unvented gas heater.

If the radiator, piping or ductwork needs repairs, call in a plumber or heating mechanic.

ELECTRIC HEATERS

A room may be made more comfortable by the use of an electric heater to supplement the heating system of the house. It usually does not need much maintenance, except for the occasional repair or replacement of a defective switch, worn cord or burned-out heating element.

The following are the three most common types of electric heaters:

Portable heater, which may be carried from one room to another. It should have extension cords with adequately protected wires.

Portable electric steam radiator, which needs careful checking to see that it contains sufficient water to cover the electric heating element.

Radiant electric heater, which should not be placed too near curtains, draperies or furniture, since it may overheat and ignite nearby combustible materials. Never use the radiant heater to dry laundry that is put over it; this can be a fire hazard.

COAL FURNACES AND BOILERS

Do not let ashes accumulate in the ashpit to the point where they touch the bottom of the grate. Keep them to a minimum by constant cleaning out.

If clinkers are formed in the firebox, they must be removed as soon as possible. Use care in their removal to avoid damaging the grates. In some furnaces clinker doors are installed just above the level of the grate; however, in other furnaces the clinkers have to be taken out through the firing door.

Do not permit the water level in a hot-water or steam boiler to become low, since this can cause warping or burning of the grate.

AUTOMATIC COAL STOKER

The purpose of a stoker is to feed the furnace or boiler with coal, relieving you of the manual operation. The underfeed type is the most popular; it has a coal-feed screw that is driven by an electric motor, and it feeds the coal into the fire pot of the furnace from either a storage bin or hopper. By means of a motor-driven fan the air that is necessary for combustion is forced through openings in the fire pot.

In the shaft is a shear pin that may become jammed by a large piece of coal. When this happens, remove the piece of coal and replace the shear pin.

The "hold fire" control in the stoker may sometimes feed insufficient coal into the fire pot, causing the fire to go out, or it may feed too much coal and cause overheating. If this happens call in an experienced work-

man to make the necessary adjustment of the control.

If you use anthracite coal the stoker pushes the ashes aside to the outside edge of the fuel bed, and they fall into the ashpit for removal. However, if you use bituminous coal, clinkers may form, and these will need to be removed through the door of the furnace.

At the end of the heating season, remove clinkers, coal and ash from the furnace and clean out the stoker. Coat the coal-feed screw and inside surfaces of the hopper with a lubricating oil to prevent rust. A few weeks before you put the heating system into operation, inspect the stoker and make any repairs or adjustments that may be necessary.

Coal stoves

A coal stove has no mechanical moving parts and is therefore usually a simple matter to keep in good condition.

REPAIRING CRACKS

The iron casing of the stove may develop a crack. The way to repair it is by filling it with a commercial iron-repair cement made of water glass (silicate of soda) and iron filings. You may also use stove putty. With a putty knife or a small trowel, force the paste tightly into the crack, then plaster over the surface of the crack with the same material. The heat from the stove will harden the cement and make a tight joint.

STORING THE HEATING STOVE

If the coal stove is used only for purposes of heating, you may want to store it in the summer. First clean and polish the stove; then wrap it in burlap, an old carpet or newspapers, tie it with cord and store it in a dry place.

Several weeks before you are ready to take the stove from storage and put it to use for heating, inspect the lining and the grates so that if any repair or replacement is needed it can be done before the onset of cold weather.

STOVEPIPE

Keep the stovepipe surface polished to prevent rust.

Periodically clean the inside of the pipe to get rid of soot accumulation. Spread a cloth or newspaper on the floor to protect it. Remove the pipe, and if possible take it outdoors to clean it. If this is not possible, be sure the soot removed from the pipe does not land on any of your house furnishings or your clothes. Do not pound the pipe too hard, since this may cause dents. Do not bend the ends, because it may be hard to fit them together again.

When storing the pipe for the summer take its sections apart, wrap burlap or newspaper around each section and keep them in a dry place.

Chapter Twenty

ELECTRIC FIXTURES AND EQUIPMENT

Buying equipment

ALTHOUGH YOU MAY be able to make minor repairs or emergency replacements in electric equipment, you will be better off requesting the services of a licensed electrician unless you are absolutely sure of your knowledge and skill in these matters.

In some localities electric repairs may be strictly regulated, and before you attempt to be your own electrician find out what the local ordinances stipulate. Before you buy or install any new equipment get a copy of the National Electrical Code, which specifies minimum standard requirements. You can obtain it from the National Board of Fire Underwriters; if there is no branch near you, ask your fire insurance agent to supply the address. The National Electrical Code includes information on the sizes of wiring suitable for various kinds of work, which will help you before you buy any wiring.

Never buy any electric equipment or appliances unless they carry the seal of approval of the National Board of Fire Underwriters. If they need special handling and maintenance, obtain directions from the dealer or manufacturer and familiarize yourself with them.

While electricity is one of man's great boons and so easy to use, it may also prove hazardous if carelessness is shown in handling wires and appliances. Electric safety warnings are included in Chapter 29.

A.C. OR D.C. CURRENT

Most electric appliances now operate both on A.C. (alternating current) and D.C. (direct current), and most buildings have A.C. In some old buildings or in certain areas D.C. current is still used, and some appliances still operate only on A.C. current. Therefore make sure of the current in your house before you invest in any new appliance.

Disconnecting the current

The main switch to the supply of electric current to the house is generally located in a metal box near the electric meter in the basement. The entire supply to the house may be disconnected merely by pulling the main switch.

It is a good idea for every adult in the house to know where the switch is located and how to disconnect it in case of emergency. The way it is done depends on the type of equipment you have. In some cases a handle protrudes from the enclosure, and all you need to do to disconnect the circuit is pull the operating lever downward. If you have a pull-out type switch or circuit breaker, either printed or written-out directions to disconnect the circuit should be attached to the outside of the enclosure box.

The main switch should be pulled when the house will be unoccupied for a long period, or in an emergency such as a fire.

Repairs

REPLACING FUSES

A fuse may blow out if you have too many appliances overloading the electric circuit or if there is a damaged electric insulation. If fuse trouble occurs too frequently, call in an electrician to determine the cause and correct it.

Before you start to replace a fuse, bear in mind the following safety rules:

1. Stand on a dry surface and have your hands dry.
2. Pull the main switch handle to the "OFF" position.
3. Open the fuse box.
4. Examine the fuses to discover which one has blown.

118

5. Replace the blown fuse with a new one of the proper size.

6. Close the fuse box and pull the main switch to "ON."

In a convenient place near the fuse box, keep an extra supply of fuses for emergencies. Also keep candles in the house, so you may light them during the temporary darkness before a new fuse is put in.

REPLACING PLUG CORDS

Electric cords must be handled with care; they should never be twisted or bent sharply since tears or breaks may result. If a cord needs to be replaced in a socket, examine Figs. 20.1a and b and use the following procedure:

1. Loosen the screws inside the plug cap, removing any short pieces of wire or thread remaining on the screws.

2. Insert the end of the new cord by pushing it through the hole in the cap from its outer (or under) side, leaving the cord end protruding about one inch above the cap hole.

3. Use a knife to split the end of the cord, so that you have two wires, and scrape off the outside braid on each of the split ends.

4. With a knife remove the first half-inch of insulation from each end of these two wires.

5. In each wire, twist the strands to form a little coil to hold them together.

6. Form each of the twisted wires into a loop, and set each loop around the blades of the plug, shown in

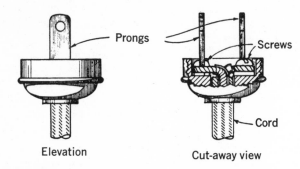

Elevation   Cut-away view

Fig. 20.1a

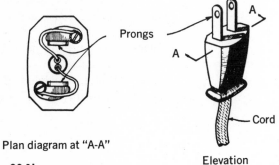

Plan diagram at "A-A"   Elevation

Fig. 20.1b

(b), and with a screw driver tighten the looped wire ends under each terminal screw.

You must take care that the bare wires do not come into contact with each other.

SPLICING CORD

Splicing is recommended only as a temporary way to join two ends of cord to lengthen them, or to repair a worn or torn cord. It is better to buy a new cord. The following is the procedure for splicing (joining), as shown in Fig. 20.2:

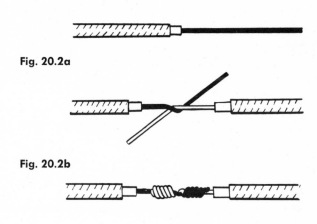

Fig. 20.2a

Fig. 20.2b

Fig. 20.2c

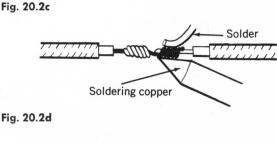

Solder

Soldering copper

Fig. 20.2d

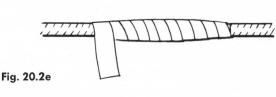

Fig. 20.2e

Scrape the two wire ends (which are to be joined) with a knife until the covering is removed to about three inches from the ends (a). Use sandpaper to clean and smooth the wire ends if they are rough.

Cross the wires 2½ inches from the ends (b).

Make five short turns with each end of the wire. Use pliers to squeeze the ends together and to make sure there are no sharp ends protruding (c). If you have soldering equipment, you may strengthen the splice with solder, although this is not absolutely essential (d).

Wind rubber tape around the splice, carefully and evenly. Wind friction tape tightly over this to produce an insulated cord repair (e).

APPLIANCE PLUG CORD REPAIR

To repair or replace a cord in an appliance plug (as shown in Fig. 20.3) use the following method:

1. Loosen bolts and take the plug apart.

2. Lift out the terminals and spring guard.

3. Trim away any loose or worn insulation, or cut the cord off and start with new ends of wire if necessary.

4. Remove the outer covering so that 2½ inches of the rubber-covered wires will be exposed.

5. Remove ¾ inch of the rubber insulation from each wire.

6. Scrape and solder the ends of the two wires.

7. Put the cord back through the spring guard.

8. Make hooks at the ends of the wire, as shown in the small drawing.

9. Place each hook under a terminal screw, in the same direction as the screw tightens. Tighten the screws.

10. Reassemble the plug.

Fig. 20.3

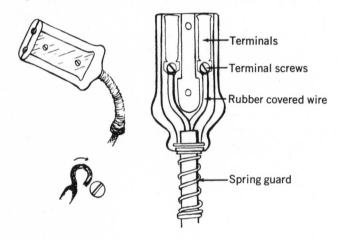

WIRING A LAMP SOCKET

1. Pare off about three inches of the outer fabric or rubber insulation on the cord. In the case of a molded rubber cord, simply split the cord back three inches, taking care to avoid cutting the insulation on the individual wires.

2. Remove three-quarters inch of insulation from the end of each wire, cutting the insulation on a slant. Scrape the wires with the back of a knife.

3. Twist the exposed strands in each wire tightly together, and cover with a hot coat of solder.

4. Thread the wires through the cap.

5. Make a hook in each wire to fit around the terminal screw.

6. Place the hook under the screw. Tighten the screw over the wire.

7. Put the lamp socket together. Place the paper shell inside the brass shell. Put the central section in-

side the paper shell. Clamp the cap down over the brass shell. (See Fig. 20.4.)

MISCELLANEOUS REPAIRS

When lamp sockets or wall switches become defective, call in an electrician to repair or replace them, since a nonprofessional job may not prove safe enough.

Fig. 20.4

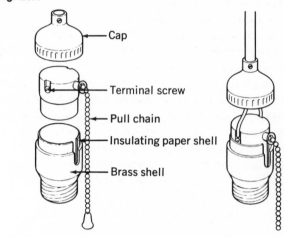

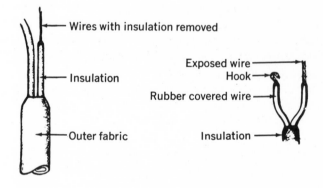

Door buzzers, bells and chimes

These mechanisms may be operated by batteries or by transformers connected to the house opening. If you have D.C. current you must not use a transformer, as the system could overheat and a fire be started. Transformers are used only on A.C. current, and if one is used it should be connected to the house wiring by an electrician.

Figure 20.5 shows an electric bell system that is operated by dry cell batteries, so that you may become familiar with the way in which it functions.

The system may fail in any of its parts, such as a worn-out battery; a loose connection in the transformer, bell or push-button terminals; a short-circuit or broken-circuit wire; or corrosion of the push-button, bell or buzzer contacts.

It is necessary to find out the cause, and the following suggestions may be of aid to you:

To examine the push-button faults, you may need to unscrew the whole mechanism from the wall or just remove the outer shell (depending on the type of button you have). The contact may be corroded from weather exposure or there may be dirt accumulation; in either case use sandpaper to clean out the contact points.

If connections are loose in the push button, bell, battery or transformer, they need to be tightened.

Should the bell parts be deranged, all that may be necessary is to clean the contact or tighten the adjusting screw. This screw is inside the bell box, and sometimes it needs to be moved either farther away from or closer to the spring. Should the spring be too stiff, bend it slightly toward the coils to loosen it.

Should the bell still not work properly after these adjustments have been made, examine the system to see if a broken wire or a short circuit exists. Sometimes a short circuit can occur because of a piece of metal inadvertently lying across the terminals or lead wires, or a staple touching both lead wires at a point where the insulation is badly worn. If you find any worn places on the insulation, wrap friction tape around them.

You may not be able to find a broken wire too easily. Look for the break where the wire is fastened with staples or where there is a sharp bend. But if you cannot find the break, you may need to make tests to locate the source of trouble. An A.C. meter (as shown in Fig. 20.6) is used for tests where the current supply is a transformer; but where a dry or storage battery is used a D.C. meter should be used.

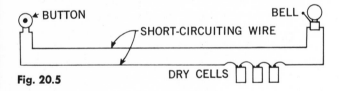

Fig. 20.5

Electric motor maintenance

Periodical inspection of and major repairs to a motor that provides power for your house lighting and appliances, or the motor in your freezer, refrigerator or vacuum cleaner, should be done by a licensed electrician.

To understand the motor and its maintenance, get a manual or other printed material that contains directions for the specific type of motor you have from the manufacturer or dealer.

When the motor stops working, the cause may lie in the wall plug, appliance plug or the electric cord. Examine these first and, if they are damaged, they should be repaired or replaced. If you find them in good condition, the next step is to inspect the brushes inside the motor. If a brush is worn out, you may take it out by removing the plastic cap and pulling out the brush with the spring attached to it. Place a new brush in the spring, then put it back into its opening, where the spring is kept in place by the plastic cap. If you cannot conveniently obtain a new brush right away, you may be able to get further temporary use from the old brush by giving it a new surface; use a fine sandpaper to do this so that you won't get any particles (if you use emery or rough sandpaper) into the bearings.

The belt on the motor should also be examined to see that it is not worn or slipping. If either is true, buy a new belt; as a temporary measure you can cover the worn places with friction tape. Take along the old belt when you go out to purchase a replacement to make sure you obtain the identical thickness and size.

Sealed bearings in the motor do not need periodical oiling. But if the motor has oil cups you must keep them oiled in order to prevent burning out the bearings. For this purpose a heavy oil is best and it is important to keep the oil cups well filled.

The motor surface must be kept clean and dry. Use a soft cloth to wipe off any dust and grease on its exterior, but never use water or any other liquid to wash motor clean. The inside of the motor must also be kept free of dust, which may be removed with the nozzle of a vacuum cleaner.

A motor needs ventilation, and even though it may be self-cooling it should not be kept where there is insufficient circulation of air.

An overheated motor is a signal that something is wrong, and it should be inspected by an expert for possible repairs or part replacements.

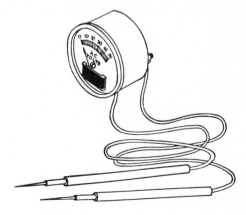

Fig. 20.6

Chapter Twenty-one

MAKE THE MOST OF CLOSET SPACE

THERE SHOULD BE no waste space in a closet, since its prime function is to provide storage for clothes and household items, in order to make the rooms of the house less cluttered, more comfortable and easier to keep clean.

The length of the rod in a closet, the number of hooks, the amount of shelving and the arrangement of the fittings should be suited to the needs of your family. For a closet that will be used by different persons from time to time, adjustable fittings are convenient. For instance, if hooks and rods in a closet for a child's clothing are adjustable, the closet can grow up with its owner. Shelves, too, may be made adjustable by the use of vertical wood strips fitted on the wall with movable pegs. Ready-made metal strips with adjustable brackets may be fastened to the walls to serve the same purpose.

Natural and artificial lighting of closets should be sufficient to make the contents plainly visible. If light from the room does not make garments or other articles in the closet easy to distinguish, an electric light fixture inside the closet is desirable.

One way to make the floor of a closet easy to clean is to lay linoleum or other washable covering over the wood surface, preferably to match the floor in the room. If you wish the closet to harmonize with the room, the walls of the closet may be painted the same color as those of the room. Wallpapering a closet is not feasible, since it is best to have walls which may be easily cleaned and washed down periodically.

Clothes closet

The closet shown in Fig. 21.1 may serve as a suggestion for your own needs. One or two shelves may be built across the width of the closet. A row of narrow shelves may be built at one side of the closet when space permits. You may also buy ready-built stacks of narrow shelves, if you don't want to make them yourself, and place these units on the floor of your closet. A row of hooks can be screwed to the lower shelf of closet, or a rod installed under the shelf, to take care of the clothes hangers. In the drawing double doors are shown; if your closet is not as wide, it will have only one door. On the inside of the door hooks can be added on which to hang miscellaneous articles, or a full-length mirror can be attached if there is none in your bedroom.

CLOSET FOR A CHILD

If you cannot spare an entire closet for the clothes of the

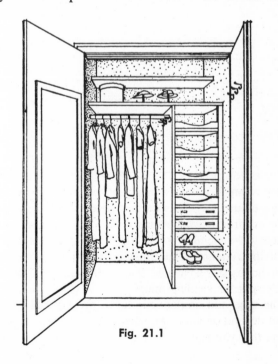

Fig. 21.1

122

youngster, you can convert an existing closet into combination adult-child use. In Fig. 21.2 you will see how a lower shelf and rod were attached, to allow for hanging of shorter clothes and to provide a separate shelf for the child's hats and so forth. The dimensions given in the illustration are merely suggestions to show how to proportion the heights of the different shelves.

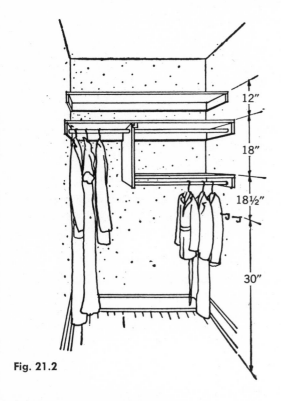

Fig. 21.2

VENTILATING CLOSET

Good ventilation is needed in a clothes closet to keep garments fresh-smelling and free of any dampness. Some closets are fortunate in having windows; but if yours doesn't have one, provide for air circulation by making openings in the top and bottom of the door or by using a louvered door.

Living room closet

If you have a closet in or near the living room, convert it into a storage place for the miscellaneous items used in that room. You may want to store folding card tables, folding chairs, trays, musical instruments, books, phonograph records, portable record players, sheet music or whatever the members of your family usually bring into the living room. Or there may be a stamp collector or other hobbyist who would find such a storage closet a handy spot for keeping things.

The type and amount of shelves you install in this closet depend on your own needs, but Fig. 21.3 suggests a plan that you may use as a guide.

Fig. 21.3

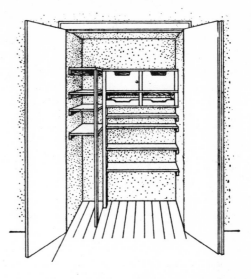

Dining room closet

A closet in the dining room is helpful for storing the dishes, silverware, linens and all articles used at mealtime. It is also useful to provide a place for the electric appliances that you use at or near the table when serving.

If there is already a closet in the room, you can install shelves on which to harbor all the dining room articles. If no closet is available, a corner closet can be built in, of whatever depth is desired. A good suggestion to follow is given in Fig. 21.4a, which shows the placement of the various items; Fig. 21.4b is a plan.

You will notice that a drawer is provided for the silver, since silverware should not be kept on an open shelf. You will also see that narrow double doors are suggested, since they may be more convenient to open than one full door. However, the size of your room will determine that for you.

Sewing closet

The woman who enjoys sewing would like to have a closet, if there is one to spare in your house, set aside for sewing equipment and materials. The closet should have shelves installed on which to keep boxes for trimmings, patterns and sewing accessories. A surface should be provided (perhaps one that can be pulled out and let down) for cutting from patterns. Cabinets may be bought (or made in your workshop) and placed on the floor. A rod should also be installed across the closet on which to hang clothes that are in the process of being sewed or mended. Space must also be provided to roll in a large sewing machine, or a surface on which to place a portable machine.

Fig. 21.4a

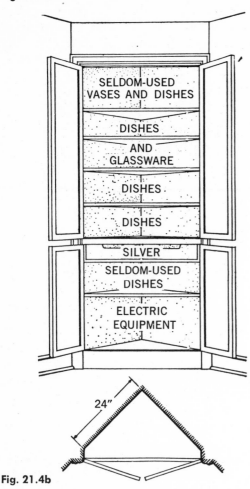

Fig. 21.4b

You may be guided by Fig. 21.5 in choosing the kind of sewing closet to install.

Your home office

If you have a narrow closet that you can turn into an "office" to hold papers pertaining to the running of your home, Fig. 21.6a suggests a way of building shelves and a receipt filing box. You may find this a useful aid in making your own business center.

This drawing gives suggested dimensions and an efficient way to section off the closet; Fig. 21.6b shows the detail of the drawer in which to keep your receipts.

Closet under stairs

This closet may be built in under the stairway leading to the basement and be used as a utility storage space, or it may be installed on any floor in the house as a handy extra closet if one is needed (Fig. 21.7).

Build a framework, using 2 by 4 inch wood strips, to support the walls. If the closet is to be built in the base-

ment on a concrete floor, secure the strips to the floor with toggle bolts.

If the house wall is finished, it may be used as it is; but if the wall is unfinished or has any inclination to dampness, the framework should also be built against that wall.

The upright strips must fit tight under the stairway and be set sufficiently close to maintain a strong wall. Nail the strips in place, at top and bottom. Over the framework nail the side walls, which may be of composition board or plywood. Or, for a paneled effect and a stronger construction, you may use tongued-and-grooved boards.

The door (which you may buy or make) should then be installed with hinges.

If the floor is concrete, you can lay a wood flooring over it, raised about an inch above the floor. Or you can lay linoleum over the floor.

The shelves should be cut of board of sufficient strength to hold whatever supplies you store on them. Nail cleats on the two sides of closet (running from the door to the back of the closet), then fasten the shelves onto the cleats.

You may want to leave free standing space in the closet if you wish to place upright tools (such as garden tools, vacuum cleaner and so forth) in it, and just have a shelf or two at the top.

For convenience, you may want to install an electric light fixture inside the closet.

Fig. 21.5

Fig. 21.6a

Fig. 21.8

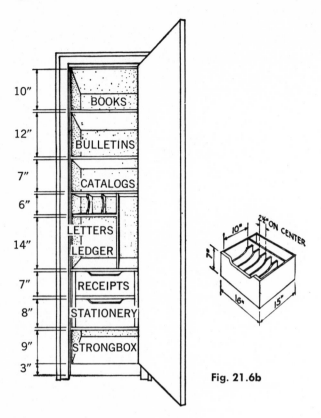

Fig. 21.6b

Room divider closet

A partition with a twofold purpose is one that extends part way across the room and gives you two separate smaller rooms, at the same time providing extra closet space.

A suggested way of making one is shown in Fig. 21.8. Here the divider goes up to the ceiling and extends about two-thirds of the way across the room. You may make the divider only three-fourths the height of the room to

admit light (should there not be sufficient window light for both the smaller room sections that the divider now makes). You may build the divider as narrow or as wide or as long as suits your purpose.

The divider can be used as a large closet with shelves and hooks inside it; or it can be used partially as a closet with open shelves added for decoration, and partially as a cupboard under the shelves, as suggested in the illustration.

First locate the studs in the wall to which the divider will be attached, bearing in mind that studs are usually sixteen inches apart; it will save you extra work if you plan the divider to be sixteen or thirty-two inches wide (or whatever the distance between studs in your wall may be). Mark the floor and the wall where the divider will go.

Using 2 by 4 wood strips, build the framework and nail it securely to the floor and the wall (and the ceiling, if the divider extends all the way up). Allow for a door frame on one side. Cover the framework with composition board or plywood. These boards usually come in large sheets, and it is best to buy the wall material in as large a size as possible to avoid too many joints and seams.

Install shelves and hooks inside the closet, as you desire them. Nail in cleats and nail down shelves on the cleats, if you are to include shelves in the divider.

Hang the door with hinges. A flush door is a good choice since it isn't too conspicuous. The door opening (and shelves, if you include them) should be placed on that side of the divider where it will fit in with your decorating theme and will be most convenient to you.

Finish the walls and door in the same color that is used in the room in which the divider-closet is placed. If you use different wall color in the two separate parts of the previous larger room, you may paint the divider differently on each side to match the room into which it faces.

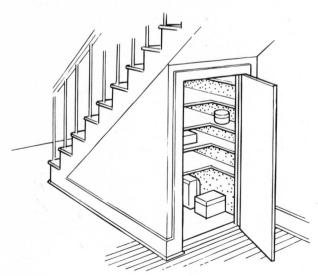

Fig. 21.7

Chapter Twenty-two

SHELVES AND RACKS

THE ADDITION OF SHELVES on the walls for decorative or useful purposes, and in closets and cupboards to gain more storage space, is not too complicated a task for the home handyman.

Shelving boards

For shelves use wood that is clear and has a good grain, such as poplar (whitewood) or white pine. You may have on hand other wood of a similar type, which will not splinter when it is being sawed and nailed, and will result in a smooth surface after you apply a coat of paint or other finish.

Wood should be strong, so that the shelf won't sag in the center when objects are placed on it. However, if you just need a short shelf that will not have any heavy articles placed on it, you can use composition board or plywood, then paint the shelf to match the wall.

To give a professional look to your shelves, make them of a board of full width. For bookshelves, boards of eight- or nine-inch width are generally used. If you have narrower boards, place them side by side, unless they are very narrow or you use more than two. In that case you can cut a narrow strip of 1 by 2 inch wood and screw it under the boards in the center of the shelf to act as a strengthener.

Always smooth the exposed edges and corners of the shelf with sandpaper or a plane. If the corner of the shelf prevents a door from opening, or simply for decorative purposes, you may want to round the corners, or cut them at a 45° angle.

Shelf brackets

When you make open shelves in the room, they should be laid over wood or metal brackets that are screwed into the wall. The edge of the bracket should not be brought flush with the edge of the board. Depending on the width and length of the board, the edge of bracket should be from one to four inches in from the edge. Always make sure there is a good balance so that the shelf will not sag under the weight of articles placed on it.

Whether you use brackets or cleats, they should be painted the same as the wall in order to be as inconspicuous as possible. Unless you have some special decorating color theme, it is well to paint a shelf (especially its underside) to match the wall, too.

Several ways to install the shelves on their supports are illustrated in Fig. 22.1:

Fig. 22.1a shows how to attach wood cleats to a wall and lay shelf board over them. If you are making open shelves, and one end fits into a wall corner, you can nail the cleat on the wall at that end; the board will rest on the cleat, then you need only one bracket at the other end of the board.

Whether you use one bracket, as suggested in the preceding item, or two brackets (one at each end if the shelf is free-hanging), the usual types are shown; (b) and (c) are wood brackets you can make yourself, and (d) is the metal bracket to be purchased at the hardware dealer.

If you want the shelves to be adjustable (not fixed in height) so that you can space them wider or narrower to suit the height of the books or objects you place on them, the simplest way to achieve this is to buy adjustable metal shelf standards and supports (e). These are obtainable at the hardware dealer. You will need four standards (one for each corner of the shelf). Before buying, measure the height of your bookshelves so you will know how many to purchase. You will also need

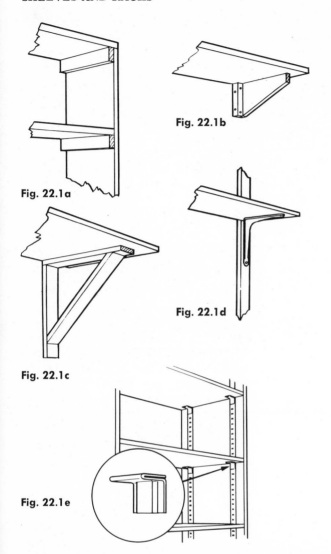

Fig. 22.1b

Fig. 22.1a

Fig. 22.1d

Fig. 22.1c

Fig. 22.1e

Bookshelf

A bookshelf serves the dual purpose of being decorative as well as useful. Therefore use a good-quality wood. Generally the board is ¾ inch thick by 8 or 9 inches wide, and the uprights may be 1½ by 1½ inches. Figures 22.2a and b will suggest to you the way in which the shelves are made.

Cut all the boards at one time, to make sure they are of identical size; then cut out a notch at each corner of the boards (except the top one). These notches must be the same width as the upright posts, so they will fit in properly (a).

Cut the four uprights the same height. With a pencil mark the point on each upright where the bottom of the shelf is to go. Lay two uprights on a flat surface and space them so that their outer edges will delimit the width of the shelf board. Cut cleats the same width as the shelf. On the markings where shelves are to be placed, nail the cleats to the uprights, being sure the top of the cleat comes to the pencil marking (not over or above that mark). Then lay the other two uprights down, and nail cleats in a similar manner (b).

Stand the uprights erect, then nail down the top board, keeping all edges at the four corners flush with uprights.

Lay the shelves over the cleats, making sure their notched-out corners fit tightly at the uprights. You don't need to nail down the shelves, but if you want to do so, drive nails into the cleats. You may prefer to have the bottom shelf on the floor; or it may be raised (on cleats) an inch or higher from the floor, as you desire.

The uprights should be sturdy enough to be placed against the wall; but if you want to add a backing you may nail a sheet of plywood or composition wallboard to the back of the two uprights, making sure the edges are flush all around.

four supports for each shelf (a typical support is shown in the small drawing). These are put on the underside of each corner of the board. Your dealer will provide you with instructions on how to install the standards on your wall and the supports under the shelf. The finished product is attractive in appearance as well as very easy to manipulate when you want to raise or lower a shelf.

Single shelf

If you want to make one or more individual shelves, consider first your wall space. Measure it to see how long your shelf may be. On the wall make a pencil mark where the bottom of the shelf is to go, and allow one inch—or whatever the width of the board is—so you will know that the top of the shelf will be that much higher than the mark on the wall. If you are to have two or more individual shelves, it may be a good idea to start measuring the wall from the bottom, so you may better gauge the placement of the shelves.

Fig. 22.2a

Fig. 22.2b

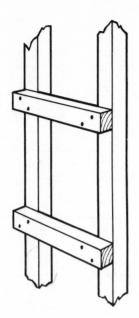

Fig. 22.4

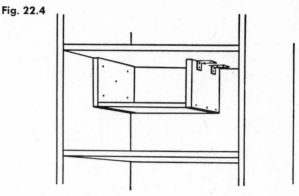

Sliding shelf

You may have shelves in a deeply recessed place (a closet or storage cabinet) that is not easily accessible. The sliding shelf is the answer to this problem. Figure 22.3 shows the two ways to make this shelf.

On both walls or both solid wood uprights, at each side where the shelf rests, install two cleats for each shelf (a); allow enough distance between the two cleats for the shelf to be slid easily in and out.

Instead of cleats, you can use solid boards (b), allowing the correct distance between them for sliding the shelf.

Inserted fixed shelf

Narrow shelves may be added where the present shelves are far apart (Fig. 22.5). These shelves may be held in place by narrow strips of wood (cleats) nailed in place; metal brackets or angle irons; large screw eyes placed so that the shelf will rest on the flat surface of the screw eyes; pegs inserted in holes bored in the side of the cupboard; or adjustable metal shelf standards and supports.

Shelves eight to ten inches apart may have one narrow shelf in between. If shelves are twelve or more inches apart, two narrow shelves may be added. The articles to be stored in the space will determine the width of the shelves and the distance between them.

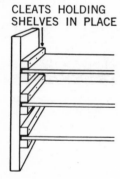

CLEATS HOLDING SHELVES IN PLACE

SOLID BOARDS BETWEEN SHELVES

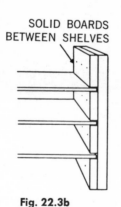

Fig. 22.3a

Fig. 22.3b

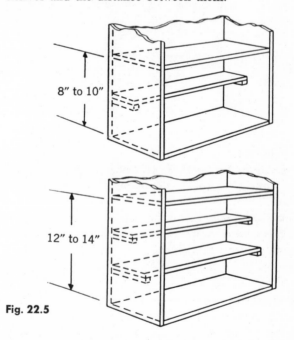

Fig. 22.5

Inserted hanging shelf

If your cupboard has spaces between shelves that are too wide for your purposes, and if you could benefit by more shelf space, you can make an extra shelf to hang onto the underside of an existing one. Figure 22.4 shows how this may be done by screwing in the inserted shelf with small angle irons.

Shelf under cupboard

If the kitchen or workroom needs more shelf space, and if there is adequate room on the wall between the top of the table or floor cabinet and the cupboard overhead, you may insert one or more narrow shelves of the same or of varying widths. Attach them to the wall with small metal brackets or angle irons (Fig. 22.6).

Fig. 22.6

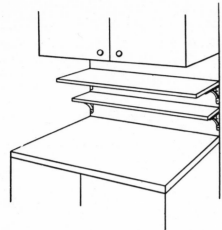

Fig. 22.8

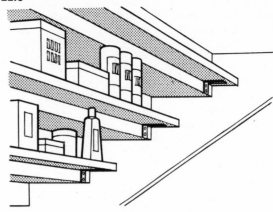

Wall hanging shelf

First make sure the wall is strong enough to hold the weight of the shelves and their objects. This shelf is a popular way of holding cookbooks, small spice jars and other necessities near the kitchen range. It is also suitable for books in youngsters' rooms. The shelves should be nailed to solid side pieces, then hung with screw eyes and hooks (Fig. 22.7).

Fig. 22.7

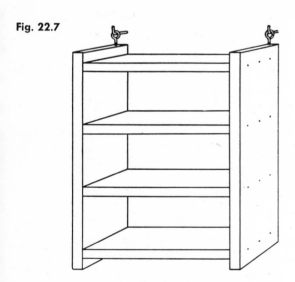

Shelf under stairway

If your storage shelves are not sufficient for many of the items used in the kitchen, workroom or basement, you may utilize the underside of the stairs that lead to the basement.

Figure 22.8 suggests doing this by cutting four to six inch wide boards the full width of the stairs. Attach them to the back of the riser with angle irons, or small metal brackets, keeping the bottom of the iron flush with the bottom of the riser. If the stairs are wide, you may need an extra angle iron in the center of the shelf in addition to the two that are placed near either end.

If the stairway is enclosed on both sides or rests against walls, for added strength you can nail cleats on the wall on which to rest the shelf.

Storage rack

There are many small items in a household that may be stored, to avoid cluttering, in built-in racks that you may make in your own workroom or buy ready-made.

A rack may be built from a solid piece of wood or of strips that you may have available. Depending on the weight of the articles you plan to put into the rack, use wood of sufficient thickness.

If the rack is to be on the inside of a door, make the rack narrower than the door itself so that the door may be opened easily. Sometimes the rack juts too far into the room; care must be used to build it narrow enough not to interfere with the room area when the door is closed.

In planning the rack, have the front of it high enough so that none of the articles will fall off when the door is opened or closed. If the rack is on the wall (not on a door), take the same precaution, because a person passing close to the rack may inadvertently cause some article to drop out. Sometimes all you need to do is provide a narrow wood strip across the front of the rack, as shown in the spice rack in Figure 22.9a.

The size and weight of the rack determine how it should be fastened to the wall or door. The rack may be screwed on; this is done by first boring holes near the top edge of the rack, at both sides, and inserting screws through these holes. If the rack is heavy, in addition to screws use one or two angle irons at the bottom for extra security. Should you have a very heavy rack on a door whose hinges are not sufficiently strong, it may be necessary to add another hinge.

Generally the rack is painted the same color as the wall or door on which it is secured. However, your decorating theme may be such that you will want to use another color or simply a natural finish.

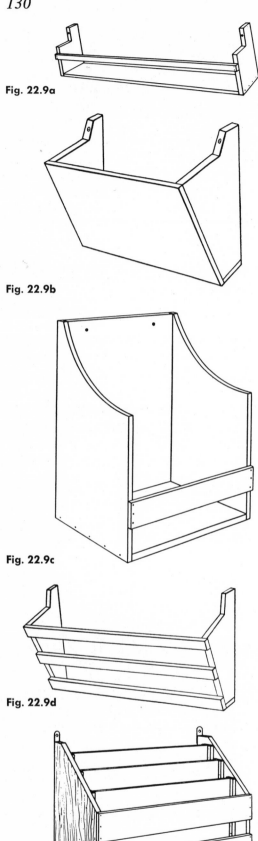

Fig. 22.9a

Fig. 22.9b

Fig. 22.9c

Fig. 22.9d

Fig. 22.9e

You will build whatever racks you feel are necessary; as a guide, Fig. 22.9 shows the various racks that are handy in a household: for spices or cosmetic jars and boxes (a); for paper bags, lids for pots and pans or trays (b); for a garbage can, usually placed inside the door of an undersink cabinet (c); for magazines, books and newspapers (d); and for platters, trays or lids for pots and pans (e).

Boxed knife rack

For safety's sake you may prefer to keep the kitchen knives in a rack, placed high on the wall out of the reach of a child. Figure 22.10 shows how you may make a rack from a wooden box (perhaps a cigar box).

Cut a block of wood, from any board you have available, to fit the end of the box. Mark the wood where you will insert the knives. Stand the box on end, and open its lid so you may have comfortable space to work in. Now nail the wood block onto the top of the box end,

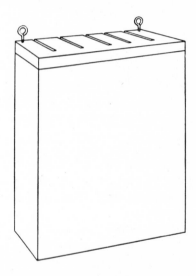

Fig. 22.10

starting the nailing from inside the box into the bottom of the block in order to avoid having the nailheads visible on the surface. Be sure no nails are driven at any place where the marks for the slots are made. Then saw the slots through the block of wood and through the end of the box. Nail down the lid of the box so that it won't interfere with the smooth hanging of the rack on the wall. It is hung by screw eyes at each side of the rack, onto hooks fixed into the wall.

Open knife rack

Figure 22.11 shows how a simple rack may be made out of a strip of wood about one inch thick by two inches wide. Cut the strip whatever size you need to hold the knives, and allow about four inches extra (two inches each end) for fastening the rack to the wall. Cut the length of strip on the lengthwise grain of the wood, for more strength. Shape the two ends of the strip to narrow them, so that screw holes may be made there to allow for screws to be inserted when the rack is hung up.

Cut a strip of board one inch wide the length of the rack (not including the two shaped ends) and about one-half inch higher than the rack strip (to keep the knife handles from slipping out). Nail this strip to the first strip, as shown in Figure 22.11.

Mark the front of the strip where the slots are to be cut. Make two markings for each one, one-quarter inch apart. Clamp the rack to the edge of a table with a C clamp or put it in a vise, so it will be steady when you saw through the slots. Remove the wood between the one-quarter inch spaces you have sawed out.

Insert screws through the two holes drilled at each end of the rack, and hang it up on hooks provided for the purpose on the wall or door.

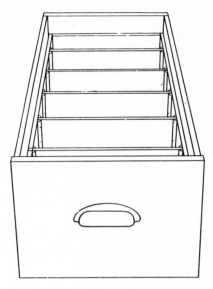

Fig. 22.12a

Fig. 22.11

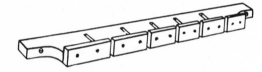

Filing rack

Horizontal and vertical files, which may be set into a drawer or closet, or kept on top of a table surface, are very handy for storing small articles that might otherwise cause cluttering.

The framework may be made of slightly heavy wood pieces, but the partitioning pieces can be made of plywood or composition wallboard, or even of pieces of metal if you have any you want to cut up for the purpose.

The easiest way to hold the divider pieces in place is by nailing down a piece of wood between them; you can use any narrow strip of wood you have available, or pieces of quarter-round molding. If you want to do more work on the rack, you may cut grooves in the wood to be used as a base for the dividers, and then slide the dividers into the grooves.

Figure 22.12 shows suggestions you may follow.

A deep drawer is turned into a vertical file by upright dividers, (a) held in place by strips of wood or by grooves.

This horizontal file has a top and two sides (b), and you may add a bottom piece and a back if you desire. You will notice that the shelves slant downward toward the back; but the same file rack may be made with straight shelves.

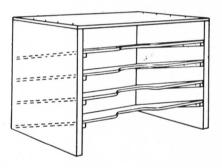

Fig. 22.12b

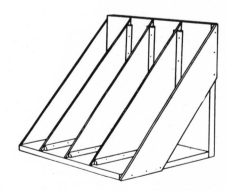

Fig. 22.12c

This type of vertical file (c) is useful for storing lids for pots and pans, trays or other articles that you need to grasp quickly by hand. All that is needed here is a back and a bottom piece.

Drawer divider

You may want to partition a drawer to keep small articles in orderly arrangement (Fig. 22.13). You may use a thin wood for the purpose, cutting the divider pieces shorter than the height of the drawer so they won't interfere with its sliding. Cut one strip the full length of the drawer, to fit in snugly so it won't slide. Then cut the divider pieces the width of the drawer.

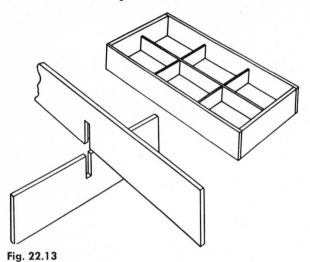

Fig. 22.13

On the long strip, mark off the places for slots where you will put the partitioning pieces (marks to be half the height of the wood); then on the smaller pieces mark off in the same way where they will join the larger strip.

Cut the slots evenly, so the pieces will fit together where they are joined.

Dishpan sink rack

If your sink is too low for you to work comfortably at it, you may raise the surface by building a rack (Fig.

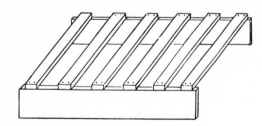

Fig. 22.14

22.14). Of course the wood must be strong and able to withstand the wear it will receive as a platform for the dishpan, and it must not be splintery.

First find the most suitable height at which you want to set this rack into the sink. Put some blocks of wood of varying heights into the sink; then set the pan on them and keep testing until you find the right height. Then cut the two side pieces and the slats, and nail them down so their edges are flush with the side pieces.

Add a water-resistant finish to the rack to keep it from warping.

Shoe rack

You may provide space for holding shoes inside the closet, or on the back of the door. Figure 22.15 provides two suggestions; the dimensions given in the drawings are tentative and you will alter them to allow for whatever space you have available:

For use on the floor of the closet, build a slanted shelf raised in the back (Fig. 22.15a). Nail a narrow wood strip or a quarter-round molding on top of the shelf, against which to rest the heels so the shoes won't slide down. The width of the rack will depend on your shoe size.

Figure 22.15b shows the rack generally used on a wall or on the back of a door, when no floor space is available. It is made of two bars, and the heels rest on

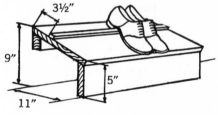

Fig. 22.15a

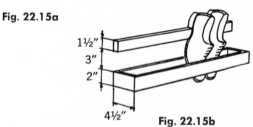

Fig. 22.15b

the upper rod. It is a good precaution to make the lower section with two rods, with sufficient space for the shoe, and to cover the inside with a piece of felt or flannel as a protection for the shoe toes.

Another way of making a shoe rack is to screw two flat-shaped metal curtain rods on a wall or inside a door, using a narrowly curved rod for the upper bar on which the heels rest, and a wider curved rod for the lower bar to give enough space for the shoe fronts.

Chapter Twenty-three

PLANNING THE KITCHEN, WORKROOM AND LAUNDRY

THE WORKING ROOMS in which the homemaker prepares the meals and does the laundry and sewing should be planned with as much efficiency as a business firm plans its offices and factory layouts. Too often a kitchen is laid out so inconveniently that many needless steps must be taken by the homemaker, and cabinets are placed too high or too low for most efficient use.

Work centers

To achieve maximum efficiency, three work centers should be planned, in the following order:

STORAGE CENTER

This area is where the refrigerator and freezer, and the pantry or closet where you put the foodstuffs, are placed. The storage center should be as near as possible to the door through which food deliveries are made to the kitchen.

PREPARATION CENTER

In this area, which is next to the storage center, food is prepared for cooking and dishwashing is done. The sink is the focal point of this center, and floor cabinets that have adequate counter surfaces as well as overhead cupboards are added as necessary. This area is also the place for the automatic dishwasher and garbage disposal unit (if your kitchen includes such equipment).

COOKING AND SERVING CENTER

The kitchen range and the counter space (tops of floor cabinets or tables) that is needed for serving food are placed here. In this area also place cupboards for pots, pans and other cooking utensils. Seasonings (spices and condiments) should also be kept here—perhaps on a small shelf built for the purpose.

Planning the layout

The size of your kitchen, as well as the needs of your family, will determine the type of equipment you use and the way in which you place all the equipment in the room. You may have cupboards between the refrigerator and the sink, and between the stove and the sink, so arranged that you will have convenient table-top space in each working center. You may also build cupboards on the wall, as well as underneath the sink and extended at its sides so you will have more counter space. Shelves may also be provided on the walls if you desire them.

Figure 23.1 shows the four basic kitchen arrangements as suggestions for planning work centers.

A one-wall unit (a) is suitable for a small, narrow room. This compact arrangement may be put to further use by building overhead cupboards.

An L-shaped unit (b) is suitable in a kitchen where

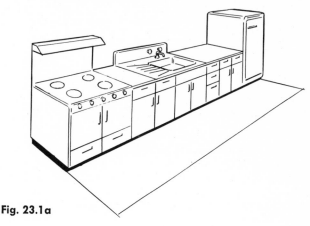

Fig. 23.1a

133

Fig. 23.1b

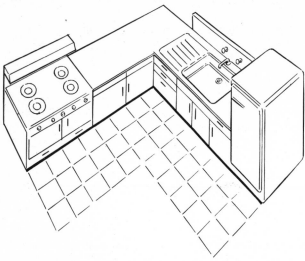

Fig. 23.1d

you want to use only two walls, leaving the other walls free for a dining nook or to place a table and chairs for mealtimes. Should your kitchen have two doors, place the refrigerator nearest to door through which you bring the groceries, and the stove near the other door.

A corridor unit (c) is suggested for a square, small kitchen. Along one wall place the storage and preparation centers, along the opposite wall the cooking and serving center. If there is sufficient space along the wall, you can include a dining spot.

A U-shaped unit (d) is regarded as the most desirable plan if you have sufficient kitchen space. The preparation center is placed at the top of the "U," with the storage center along the wall that has the door and the cooking and serving center along the opposite wall. If the kitchen is large enough, along the fourth wall you can place a table and chairs for dining, or for ironing, sewing and other chores.

Laundry and sewing room

If there is space in your house to allow for a utility room, place it as near the kitchen as possible. The size of this workroom and the equipment you install in it will depend, of course, on the room; and the work the homemaker wishes to do in it will determine the kind of equipment you install.

Figure 23.2 may serve as a guide in your planning. But the following are practical suggestions regardless of the size and type of the room:

1. Place the washing machine next to the stationary tub or large basin (if no tub installed).

2. On top of the washtub have a hinged cover that will serve as a working surface when you let it down.

3. Install shelves above the washing machine and tub to accommodate soap flakes and other laundering items.

4. The hamper or bin (portable or built in) should be close to the washing machine. If possible more than one hamper or bin should be used, for easy sorting of soiled clothes.

5. The sewing section should not be too close to the laundry, and should be placed preferably at the other side of the room. Provide a sturdy table in this area, preferably with many drawers in it to hold needles, threads and other sewing accessories; or else provide a cupboard, on the floor or attached to the wall, to hold these items.

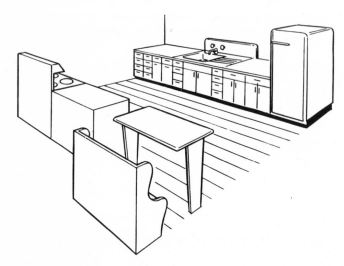

Fig. 23.1c

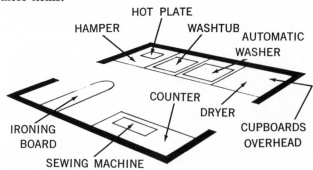

Fig. 23.2

Comfortable work heights

Although most equipment comes in standard sizes and heights, you may want to provide working surfaces to suit the homemaker who is below or above average height. Figure 23.3 shows equipment accommodated to a woman whose height is five feet four inches, and suggests the most efficient manner of storing articles that are used either frequently or seldom.

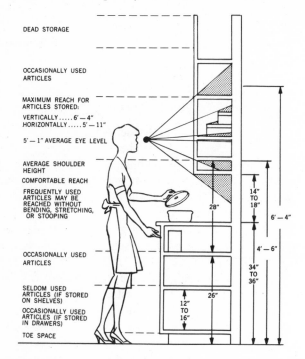

Fig. 23.3

Compact kitchen storage

To achieve greatest efficiency, especially in the food preparation area, you can install cabinets on the wall as well as on the floor that are as well planned as a filing system in an office. Figure 23.4 shows how you may plan such an installation, which of course you may adapt to your own space and needs.

Good lighting

Natural lighting helps to prevent fatigue, decreases accident hazards and adds cheerfulness to the room. The window area in a kitchen should be at least fifteen to twenty per cent of the total floor space. You will need artificial light, too, but nothing takes the place of light from outdoors.

Artificial lighting should consist of a central ceiling fixture, with the addition of direct lighting where you need it most. Incandescent and fluorescent lights can be combined to great advantage, because together they cast a flattering glow on both you and your decorative scheme.

Adequate lighting is a real economy in your laundry. Scorch marks and spots are easily seen in daylight or can be detected under light from a 4500° fluorescent lamp.

The Illuminating Engineering Society suggests a two hundred-watt ceiling light or two forty-watt fluorescent tubes as sufficient for general illumination in an average size kitchen. For limited-area lighting, twenty-watt fluorescent tubes above each work center (attached to the underside of the wall cabinet) are usually enough. Above the sink where the light location is normally high, higher wattage is suggested.

Work surface coverings

A covering on the countertop of a cupboard or the top of a table should be smooth and easily cleaned. Stainless steel, plastic, heat-treated glass, acid-resistant porcelain enamel, linoleum and wood are generally used; but in many cases tops are already finished with a working surface when you purchase the equipment, so you do not need to add any other covering. If one is needed and you are in doubt about a choice, linoleum is very good for working surfaces because it is a resilient material and helps to keep down breakage of dishes.

For cutting and chopping foodstuffs, you may set a flat, sturdy piece of wood (birch or maple) in one part of the countertop.

Floor coverings

The prime requisite in covering the floor of the kitchen and workroom is that it be resistant to dust and grease. Select for your covering linoleum, asphalt tile, rubber tile or vinyl plastic. Covering that has a design in it usually shows less wear than solid color.

Make sure the floor is smooth, to get best service from the covering. Some brands have a felt padding built into the back of the material; if the covering you buy does not have such a backing you may want to use a special felt padding, cementing it to the floor to reduce cracking from expansion and contracting. Ask your dealer about this when making your purchase.

Do not use carpeting in the kitchen or workroom. Avoid all scatter rugs, regardless of their material, since they are accident hazards.

Wall coverings

Your taste and budget will guide you in your choice. You may use paint, wallpaper, thin-gauge linoleum or tiling.

Fig. 23.4

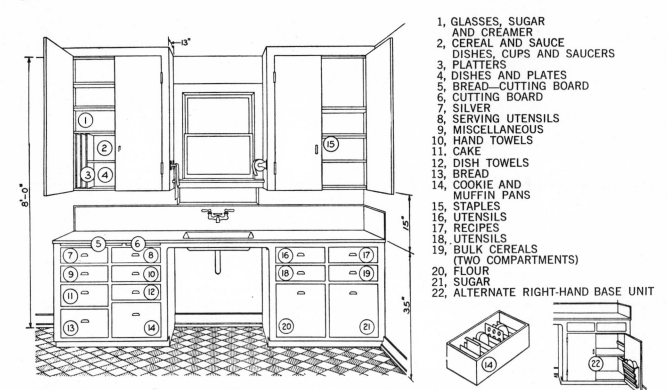

1, GLASSES, SUGAR AND CREAMER
2, CEREAL AND SAUCE DISHES, CUPS AND SAUCERS
3, PLATTERS
4, DISHES AND PLATES
5, BREAD—CUTTING BOARD
6, CUTTING BOARD
7, SILVER
8, SERVING UTENSILS
9, MISCELLANEOUS
10, HAND TOWELS
11, CAKE
12, DISH TOWELS
13, BREAD
14, COOKIE AND MUFFIN PANS
15, STAPLES
16, UTENSILS
17, RECIPES
18, UTENSILS
19, BULK CEREALS (TWO COMPARTMENTS)
20, FLOUR
21, SUGAR
22, ALTERNATE RIGHT-HAND BASE UNIT

Between the bottoms of the wall cabinets and the countertops of the floor cupboards or tables, linoleum or tiling is often used, even though the rest of the room is painted or papered. The reason for this is to avoid wall damage and stains from spattering food.

You may exercise your creative urge by painting or using other wall covering of a solid color at the work centers, and using a patterned wallpaper at one wall where there is no activity going on.

Safety in the use of gas

Buy appliances that carry the seal of approval of the American Gas Association.

Gas installation should meet approval requirements of the National Board of Fire Underwriters.

Equipment should be supplied with an automatic shutoff device that operates when the flame goes off.

If you use liquid gas or natural gas that has no odor, supply a warning odor (ask your gas company about this) to prevent a hazard in case of gas leaks.

Safety in the use of electricity

Buy equipment (all appliances, cords, plugs) that car-

ries the seal of approval of the Underwriters' Laboratories, Inc.

Wiring done by an electrician should conform to the Code of the National Board of Fire Underwriters.

Protect each circuit, including the main circuit to the house, with fuses or circuit breakers of rating to agree with the carrying capacity of wire, to prevent any overloading of the wires.

Plug-in outlets should have ground connections so all electric appliances may be grounded; use three-prong plugs to fit the outlets.

Provide light switches near the room entrance.

Flush plates of outlets should be of nonconducting material.

Install outlets as far from water faucets as possible, so you won't inadvertently touch both the faucet and the outlet at the same time.

Install outlets high enough to keep cords off the floor, and close enough to the area where the appliances are to be used to avoid unnecessarily long cords.

Use rubber covered cords if the appliance is used in an area where the cord may get wet.

Provide round pegs on which to hang cords when not in use; this will prevent wear on cords.

Provide an insulation link in all pull-chain switches.

Chapter Twenty-four

BATHROOM PLANNING

YOU MAY WANT TO ADD or replace fixtures in the bathroom, build an additional bathroom to provide for a growing family or perhaps add an extra washroom to the house. The prime thing to bear in mind is that bathroom fixtures are permanent, so you must get the best quality you can afford and see that the installations are done in an expert manner.

Placement of the bathroom

The best location, from a plumbing point of view, is to put the bathroom next to a room that already has water fixtures (such as the kitchen or laundry), or on the floor above that room over the spot where the plumbing exists. In this way you don't need to install more extra piping than is absolutely necessary.

If you have two bathrooms or a separate washroom (one on each floor of your house), the most economical procedure is to have each situated at the same spot (one over the other) to save extra work and extra plumbing costs.

For sake of family convenience, the bathroom door should open into a hallway rather than into a room; in this way everyone may have access to the bathroom without needing to cross any room. Of course your house may be large enough to have a separate bathroom that is entered through the master bedroom and a second bathroom opening into a hallway for the rest of the family or for guests to use.

Selecting fixtures

Bathroom fixtures are made of vitreous china, enameled steel or enameled iron. The most expensive is vitreous china, which is used for water closets and often for lavatories. It is very strong, does not damage or stain easily and is resistant to acids.

Pressed or cast-iron steel, coated with regular or acid-resistant porcelain enamel, is used for bathtubs and lavatories.

Acid-resistant enameled fixtures do not damage or stain easily, and of course they are not affected by acids. If the enamel finish is not acid-resistant it may be subject to stains and damages, and if the enamel wears away it cannot be repaired.

Plumbing details

Water pipes are placed in the wall and under the floor to hide them from sight. If it is not feasible to put the vertical pipes into the walls, build a box around them and paint it the same color as walls.

Cold climate is hard on water pipes, which may freeze

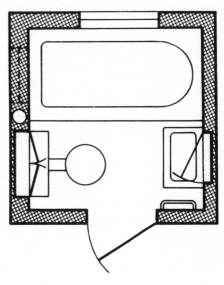

Fig. 24.1

137

even if they are placed in the outside walls. Such pipes should be covered with special pipe insulation, and it is best to ask your dealer to recommend the type of insulation and the way to apply it.

If you are to install new fixtures, remember they are usually heavy and that you must be sure the floor joists are big enough to hold them. You may need larger or additional joists, and it may be wise to consult a builder.

If you are installing a wall-hung lavatory (wash basin), the wall needs to be of sufficient strength to carry it.

When installing a bathtub, place the fixture end of the tub on an inside wall. Install a removable panel in the wall, as shown by the dotted line in Fig. 24.1, so that when pipes need to be repaired you will have easy access to them.

Fig. 24.2

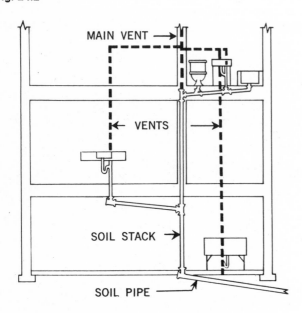

Waste pipes

The waste is carried away from the bathroom in a three-inch vertical soil stack, as shown in Fig. 24.2. To make the wall stronger at the point where this pipe is placed, use six-inch studs rather than the usual four-inch studs.

The wash basin (lavatory) is connected to the soil stack by a 1¼-inch waste pipe, and to the bathtub by a 1½-inch pipe.

The water closet (toilet) waste pipe is the same size as the soil stack, as a rule. Therefore place the water closet as near the soil stack as possible.

Figure 24.3 shows how the distance of the pipe is limited by the size of the floor joists. Place the water closet so that the large waste pipe goes between and parallel to the floor joists, rather than having to cut

Fig. 24.3

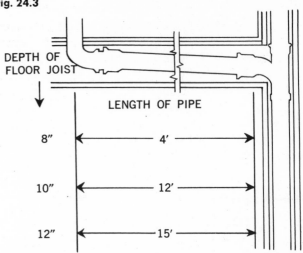

through them. This will save you the work of cutting the joists as well as the expense of having to put in floor framing. A good way to save on the cost of piping is to place all the fixtures along one wall, if that is possible.

TRAPS AND VENT PIPE

Each fixture must have a trap and be connected to a vent pipe, to prevent the sewer gas from leaking into the bathroom. Locate the fixtures so they can all be vented through a single main vent that extends through the roof. The main vent is an extension of the soil stack.

The trap to the water closet is built into the bowl. The traps to the lavatory and bathtub empty into the waste pipe.

Fig. 24.4

Space for baby's bath

Allot an available wall space in the bathroom for a special baby bath section. As a suggestion, Fig. 24.4 shows a bath table between two cabinets that contain the baby's clothes. The table may be made with a shelf below the top to hold the small bathtub, with space beneath it for a pail or tiny hamper to contain the baby's soiled clothes.

On the wall attach shelves or a cabinet to hold bath supplies.

Heating

Be sure to include a place for a register, radiator or heater, and plan to place it out of reach in a small bathroom.

A portable heater may be hazardous; if a heater is needed, it is better to get a built-in or wall-panel electric heater. An electric heater must be grounded for safety, and a gas heater must be vented to the outside of the house. A heater must be located where it will not set any blowing curtains, towels or clothing afire.

Lighting

An overhead light is needed, as well as a mirror light. For purposes of shaving and applying cosmetics, use side brackets at the mirror with the electric bulb about 5½ feet from the floor. In a very small space you may not be able to install side brackets, but you may be able to put one good light above the mirror. Adjust the lighting so that it shines full on your face and not in the mirror.

Don't use pull chains on electric lights; wall switches are safer.

Wall finish

In choosing a wall finish you must consider whether or not it is easy to keep clean, how long it will last and how easy it is to install.

You may select either waterproof paint and enamel, oilcloth or other coated materials, wallboard with a waterproof finish or tiles made of plastic, enameled metal or ceramic (glazed or unglazed). If you are going to apply any of these materials to the wall, get the manufacturer's directions on the easiest way to do so.

Good wall finishes that fit into the bathroom but must not be used in the shower stall or if there is danger of sprinkling (if the shower is over the tub) are washable wallpaper, wall linoleum and enameled wall coverings. Do not select any of these if there is a possibility of wetting from the shower.

Floor covering

There is a large choice of materials for floor covering, and it is best for you to consult with a dealer first to get his opinion on the durability and the installation of any of the following: tiles made of asphalt, rubber, cork, unglazed ceramic, unglazed clay or plastic; linoleum tile or sheet; wood with a water-resistant finish.

Do not use scatter rugs of any kind since they may cause you to slip and get hurt. If you use an absorbent bathmat on the floor to step on when you come out of your bath, pick it up the moment you are ready to leave the bathroom.

Safety check list

The bathroom is, unfortunately, a popular spot for accidents. To avoid such occurrences, observe the following safety rules:

1. Provide grab bars at the tub and shower.
2. Keep floors dry; immediately mop up any dripped water.
3. Install a bathtub with a flat bottom, to reduce the danger of slipping.
4. Place the medicine cabinet high on the wall and keep it locked to prevent a child from opening it.
5. Keep electric light switches out of reach of anyone who is using a water faucet or taking a bath.
6. Use wall switches instead of chain pulls for all lights.
7. Keep the gas or electric heater properly located and shielded to prevent fire or burns.
8. Install faucets that combine hot and cold water in the tub and lavatory. A separate hot-water faucet may cause scalding.

Fig. 24.5

9. Install a mixer valve, to combine hot and cold water, for the shower bath.

10. Use faucet handles of metal; avoid porcelain ones, which may crack and break.

11. If anyone in the family is not sure-footed, place a rubber mat on the floor of the stall shower or on the bottom of the bathtub, to prevent slipping when taking a shower.

Extra facilities

Your house may require an added toilet and washroom. These may be located under a stairway, or a closet may be converted to accommodate the wash basin and water closet. Before you decide where to place the new room, study the location of existing water pipes and soil pipe in order to keep new plumbing to a minimum.

Figure 24.5 shows how this added room may be fitted under a stairway. If the stairs are not enclosed (as may be the case when they lead to the basement), you may build an enclosure of composition wallboard or plywood, and fit a door to it.

For a floor covering, use linoleum, which is easy to install. Paint or wallpaper the inside of the room in a light color, to give it a more spacious look. The outside can be painted or wallpapered to harmonize with the adjacent walls.

Chapter Twenty-five

FOR THE GARDEN OR BACKYARD

A WELL-KEPT GARDEN or lawn, or even a little backyard greenery, enhances the appearance of the house, and the proper maintenance of the grounds provides a good form of outdoor exercise.

Tools and equipment

You do not need to buy every garden tool listed in a catalogue or on display in the shops; start off with the barest essentials and then add to the equipment as more tools become necessary. There is no bargain in buying cheaper-grade tools; it is wiser to get equipment of best quality rather than an inferior sort that won't last long. Start off with the following:

Bucket	Lawn mower (manual
Cord (to lay out rows for	type)
planting)	Shovel
Garden hose, long enough	Spade or spading fork
to reach entire area	Steel bow rake
Hoe (7-inch, with socket	Trowel
handle fitting)	Watering can

If you have a large garden and lawn, you may prefer to get a hoe with a wheel, to push around, a power lawn mower and a sprinkler-type watering hose, instead of the three simpler corresponding items in the first list.

Care and repair

In the same way as you make periodical inspections of your house, you should use care in examining the garden equipment to see if it needs any attention.

The handles of all garden tools should be painted a bright color, such as yellow or orange, in order that they may be seen easily if they are resting on the ground. Handles that are painted green or brown are not sufficiently visible, and someone may trip over them and be hurt by the sharp metal edges of a tool.

Painting also preserves a wood handle. The metal part of a tool which is put into the ground should not be painted. However, the metal part of a tool which does not come into contact with the earth should be painted. Apply a priming coat of red lead on the metal part, and over that base apply two coats of exterior paint.

If you have a wheelbarrow, keep the moving part oiled so it doesn't rust or squeak, and preserve the wood by a good-quality paint. Repair any breakages in the wood or metal parts as soon as they occur.

A broken wood tool handle may be replaced and is no reason for discarding the tool. If you're a handyman you can make a new wood handle and attach it to the tool. Many hardware shops carry standard types of wood handles, and you may be able to match one to the tool.

However, should the wood handle be cracked and not completely broken off, you can put a "bandage" on it by winding a thin wire or a strong cord around the crack, then covering it with adhesive tape.

A wood handle that becomes splintery and rough may be smoothed down with sandpaper. This not only protects your hands but also prevents cracks from spreading from the splintered part.

The edges of shovels and hoes should also be examined for nicks, and if any exist they should be smoothed off with a metal file. Any rough surfaces on the metal should be smoothed off with steel wool. Straighten out any dents.

Outdoor metal equipment, or the metal parts of wood tools, should be coated with petroleum jelly or a similar oily preparation before the equipment is stored for the cold months. This prevents rusting. Also, if any repainting is needed on the tools, do that before storing so you will have them all ready for use when you take them out in the spring.

The lawn mower needs constant care. After each grass cutting, wipe the blades dry with a cloth. If any dirt has accumulated at the oil holes, use a thin wire to

141

clean out the hole and drop in a bit of oil. Be sure to keep the mower in a dry place since dampness may be harmful to it. Before you store the mower for the cold weather, remove its wheels, clean the mower carefully, then coat the metal parts with an oily substance.

The garden hose will last longer if you give it good care. Be sure the hose is drained dry every time you finish watering the garden. Do not fold the hose at any time, because it may cause cracks in the creases. The hose should be coiled and hung; but never hang it on a single nail or peg. Some hose comes with its own roll-around stand on which to coil it when not in use; but if you don't have one, insert two or three rounded pegs in the wall, spaced about twelve inches apart, and hang the coiled hose on these pegs.

To repair a leak in the garden hose, cut through the hose where the hole appears. At a hardware shop buy a coupling that is especially made for this purpose. Attach the two parts of the coupling to the two ends where the hose was cut through (following the same method used at the top of hose where the fitting is put on). Then screw together the two couplings to join the hose.

If you use any chemical spray equipment in your garden, give the hose a thorough washing before putting it away. If chemicals are left in the sprayer, they may clog or rust it.

Where to keep tools

Letting tools lie carelessly around the garden or in the garage may prove hazardous to personal safety and may also cause damage to the tools. It is essential to provide a safe place for outdoor equipment.

First find the most convenient location. This may be the basement, garage or a lean-to on the house, or you may want to build a special closet for the purpose.

WALL RACK

For a small garden and few tools, you can build a rack to harbor all the equipment, along the lines suggested in Fig. 25.1.

1. Use two upright pieces of wood for the sides and a board for the top, and join them to make a frame. Nail the frame securely to the wall.

2. Lay four or five cleats on the floor. On these cleats lay a board (wide enough and strong enough to accommodate heavy equipment, such as a lawn mower), then nail down the board.

3. Cut a wood strip the same length as the top of the frame, and nail it to the wall about eighteen inches below the top board. Then nail each end of this strip to the side upright boards of the frame.

4. Into the top board and the lower board screw sturdy hooks and clamps on which to hang your tools.

5. For added strength, nail a diagonal wood brace to

Fig. 25.1

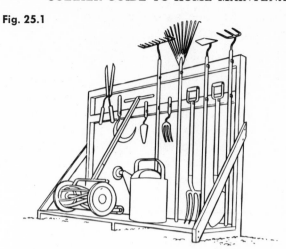

the bottom board and to the uprights on each side. Saw both ends of these braces at an angle so they will be flush with the floor board and the uprights.

WALK-IN CLOSET

If you have a closet near the garden, which is not being used, you can turn it into a tool closet. However, you may need or want to build a new one for the purpose.

Figure 25.2 may be helpful as a suggestion. The closet shown is five feet deep and three feet wide. You will notice racks on the wall for small items and boxes on the floor to hold tools or children's outdoor toys. Hooks on the wall hold larger tools, and pegs are provided for the coiled garden hose. Shelves may be put around the walls, but always within easy reach.

In building this closet, you can use wood, gravel or concrete for the floor (depending on where the closet is located). The material for the walls should be the kind that will hold the hooks and shelves very securely.

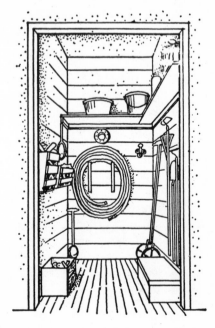

Fig. 25.2

It is a good idea to provide a light in the closet if electric wiring permits it.

Window plant box

When making window boxes be sure to buy well-seasoned wood that will withstand all sorts of weather. Although it is easier to buy a metal box and set it on the outside of your window sill, metal does not fare well under hot sun rays and may rust in wet weather.

Use a 1 by 8 inch board, 12 feet in length. Proceed as follows, using Fig. 25.3 to help you:

1. Cut three pieces the same size, each three feet four inches long. Mark them *back, front* and *bottom*. Square the ends of the boards.

2. On the bottom piece, plane off a one-quarter inch bevel on one edge.

3. On the front piece, plane off a one-quarter inch bevel on both edges.

4. For the ends, cut a two foot long piece from the remaining board, then square its edges.

5. Lay the board flat (with its grain running right and left). From the left end, measure 10½ inches to the right along the far edge of the board, then make a mark at that point.

6. From the mark made in step 5, measure another 8½ inches to the right and make a mark at this point. Then, with the help of a square, draw a line (at this point) across the width of the board.

7. From the left end of the board, measure 8½ inches along the near edge, to the right, and make a mark at this point.

8. With a line connect the points marked in steps 5 and 7.

9. Saw the wood along the lines drawn in steps 6 and 8.

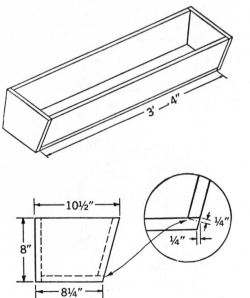

Fig. 25.3

10. Place the two end pieces in a vise in order to true their edges so that both are exactly the same.

11. To assemble the parts, use four No. 8, 1½-inch flathead wood screws to fasten the bottom to the back piece. Countersink the screw heads so that they are even with the wood surface.

12. Use ten No. 8, 1½-inch flathead wood screws to fasten the ends to the back and bottom. Be sure that all the edges are kept even.

13. Use six No. 8, 1½-inch flathead wood screws to fasten the front piece in place.

Now that the box is completed, finish it by shellacking all the knots in the wood. Then use a good-quality paint to cover the outside of the window box in whatever color you desire to harmonize with the trim on the house. The inside of the box should be covered with a good-quality paint, too, to protect its surface.

Making a trellis or arbor

If you have sufficient outdoor space you may want to add a trellis or arbor for an added touch of beauty to your grounds. There are some ready-made ones, at garden supply dealers, which might fit into your garden, and all you need to do is sink the posts into the ground and then paint the pretty structure. However, if you want to make your own, the following are general suggestions:

TRELLIS

It is best to use 2 by 4 lumber to make a trellis. Depending on how wide the trellis is to be, and allowing two feet of space between the wood uprights, you will decide how many uprights to cut. For instance, for a trellis six feet wide you will cut four uprights—that is, one at each side and two in between, spaced two feet apart.

1. Cut lumber into the desired number of uprights, to whatever height is desired, allowing about two feet for sinking them into the ground. For example, if you want the trellis to be seven feet high you will cut the uprights nine feet high.

2. Dig holes in the ground about two feet deep, one for each upright.

3. Press down firmly into each hole two inches of gravel or very small stones.

4. Coat with creosote or tar the part of the wood uprights that will go into the ground, to prevent the wood from rotting.

5. Sink the uprights into the holes, and make sure that each one is sunk into the ground to the same depth, so they will match in height above the ground.

6. When all uprights are in the ground, nail wood strips (cut to the full width of the trellis) across the top of the uprights to form a framework.

7. Using 1 by 1 inch wood, cut strips to nail to the framework to form the trellis. You may nail the strips all one way diagonally, or crisscross vertically and horizontally, or crisscross diagonally, or in whatever other way you wish to form the design.

8. Paint the trellis either to match your house or fence color, in green to match the lawn, or however you may prefer.

ARBOR

An arbor is made in the same way as a trellis, except that it is usually sturdier and larger. It is best to use 4 by 4 inch lumber. Generally only two uprights are used, spaced about six feet apart. You may arch the top or, to save yourself time and work, make a straight-across top. Here, too, your own taste will dictate the style of the arbor and the color you paint it.

Fence and gate

A fence is both useful and decorative, and the style you choose depends on your house and on the space you want to enclose. If you decide on an intricate style you may want to use the professional services of a brick-layer for a brick fence or a carpenter for a wood fence. However, if you want a simple fence, you will enjoy making it yourself.

BRICK FENCE

Study the many designs in bricklaying before you choose the one you prefer. You may like the basket weave, which is made by alternating three bricks horizontally and three bricks vertically; or you may want to lay all the bricks horizontally, with regular or random spacing between each brick. Before buying the bricks, consult with the dealer to find out what color, size and type would be best for your purposes.

WOOD FENCE

For a simple fence made of horizontal boards, use 4 by 4 inch lumber for the square supporting posts, and 1 by 4 inch lumber for the horizontal strips.

1. Mark the line on the ground where you will put the fence; you can do this by driving small wood pegs into the ground at intervals of about six feet, then tying a cord at each peg, going all around the area where the fence will be placed.

2. Dig holes about one foot deep and six inches in diameter, spaced about five feet apart.

3. Press down firmly about two inches of gravel or very small stones into each hole.

4. Coat the bottom part of the post which will go into the ground) with creosote or tar to prevent rotting of the wood.

5. Cut supporting posts about five feet in length (or whatever height you want the fence to be) and allow one foot extra for sinking them into the ground. Thus, for a five-foot supporting post you will cut the wood six feet in length.

6. Cut horizontal strips to measure twice the distance between posts. For example, if supporting posts are spaced five feet apart, cut horizontal strips ten feet long. However, if you have only shorter lengths of wood, cut the strips the length of the distance between two posts. Cut as many horizontal strips as you need to make your finished fence look as open or closed as you desire.

7. Sink the posts into the holes, making sure that all posts are sunk to the same depth so they will match in height above the ground.

8. Nail the horizontal strips to the posts, either on the outside or inside of the posts, depending on where you want the fence to look "finished." If you use long strips cut twice the distance between posts, you can produce a more attractive fence by staggering the placement of the strips, so that each row of strips is nailed to alternate posts.

9. Whether you paint the fence or leave it in its natural state is up to your taste. If you paint it, be sure to use only the best-quality paint for long usage and protection of the wood.

GATE

A gate is not always included with the fence; but if you want to add a gate, you can follow the same design as the fence. First build a frame, then add the strips. The gate is attached to the supporting post of the fence with hinges that you can buy for this special purpose. For a brick fence, you may add a wooden gate designed to fit the type of house you have, or you may want to buy a ready-made gate.

MAINTENANCE

If a post in the fence becomes loose, put it back into its vertical position, then insert a brace of iron or wood against it and sink the brace deeply and securely into the ground. Screw the brace to the post about ten or twelve inches above the ground.

Should a post in the fence or gate be very old and beyond repair, you may need to set a second post in back of the old one to brace it, or else replace it with an entirely new post.

If gate hinges or screws grow rusty, it is a good idea to replace them with new ones of weatherproof sturdiness. If the gate becomes warped or the wood shows signs of wear, smooth it with a plane to bring it back into good shape.

Chapter Twenty-six

SIDEWALKS AND DRIVEWAYS

ALTHOUGH SIDEWALKS AND DRIVEWAYS are usually completed and are included in the price of a house, there are times when you may want to rearrange their placement or need to provide new ones. The first requisite is that all walks and driveways be convenient to the occupants of your house and to your guests; there should be easy access to the service entrance and the main doorway of the house, as well as to the garage. Following are suggestions intended primarily for small town use, but you may find them adaptable to your own situation.

Location of the driveway

The driveway should be placed on the service side of your house, as shown in Fig. 26.1. All service entrances to the house and grounds should be on the same side of the house for convenient delivery of household supplies.

Allow room for a pass court and perhaps for planting of shrubs, and place the driveway approximately nine feet from the side of your house. The driveway should be made in a straight line; if you need some curve at the entrance to the garage, make the curve as slight as possible. In Fig. 26.3 the dotted lines show an alternate arrangement. In the illustrations in this chapter the dimensions shown give ample turning space for most cars; however, try turning your car in the area to make sure you have sufficient space.

The pass court should be long enough to accommodate one or more cars. Place the court near the main entrance to the house for the convenience of guests, as shown in Fig. 26.2. It is best to construct the pass court on a level part of the driveway. The dotted lines in Fig. 26.2 show an alternate arrangement. You may need to provide a wall, as shown in Fig. 26.4, if the driveway slopes.

Construction of the driveway

To prevent the surface of the driveway from becoming soft and sticky in hot weather, use coarse stone for the foundation, then finish the surface with finer stone or concrete, or any black-top surface. Follow the details shown in Fig. 26.5.

Grade the roadbed (A) to an easy slope. For a stone road excavate 10 inches deep, for a concrete road 9½ inches and for a black-top road 12 inches.

At the bottom of the excavation (B) place a layer of coarse stone. Then press the stone down compactly with a roller or whatever else you have for the purpose. For a concrete road the layer of stone should be four inches deep; for a stone or black-top road the layer should be eight inches deep.

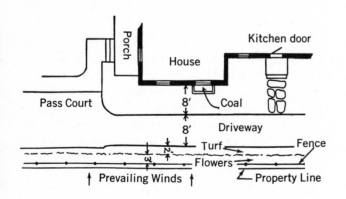

Fig. 26.1

145

Fig. 26.2

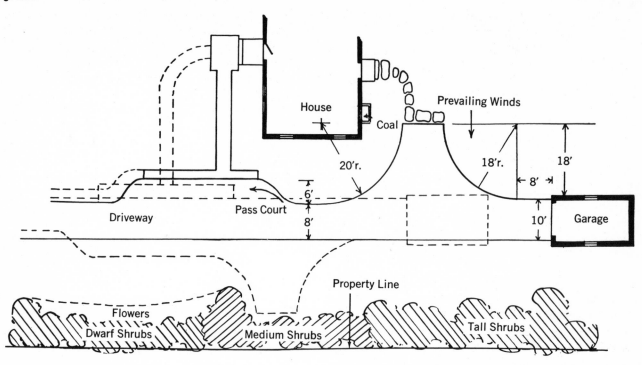

To make the surface of a stone road, place a layer of two inches of fine crushed stone (one-quarter to one inch size) on top of the coarse stone foundation. Roll the surface (C) firmly, keeping a crown in the center for drainage purposes.

For a black-top road, place a layer of two inches of fine crushed stone on the foundation (D), keeping a two-inch crown in the center; then roll over it firmly. On top of this put a two-inch layer of an asphalt mix (E), then roll firmly. You can purchase an asphalt mix in a building or hardware supply shop.

For a concrete road, you will use concrete mix (1-1-3½ mix). Make side forms 5¼ inches high and place them between 6 by 6 inch No. 3 highway wire. Pour the concrete mix between these forms (F) and embed the wire when doing so. Make a crown at the center of the surface, then smooth down the concrete with a wood-float finish. The expansion joints should be fifty feet apart.

Grading the road

Grading with allowance for drainage construction is necessary, regardless of the kind of material you use for making a driveway.

If your ground has a natural slope, build your driveway so that it has a gentle downward slope from the center of the road toward both sides. The driveway should always be higher than the adjacent grades (G) in order to prevent water from remaining on the surface.

If the natural grade (H) is slight, make smoothly rounded, shallow grass gutters to carry the surface water to a suitable outlet.

If there are low, wet places, install concrete catch basins with a tile (I) to carry the water to a suitable outlet. Or construct a ditch with a tile at its base (J), which can be covered with gravel, and it will serve to carry away the excess water.

Fence or shrubs to protect the driveway

If you want to put a fence or to plant between the driveway and the edge of your property line or lawn, take

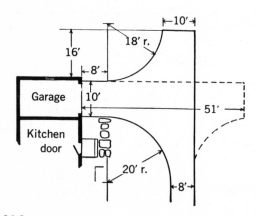

Fig. 26.3

Fig. 26.4

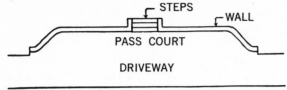

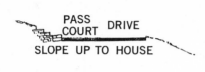

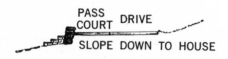

curve it slightly to the pass court or driveway (as shown in the dotted lines in Fig. 26.2).

When the house is close to the road, lay the walk from the main entrance of the house to the roadside or the street sidewalk, as shown in Fig. 26.8.

Fig. 26.6

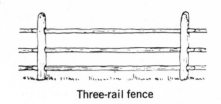

Three-rail fence

Fig. 26.7

Three-board fence

into consideration the width of the area as well as the prevailing winds. Should the winds from your property line or lawn come toward the driveway, you can prevent snowdrifts from forming in the driveway by installing a three-rail fence as suggested in Fig. 26.6, and growing vines on the fence, or a hardy shrub against the fence.

But if the prevailing winds blow from the house toward the driveway, a three-board picket fence, as shown in Fig. 26.7, is suggested. Or you may want to plant woody shrubs as shown in Fig. 26.2.

If the space between driveway and your lawn or property is very narrow (from two to eight feet) it may be better to build a fence; if the space is wider, a shrub border may be sufficient without a fence.

Entrance walk and sidewalk

When you make a walk from the front or main entrance of your house to the pass court or driveway, extend it either parallel to the front of the house and keep it more than six feet from the foundation (see Fig. 26.2), or

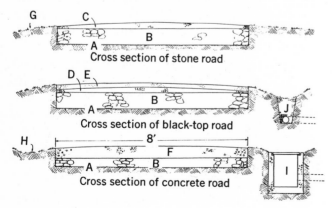

Fig. 26.5

You may desire to lay the walk in a slight gradual reverse curve, or in an arc in the direction most often used to and from the house entrance. This arrangement is shown in Fig. 26.9, which also shows an alternate arrangement in the dotted lines.

If you prefer to allow for parking space, you may follow either plan in Figs. 26.8 or 26.9, and then widen the highway shoulder.

The walk may be made of concrete, of concrete faced with flagstones with grass coming up in the joints (see Fig. 26.10) or with a black-top surface.

The surface of the walk should be made flush with the lawn. Try to keep the minimum width of the main walk to about 3½ feet.

CONSTRUCTION OF THE SIDEWALK

The sidewalk is made in the same way as described under Construction of Driveway, except that it need not be made so heavy. For an asphalt or concrete sidewalk the base should be only four inches deep, and it may be made of sand, cinders or gravel.

For a concrete sidewalk, place a four-inch concrete mix (1-2-3½ mix) on top of the foundation. Smooth it down with a wood-float finish. Place expansion joints fifty feet apart, making the creases five feet apart with a joining tool.

For an asphalt sidewalk, place a two-inch asphalt mix on top of the base. Roll it firmly. Be sure to use material that will not become soft or sticky in hot weather.

To make a flagstone walk, lay the stone on top of two

Fig. 26.8

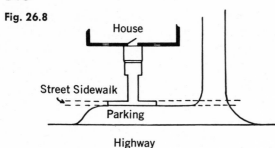

Fig. 26.9

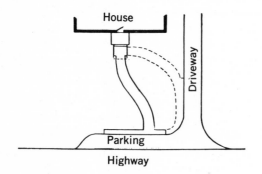

or three inches of sand or cinder base. For this walk you need only make a shallow excavation, just deep enough to allow the stone surface to be flush with the lawn surface.

No walk should ever be lower than the adjacent grade, in order to prevent water from standing on it. If the ground slopes, one edge of the walk should be made to accommodate this slope by being one-quarter to one-half inch lower than its opposite edge.

SERVICE-ENTRANCE WALKS

You may find it convenient to extend walks from the service entrances at the rear or side of the house, so that you have easy access to the garage and driveway or garden. Such walks need be no wider than two feet if space is scarce. Generally, stepping stones set in the ground are sufficient for this purpose; the tops of the stones should be flush with the lawn. However, if you desire more solid construction, these service walks may be made in the same way as the sidewalks.

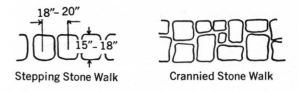

Stepping Stone Walk   Cranied Stone Walk

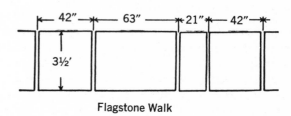

Flagstone Walk

Fig. 26.10

Chapter Twenty-seven

KEEP YOUR HOME SAFE

ACCIDENTS AND FIRES that bring unhappy results in damage to the house and its occupants may be avoided, in most cases, by taking the necessary precautions to prevent them. Each member of the family must be made to feel personally responsible for seeing that the home is kept as safe as possible.

Teach children safety

Physical conditions should be such that children are not invited to incur hazards. Although matches, poisons and sharp tools should not be left within their reach, sole dependence should not be placed upon the inaccessibility of such objects. All children should be instructed as to the proper handling of objects and materials that are dangerous. The child should be encouraged to cultivate good habits in taking proper precautions and in keeping hazardous materials where they belong.

If the individual can be made hazard-conscious during his growing years, he will probably remain so in later life and will not take unnecessary chances or tolerate hazardous conditions.

Not only children but adults as well should have their attention called to existing hazards and their cooperation sought in eliminating those hazards or in using the care necessary to prevent a possible accident. For example, in case fire should occur, every member of the household should know how to send in a fire alarm in those communities where a fire company is maintained. Small children should be instructed to get out of the burning building immediately and avoid smoke.

Check list for safety

The following list of questions covers a good many of the common hazards that occur in the home. The answers to these and similar questions will give you a good idea of the prevailing safety conditions in or about your home.

Are all stairs provided with railings?

Is there sufficient headroom on all stairs?

Are stairs adequately lighted?

Are there any loose rugs at the foot of the stairs or at places where sharp turns are frequently made?

Are floors or steps too highly waxed or polished?

Are steps cluttered with loose material or articles?

Is the bathtub provided with a handhold?

Are porches provided with railings?

Are chairs or unsafe substitutes used in place of ladders?

Are sharp tools left where children may handle them?

Is there a fire extinguisher in the home? What kind?

What type of matches are used?

Are children permitted to play with matches?

Are incombustible ash trays provided for smokers?

Is kerosene ever used to light fires?

Are kerosene lamps ever filled while lighted?

Is gasoline used in the home for dry cleaning or other purposes?

Is stove polish used? What kind?

Are combustible materials kept away from stoves and out of contact with stovepipes?

Is there a screen for the open fireplace?

What disposition is made of wastepaper?

Is rubbish allowed to accumulate in the attic, basement or elsewhere?

Are gas pipes or fixtures used to support clothes lines, clothing or utensils?

Are gas cocks adjusted to turn smoothly but not too easily?

Are gas connections made with tubing? Does it leak?

Where are poisonous drugs kept? Are all bottles properly labeled?

Are any of the electric circuits improperly fused by a one-cent copper coin, for example?

Is the frame of the electric washing machine grounded?

Is the portable cord for electric appliances or lamps badly worn?

Is the portable cord of an approved type?

Is a stand provided for the electric iron?

Are there any metal pull chains without insulating links?

Are electric lights in the bathroom controlled by wall switches?

Are portable electric heaters or other portable electric appliances used in the bathroom?

Is the outdoor radio and television antenna equipped with a lightning arrester?

Is the automobile engine ever run in the garage with the garage doors and windows closed?

Are first-aid materials at hand?

Are porches, walks and sidewalks kept in good repair and free of ice, snow and so forth?

Are cooking utensils on the stove kept and so used that a person will not be burned by steam or hot liquids?

Are the children's toys maintained and used in a safe manner?

Are firearms kept in the home? If so, are they kept where children cannot readily have access to them?

Do you keep tubs or other containers filled with hot water where a child cannot fall or stumble into them?

Are the laundry appliances so guarded that no one will be injured in their use?

Do you from time to time instruct the children in the prevention of injuries to themselves or their playmates?

Hall and stairway

A poorly lit hall and stairway is a major accident cause. Install light switches at the bottom and top of the staircase. No loose electric cords must be permitted on the floor of the hall or on the stairs; avoid this by installing sufficient outlets.

If the stairway is not sufficiently well lighted for people with poor vision to be sure of the steps, paint both the top and bottom step with a white or light paint (in contrast to color of stairs).

A banister is a necessity, especially where the stairs lead to the basement or attic. Build a railing on the wall if there is no banister. If the stairway is free-standing (without a wall on either side) build a railing on the upright posts.

A decorative as well as functional stairway rail may be made instead of using a wood banister or rail; every two or three feet along the wall screw large upholstery rings and pull through these rings a heavy, smooth cord (which will not splinter) or a cord slipcovered with a tubing of chintz or other material. The cord should hang down about five or six inches through each end ring at the top and bottom.

Outdoor stairs and walks

Stairs leading to the house must have a handrail!

Clear away wet falling leaves, ice and snow from stairs and all walks. Do not permit them to remain longer than necessary. They are walking hazards.

Proper lighting must be provided on stairs and walks.

Window screens and bars

The screens that are put into the window to keep out insects, or the bars at the window that keep children safely inside the house, may become loosened. Avoid possible hazard by inspecting these or any other window appliances, and if loose or broken they should be repaired immediately.

Precautions with electric appliances

Careless handling of electric appliances and cords may often cause damage to people and property. To help you prevent accidents, take the following precautions:

1. Never touch the interior live metal parts of sockets, plugs or receptacles used to carry current. In handling electric devices use insulating handles provided for that purpose.

2. Avoid touching any metal part of a lamp socket, fixture or other electric device while in damp locations such as bathrooms, kitchens, laundries or any place with damp floors and where there are stoves, heaters, steam or hot-water radiators, or pipes that may be touched, because the metal part may accidentally be live. While in a bathtub never touch any part of an electric appliance cord or fixture.

3. Avoid touching bare or torn spots on flexible cords attached to electric lamps, pressing irons or other portable appliances. Handle all cords carefully in order to avoid injury to their insulation. Do not hang them on nails or over fixed wires. Always have them replaced when any injury to insulation is observed. If toasters, fans, pressing irons or other appliances are moved about so that cords receive more or less hard usage, use only cords with heavily reinforced coverings to protect the insulation. In damp places use only cords having a heavy waterproof outer or insulating covering.

4. In buying any cord or portable appliance, inquire whether it has been inspected and approved by the proper authority.

5. After using portable heating appliances, especially pressing irons, turn off the current before leaving them.

6. If combustible materials like paper or cloth are used for lamp shades, be sure they are not in contact with the bulb. Provide portable hand lamps with substantial wire guards.

7. Open the circuit before attempting to replace fuses. Lighting circuits should be protected by fuses rated at not over fifteen amperes.

8. Do not touch a wire that has fallen to the street, but warn others to keep away and notify the city electricity department, the power company, telephone com-

pany or other owner. Overhead wires with a protective covering should be treated like bare wires because the covering soon deteriorates.

9. Avoid touching the guy wires used to anchor poles to the ground or the ground wire run down wood poles. During and after storms do not touch wet poles.

10. Avoid contact with overhead electric wires. Never climb a pole or tree near which electric wires pass. Never raise a metal pole or other conducting object so that it comes in contact with electric wires. Warn children against flying kites near overhead electric wires.

11. Never touch a person who has been shocked while he is still in contact with the electric circuit, unless you know how to remove him from the wire, or the wire from him, without danger to yourself. Have someone immediately call the nearest doctor and the lighting company. Use a long dry board, a dry wooden-handled rake or a broom to draw the person away from the wire or the wire from him. Never use metal or moist objects.

Fire precautions

A general guide to help every household to prevent fire damage is given in the following suggestions:

1. Keep matches out of the reach of young children. Teach children the dangers of playing with fire.

2. Do not throw away cigars, cigarettes and matches without first making sure they are extinguished.

3. Do not allow accumulations of combustible waste materials in or near the house.

4. Keep chimneys and stovepipes clean, with all joints and connections tight. Provide separate metal cans for ashes and rubbish. Never mix the two.

5. Place substantial fire-resistant guards in front of all woodwork close to sources of heat.

6. Keep greasy and oily rags in tightly closed metal cans provided for the purpose.

7. Avoid filling lighted lamps. Avoid the use of kerosene to start fires in stoves and elsewhere in the house.

8. Do not use gasoline, naphtha or benzine for cleaning. Use some of the safer solutions now obtainable and these, if they are to be used in any considerable quantity, only out-of-doors and during the day.

9. Keep all open flames away from gas leaks. Explosive mixtures of gas and air are quickly formed at such places, and they need only a lighted match or a spark to cause disastrous results.

10. Avoid hanging curtains and draperies near gas jets or other open flames. Remember that the draft from near-by windows may cause fires to spread and make them difficult to extinguish.

11. Avoid toy wax candles. Each year a number of deaths of children and adults are due to placing candles on Christmas trees.

12. Avoid placing articles made of plastic, celluloid, Pyralin, and similar materials, such as collars, combs, toilet articles and so forth, upon or near sources of heat, since they are very likely to catch fire.

13. Permit only experienced persons to install or repair electric fittings and appliances.

14. Never leave unattended any lighted heating or cooking appliances, particularly kitchen ranges and stoves, toasters, pressing irons, waffle irons or other equipment of a similar nature.

15. Make sure that when you burn refuse you do so out-of-doors in a metal container well away from any building, and also be sure that when you leave you have extinguished all smoldering embers.

Safety inspection before closing the house

If your house will be unoccupied for an extended period, especially during cold weather, it should be inspected carefully before you leave and precautions taken to guard against possible damage while you are away.

1. The roof should be examined for possible leaks, and repairs should be made if necessary. Gutters and downspouts should be cleared of leaves and rubbish to prevent overflow.

2. All rubbish should be gathered and burned, particularly accumulations in the basement.

3. All matches should be put in glass or metal containers, or be removed from the premises, and all oil, gasoline and paint cans disposed of.

4. Most fire insurance companies require the houseowner to obtain a vacancy permit before leaving a house unoccupied for an extended period. The necessary requirements in this respect are usually outlined in the policy, or you may ask your insurance broker what they are.

5. Before you leave the house, the refrigerator should be disconnected, defrosted, cleaned and the doors left open for airing.

6. The water should be shut off.

7. The electricity supply should also be cut off.

8. The telephone service may be temporarily discontinued by notifying the telephone company.

9. The gas company should be requested to shut off the gas supply, to guard against possible damage resulting from a leaky pipe or fixture.

10. All doors and windows should be closed and locked. If there are blinds or shutters on the house, they should be closed and locked against intruders and as a protection for windows during heavy storms. Basement doors should be securely bolted.

11. It is advisable to leave a key to the house with a neighbor or at the nearest police station, so that entrance may be readily gained in case of an emergency.

GLOSSARY

EVERY PROFESSION AND TRADE has a language of its own, and the building trades are no exception. To enable you to be on speaking terms with people in those trades the following dictionary defines the most frequently used words you will encounter when buying materials or ordering services for the maintenance of your house:

Abrasive Material used for grinding, polishing and sanding, such as emery, pumice and sandpaper.

Acoustics Sound transmission through building materials and air.

Across grain At right angles to wood grain.

Adjacent Placed against or near to.

Air dry To season lumber in air (not in kiln).

Air space Open area between outer and inner wall, or any cavity in the house.

Ampere Measuring unit of electric current.

Anchor Irons of special form used to fasten together timbers or masonry.

Anchor bolt Bolt that fastens columns, girders or other members to concrete or masonry.

Anchor-nailing Nails driven at opposite angles through two or more boards.

Angle iron Iron or steel strip in the shape of a right angle, bored to take screws; used to reinforce and support a joint.

Apron Facing or covering board used along front of workbench; also casing or molding under window sill.

Aquastat Device to regulate temperature of hot water supply, such as a water-heating furnace.

Architrave Wood trim or casing.

Armored cable Metal-encased electric wires.

Arris Sharp point where two surfaces join; for example, corner of a board.

Asbestos Fireproof material, used a good deal in shingles and insulating paper.

Ashlar Kind of stonework.

Awl Pointed instrument to punch holes in wood or plastic.

Babbit Soft metal used for bearings.

Back painting Unexposed (back) surface of lumber painted to prevent moisture.

Backing Bevel on the top edge of a hip rafter that allows the roofing board to fit the top of the rafter without leaving a triangular space between it and the lower side of the roof covering.

Backsaw (also *Tenon saw*) Saw with fine teeth and thin blade, backed with steel reinforcement; used for mitering and chamfering.

Balloon frame Lightest and most economical form of construction, in which the studding and corner posts are set up in continuous lengths from first-floor line or sill to the roof plate.

Ball-peen hammer Hammer with rounded face, used for metalwork.

Baluster (also *Banister*) Vertical posts on stair railing.

Balustrade Series of balusters connected by a rail, generally used for porches, balconies and the like.

Band Low, flat molding.

Banister See *Baluster*.

Base Bottom of a column; the finish of a room at the junction of the walls and floor.

Baseboard (also *Skirting*) Molding to cover joint between wall and floor.

Base coat Equal parts of linseed oil and turpentine, used as base for stain.

Batten (also *Cleat*) Narrow strip of board used to fasten several pieces of wood together.

Batter board Temporary framework used to assist in locating the corners when laying a foundation.

Beading Narrow wood molding, used for decorative trim.

Beam Inclusive term for joists, girders, rafters and purlins.

Bedding Filling of mortar, putty or other substance in order to secure a firm bearing.

Belly To bulge.

Belt course Horizontal board across or around a building, usually made of a flat member and a molding.

Bench stop Device to hold end of board that is being planed.

Benzine Liquid used for paint thinning and cleaning paintbrushes.

Bevel Angle cut on edge of board.

Bevel board Board used in framing a roof or stairway to lay out bevels.

Bibb Faucet with threaded nozzle for hose attachment.

Board Lumber less than 2 inches thick.

Board foot Equivalent of a board 1 foot square and 1 inch thick.

Boarding in Process of nailing boards on the outside studding of a house.

Bond Bricklaying pattern.

Bond stone Stone to tie a wall together.

Brace and bit Tool for boring holes.

Braces Pieces fitted and firmly fastened to two others at any angle in order to strengthen the angle thus treated.

Bracket A projecting support for a shelf or other structure.

Brad Short nail.

Braze To join by hard solder; also to make of brass.

Break joints To arrange joints so that they do not come directly under or over the joints of adjoining pieces, as in shingling, siding and so forth.

Brick veneer Thin layer of bricks, used as finish.

Bridging Pieces fitted in pairs from the bottom of one floor joist to the top of adjacent joists, and crossed to distribute the floor load; sometimes pieces of width equal to the joists and fitted neatly between them.

Brown coat Second coat, of stucco or plaster.

Buckle To warp or lift up.

Building paper Cheap, thick paper, used to insulate a

152

building before the siding or roofing is put on; sometimes placed between double floors.

Built-up timber Timber made of several pieces fastened together, to form one of larger dimensions.

Butter To apply mortar to brick.

Bx Cable Flexible metal-covered electric wire.

Calk To fill seam or crack with plastic calking compound or oakum.

Cap Cement finish on top of chimney or brick wall.

Carriages Supports for the steps and risers of a flight of stairs.

Casement Window in which the sash opens on hinges.

Casing Trimming around a door or window opening, either outside or inside, or the finished lumber around a post or beam.

Cast-iron pipes Soil pipes (cast iron) used in sewage system.

Ceiling Narrow, matched boards; sheathing of the surfaces that enclose the upper side of a room.

Cement Adhesive material for binding objects together; also used to mix concrete.

Cement plaster Sand and cement mixture used as finishing coat.

Center-hung sash Sash hung at its center so that it swings on a horizontal axis.

Chamfer Beveled surface cut upon the corner of a piece of wood.

Checks Splits or cracks in a board, ordinarily caused by seasoning.

Check valve Valve used to prevent reverse flow of water in pipe.

Chest pull Knob or handle to open drawer or door.

Chuck Part of drill or brace that holds the bit.

Clamp Mechanical device used to hold two or more pieces together.

Clapboards Special form of outside covering of a house; siding.

Clear lumber Lumber free of knots.

Cleat See *Batten.*

Clinch To bend over material.

Clinch nail Nail of soft metal, used for clinching.

Clockwise Turning in same direction as hands of a clock.

Code Body of local ordinances and laws that regulate building and electric work.

Collar beam Board placed horizontally between two rafters, for additional support. (Also see *Tie beam.*)

Column Support that is square, rectangular or cylindrical in section, for roofs, ceilings and so forth, composed of base, shaft and capital.

Combination frame Combination of the principal features of the full and balloon frames.

Common board Board 1 inch thick, up to 12 inches wide.

Compass saw Saw with very narrow blade that turns in its frame so that it can saw at various angles.

Concrete Artificial building material made by mixing cement and sand with gravel, broken stone or other aggregate, and sufficient water to cause the cement to set and bind the entire mass.

Conductor Pipe for conducting water from a roof to the ground or to a receptacle or drain; downspout.

Conduit Pipe that carries electric wires.

Coping saw Saw with very narrow blade that turns in its frame so that it can saw at various angles.

Cornice Molded projection that finishes the top of the wall of a building.

Counterflashing Strip of metal used to prevent water from entering the top edge of the vertical side of a roof flashing; they also allow expansion and contraction without danger of breaking the flashing.

Countersink To turn screw into wood until screw head is flush with wood surface.

Coupling Plumbing device used to join sections of pipe or hose.

Course Layer of shingles or bricks.

Cove molding Molding with concave surface.

Dado Lower part of the walls of a room when finished differently from upper part.

Dado plane (also *Rabbet plane*) Plane to cut dados or grooves.

Deadening Construction intended to prevent the passage of sound.

Dimension stuff Wood 2 inches thick, up to 12 inches wide.

Dormer window Window built into side of roof.

Double-hung window Window consisting of upper and lower sash, in a frame.

Double studding Two studs nailed together to form door and window openings.

Dovetail Joint that fastens two boards with one or more interlocking joints cut to resemble dove's tail.

Dowel joint Round stick of wood that joins two pieces together. Dowel is sunk into edges of both pieces and glued in.

Downspout See *Leader.*

Dressed lumber Lumber with surface that has been smoothed with plane.

Drip Projection of a window sill or water table to allow the water to drain clear of the side of the house below it.

Dry rot Wood decay due to dampness and dryness variations.

Dry well Hole in ground filled with gravel or stones, to collect water flowing from roof.

Eaves Part of roof that extends beyond walls.

Edge Cutting end of tool.

Efflorescence White crust on bricks, generally caused by mineral salts.

Emery paper Abrasive used to smooth surfaces.

End-match lumber Boards tongued-and-grooved on ends and sides.

Escutcheon Metal plate around keyhole and knobs, screwed to door.

Excavate To dig a hole.

Expansion bolt In masonry, a bolt for anchoring.

Expansion joint Open joint to permit contraction and expansion between concrete sections.

Face Widest plane of a board; plane used for measuring width and length of board; also the front of an exposed portion, such as face of a wall or face of brick.

Fascia   Flat member of a cornice or other finish; generally the board of the cornice to which the gutter is fastened.

Felt paper   Heavy paper used for insulating and sound-deadening.

Ferrule   Metal part at base of bristles in paintbrush.

Filler   Composition material used to fill in wood pores and cracks.

Finish   Final surface of a completed job.

Firebrick   Used in furnaces and fireplaces to withstand heat.

Fire Clay   Cement that is heat-resistant, used to bind fire-bricks.

Fire-resistant   Not actually fireproof, but capable of resisting fire.

Fire stop   Studding in wall construction to prevent fire from rising through air space.

Flashing   Material used and the process of making water-tight the roof intersections and other exposed places on the outside of the house.

Flue   Opening in a chimney through which smoke passes.

Flush   Adjacent surfaces even, or in same plane (with reference to two structural pieces).

Footing   Enlargement at the lower end of a wall, pier or column, to distribute the load.

Footing form   Wooden or steel structure, placed around the footing that will hold the concrete to the desired shape and size.

Foundation   That part of a building or wall that supports the superstructure.

Frame   Surrounding or enclosing woodwork of windows, doors and so forth, and the timber skeleton of a building.

Framing   Rough timber structure of a building, including interior and exterior walls, floor, roof and ceilings.

French door   Door with panes of glass rather than wood panels.

Frost line   Depth in earth where freezing starts.

Full frame   Old-fashioned mortised-and-tenoned frame, in which every joint is mortised and tenoned. Rarely used at the present time.

Furring   Narrow strips of board nailed upon the walls and ceilings to form a straight surface upon which to lay the lath or other finish.

Gable   Vertical triangular end of a building extending from the eaves to the apex of the roof.

Galvanize   To coat metal with zinc to prevent rusting.

Gambrel   Symmetrical roof with two different pitches or slopes on each side.

Gauge   Tool used by carpenters to strike a line parallel to the edge of a board.

Gimlet   Pointed, threaded instrument to bore hole in wood.

Girder   Timber used to support wall beams or joists.

Girt (sometimes *Ribband*)   The horizontal member of the walls of a full or combination frame house that supports the floor joists or is flush with the top of the joists.

Glass block   Translucent block of glass used in exterior and interior building.

Glaze   To insert glass pane into window sash.

Grade   Pitch or slope of ground.

Grain   Lines in wood caused by yearly growth.

Graph   Plan drawn on paper with measured squares that helps freehand copying.

Green lumber   Improperly seasoned lumber.

Groove   Long hollow channel cut by a tool, into which a piece fits or in which it works. Two special types of grooves are the *dado*, a rectangular groove cut across the full width of a piece, and the *housing*, a groove cut at any angle with the grain and part way across a piece. Dados are used in sliding doors, window frames and so forth; housings are used for framing stair risers and threads in a string.

Ground   Strip of wood assisting the plasterer in making a straight wall and in providing a place to which the finish of the room may be nailed.

Ground coat   Yellow-colored mixture applied to stained surfaces before applying new coat of varnish stain.

Grout   Mixture of Portland cement, sand and water, to seal joints and cracks.

Gutter   Channel along roof to carry off water from rain and snow.

Hanger   Iron support for attaching beams.

Head   Top portion of a window or door opening.

Header   Short joist supporting tail beams and framed between trimmer joists; the piece of stud or finish over an opening; a lintel.

Headroom   Clear space between floor line and ceiling, as in a stairway.

Hearth   Part of fireplace that extends into room.

Heel of a rafter   End or foot of a beam that rests on the wall plate.

Hip roof   Roof that slopes up toward the center from all sides, necessitating a hip rafter at each corner.

Hot wire   Live electric wire through which current passes.

Insulation   Material that is a poor conductor of heat or electricity.

Jack   Device used to lift heavy objects.

Jack rafter   Short rafter framing between the wall plates; a hip rafter.

Jamb   Side piece or post of an opening; sometimes applied to the door frame.

Joint   Place where two pieces of material are fitted together.

Joint-butt   Squared ends or ends and edges adjoining each other.

     Dovetail   Joint made by cutting pins the shape of a dove's tail that fit between dovetails upon another piece.

     Drawboard   Mortise-and-tenon joint with holes so bored that when a pin is driven through, the joint becomes tighter.

     Fished   End butt splice strengthened by pieces nailed on the sides.

     Halved   Joint made by cutting half the wood away from each piece so as to bring the sides flush.

     Housed   Joint in which a piece is grooved to receive the piece that is to form the other part of the joint.

     Glue   Joint held together with glue.

     Lap   Joint of two pieces lapping over each other.

     Mortised   Joint made by cutting a hole or mortise in one piece, and a tenon (or piece to fit the hole) upon the other.

Rub Flue joint made by carefully fitting the edges together, spreading glue between them and rubbing the pieces back and forth until the pieces are well rubbed together.

Scarfed Timber spliced by cutting various shapes of shoulders, or jogs, which fit each other.

Joist Timber supporting the floorboards.

Kerf Cut made by a saw.

Keyhole saw Narrow saw with tapering blade.

Kiln dried Seasoned in kiln oven.

Knee brace Corner brace, fastened at an angle from wall stud to rafter, stiffening a wood or steel frame to prevent angular movement.

Lap To cross over; also board that extends over another board.

Lath Narrow strip to support plastering.

Lattice Crossed wood, iron plate or bars.

Leader (also *Downspout*) Pipe from roof gutter to ground.

Ledgerboard (also *Ribband*) Support for the second-floor joists of a balloon-frame house.

Level Term describing the position of a line or plane when parallel to the surface of still water; an instrument or tool used in testing for horizontal and vertical surfaces, and in determining differences in elevation.

Lintel Piece of construction or finish in stone, wood or metal, that is over an opening; a header.

Load-bearing wall Wall supporting weight in addition to its own.

Lookout End of a rafter, or the construction that projects beyond the sides of a house to support the eaves; also the projecting timbers at the gables that support the verge boards.

Louver Kind of window, generally in peaks of gables and the tops of towers, provided with horizontal slots that exclude rain and snow and allow ventilation.

Lumber Sawed parts of a log such as boards, planks, scantling and timber.

Mastic Composition cement for asphalt and linoleum floor covering.

Matching, or *tonguing-and-grooving* Method used in cutting the edges of a board to make a tongue on one edge and a groove on the other.

Meeting rail (sometimes *Check rail*) Bottom rail of the upper sash of a double-hung window.

Member Single piece in structure, complete in itself.

Miter Joint formed by two abutting pieces meeting at an angle.

Molding Long, narrow strips of wood, milled into special designs and shapes; used as trim.

Molding base Molding on the top of a baseboard.

Bed Molding used to cover the joint between the plancier and frieze; also used as a base molding upon heavy work, and sometimes as a member of a cornice.

Lip S molding with a lip that overlaps the piece against which the back of the molding rests.

Picture Molding shaped to form a support for picture hooks, often placed at some distance from the ceiling on the wall to form lower edge of frieze.

Rake Cornice upon the gable edge of a pitch roof, the members of which are made to fit those of the molding of the horizontal eaves.

Mortar Sand and cement mixture to bond bricks or stone.

Mortise Hole that is to receive a tenon, or any hole cut into or through a piece by a chisel; generally of rectangular shape.

Mullion Construction between the openings of a window frame to accommodate two or more windows.

Muntin Vertical member between two panels of the same piece of panelwork; the vertical sash bars separating the different panels of glass.

New wood Wood that has had no work done by tools on it.

Newel Principal post of the foot of a staircase; also the central support of a winding flight of stairs.

Nosing Part of a stair tread that projects over the riser, or any similar projection; a term applied to the rounded edge of a board.

Oakum Hemp fiber used for calking.

Oilstone Stone block for sharpening tool edges and blades.

Old wood Wood previously worked on by tools and used again for a different purpose.

On center From center to center.

Orange shellac Natural-colored shellac.

Out of plumb Not vertical or level.

Panel Center piece of board, generally thinner than frame into which it is fitted. Often made of plywood.

Parallel Going in the same direction, side by side.

Parapet Low wall.

Parting strip Thin wood strip nailed between lower and upper sash in double-hung window.

Partition Inside wall acting as separation.

Picture molding Molding nailed around room, high on wall, on which pictures and mirrors are hung.

Pier Masonry support, set independently of the main foundation.

Pigment Coloring material in paint.

Pilaster Portion of a square column, usually set within or against a wall.

Piles Long posts driven into the soil in swampy locations or wherever it is difficult to secure a firm foundation, upon which the footing course of masonry or other timbers is laid.

Pilot hole Hole made with drill, bit or brad awl, to be used as a guide for driving screw into wood.

Pitch Inclination or slope, as for roofs or stairs, or the rise divided by the span.

Pitch board Board sawed to the exact shape formed by the stair tread, riser and slope of the stairs and used to lay out the carriage and stringers.

Plan Horizontal geometrical section of a building, showing the walls, doors, windows, stairs, chimneys, columns and so forth.

Plank or *lumber* Material 2 or 3 inches thick and more than 4 inches wide, such as joists, flooring and so forth.

Plaster Mixture of lime, hair and sand, or of lime, cement and sand, used to cover outside and inside wall surfaces.

Plate Top horizontal piece of the walls of a frame building upon which the roof rests.

Plate cut (sometimes *Seat cut*)   Cut in a rafter that rests upon the plate.

Plumb   Perfectly straight position.

Plumb cut (also *Ridge cut*)   Any cut made in a vertical plane; the vertical cut at the top end of a rafter.

Ply   Term used to denote a layer or thickness of building or roofing paper, as for example, two-ply, three-ply and so forth.

Plywood   See *Three-ply.*

Porch   Ornamental entranceway.

Post   Timber set on end to support a wall, girder or other member of the structure.

Plow   To cut a groove running in the same direction as the grain of the wood.

Pulley stile   Member of a window frame that contains the pulleys and between which the edges of the sash slide.

Pumice stone   Finely ground stone; used as polishing abrasive.

Purlin   Timber supporting several rafters at one or more points, or the roof sheeting directly.

Putty   Material used to fasten glass panes into window sash; also used as filler for cracks in wood or plaster.

Rabbet (also *Rebate*)   Corner cut out of an edge of a piece of wood.

Rabbet plane   See *Dado plane.*

Radius   Distance from center of circle to outer edge.

Rafters, common   Those rafters that run square with the plate and extend to the ridge.

   Cripple   Rafters that cut between valley and hip rafters.

   Hip   Rafters that extend from the outside angle of the plates toward the apex of the roof.

   Jack   Rafters that are square with the plate and intersect the hip rafter.

   Valley   Rafters that extend from an inside angle of the plates toward the ridge or center line of the house.

Rail   Horizontal member of a balustrade or panelwork.

Rake   Trim of a building extending in an oblique line, as rake dado or molding.

Rasp   Coarse metal file used for smoothing rough surfaces.

Rebate   See *Rabbet.*

Red lead   First priming paint coat used on metal.

Return   Continuation of a molding or finish of any kind in a different direction.

Ribband   See *Ledgerboard.*

Ridge   Top edge or corner formed by the intersection of two roof surfaces.

Ridge cut   See *Plumb cut.*

Rise   Vertical distance through which anything rises, as the rise of a roof or stair.

Riser   Vertical board between two treads of a flight of stairs.

Roofing   Material put on a roof to make it wind- and waterproof.

Rottenstone   Fine powder; used as an abrasive to polish furniture.

Rough lumber   Lumber that has been neither surfaced nor dressed.

Rubble   Roughly broken quarry stone.

Rubble masonry   Uncut stone, used for rough work, foundations, backing and the like.

Run   Length of the horizontal projection of a piece such as a rafter when in position.

Saddle board (sometimes *Comb board*)   Finish of the ridge of a pitch-roof house.

Sash   Framework that holds the glass in a window.

Sash weight   Metal bar tied to end of sash cord, to balance window sash.

Sawhorse   Wood structure used in workshop when sawing wood.

Sawing, plain (sometimes *Slash* or *Bastard sawed*)   Lumber sawed regardless of the grain, the log simply squared and sawed to the desired thickness.

Scab   Short piece of lumber used to splice, or to prevent movement of two other pieces.

Scaffold, or *Staging*   Temporary structure or platform enabling workmen to reach high places.

Scale   Short measurement used as a proportionate part of a larger dimension. The scale of a drawing is expressed as ¼ inch = 1 foot.

Scantling   Lumber with a cross section ranging from 2 by 4 inches to 4 by 4 inches.

Scarfing   Joint between two pieces of wood that allows them to be spliced lengthwise.

Scotia   Hollow molding used as part of a cornice, and often used under the nosing of a stair tread.

Scribe   To mark one piece of wood to provide for the fitting of one of its surfaces to the irregular surface of another piece of wood.

Seat cut, or *Plate cut*   Cut at the bottom end of a rafter to allow it to fit upon the plate.

Seat of a rafter   Horizontal cut upon the bottom end of a rafter that rests upon the top of the plate.

Section   Drawing showing the kind, arrangement and proportions of the various parts of a structure. It is assumed that the structure is cut by a plane, and the section is the view gained by looking in one direction.

Shake   Imperfection in timber caused during the growth of the tree by high winds or imperfect conditions of growth.

Sheathing   Wallboard, roofing board; generally applied to narrow boards laid with a space between them, according to the length of a shingle exposed to weather.

Sheathing paper   Paper used under siding or shingles to insulate the house; building papers.

Shim   Strip of material to fill small space.

Shiplap   Way to cut edges of boards so that when they are nailed alongside each other a half-lap joint is formed.

Siding   Outside finish between the casings.

Sills   Horizontal timbers of a house that either rest upon the masonry foundations or, in the absence of such, form the foundations. (Also see *Window sill.*)

Size   To work material to the desired size; to coat with glue, shellac or other substance applied to a surface to prepare it for painting or other method of finish.

Skirting   See *Baseboard.*

Sleeper   Timber laid on the ground to support a floor joist.

Smoke chamber   Part of fireplace directly over damper.

Soil pipe Pipe used for sewer system.

Solder Lead and tin alloy, for joining and repairing metal.

Span Distance between the bearings of a timber or arch.

Specifications Written or printed directions regarding the details of a building or other construction.

Spike Very large nail (usually from 20 penny to 8 inches).

Splice To join two similar members in a straight line.

Spline Small, flat piece of wood used to fill groove made by joining rabbets.

Square Tool used by mechanics to obtain accuracy; a term applied to a surface including 100 square feet.

Stairs, box Stairs built between walls, and usually with no support except the wall strings.

Stencil Design cut out of metal or heavy paper or wood, to form pattern in painting.

Stile Upright member of door frame; side frame of panel door.

Stool Inside sill of window frame.

Stock size Lumber cut in standard sizes and bought that way at wood mill.

Straight edge Board that has a straight side and used for drawing and measuring.

Strap hinge Heavy hinge on large doors.

Stringer Long horizontal timber in a structure supporting a floor; also side of a flight of stairs.

Strut Wood used as brace or support; used for framing and where heavy pressure is exerted.

Stucco Rough plaster for exterior wall covering of building; also made fine and used for interior wall decoration.

Stud Upright beam in the framework of a building.

Studding Framework of a partition or the wall of a house; usually referred to as 2 by 4's.

Subfloor Wood floor that is laid over the floor joists and on which the finished floor is laid.

Surfaced lumber Dressed or smoothed lumber.

Tang Part of metal tool that fits into handle.

Template Short piece of wood placed under girder or other beam to add strength; beam over opening, such as doorway; pattern cut from cardboard or heavy paper.

Tenon Protruding tongue or lip cut in end of piece of wood, which is fitted into second piece of wood that has mortise cut out.

Tenon saw See *Backsaw*.

T Hinge Hinge shaped like letter T.

Three ply Three thin sheets of wood, with grain of center board running at right angles to grain of outer sheets. When glued together it is called plywood.

Threshold (sometimes *Carpet strip*) Beveled piece over which the door swings.

Throat Opening into chimney at top of fireplace where the damper is situated.

Thumbscrew Screw capable of being tightened by hand without screw driver.

Tie beam Beam so situated that it ties the principal rafters of a roof together and prevents them from thrusting the plate out of line.

Timber Lumber with cross section of over 4 by 6 inches, such as posts, sills and girders.

Tin shingle Small piece of tin used in flashing and repairing a shingle roof.

Tin snips Shears for cutting thin metal.

Toenailing Method of nailing in which nail is driven into surface of wood at an angle.

Tongue Protruding piece (lip) in one piece of wood that is cut to fit into a second piece of wood in which a groove is cut.

Tongue-and-Groove Joint that is formed by two pieces of wood, one with a groove cut into it, the other with a tongue protruding from it.

To the weather Term applied to the projecting of shingles or siding beyond the course above.

Transformer Electric device installed to reduce voltage; often used where only D.C. current available.

Tread Horizontal part of a step.

Trim Term sometimes applied to outside or interior finished woodwork and the finish around openings.

Trimmer Beam or floor joist into which a header is framed.

Trimming Putting the inside and outside finish and hardware upon a building.

Truss Structural framework of triangular units for supporting loads over long spans.

T square (sometimes *Try square*) Measuring rule shaped like letter T.

Turpentine Liquid often used as paint thinner and for various other uses around house.

Valley Internal angle formed by the two slopes of a roof.

Veneer Thin layer of wood glued over a base of another wood. Usually wood underneath is inferior grade, whereas veneer is better quality.

Verge boards Boards that serve as the finish for the eaves on the gable end of a building.

Vestibule Entrance to a house; usually enclosed.

Vitrified soil pipe Pipe made of hard-baked clay that is used for outside sewer lines.

Volt Unit that measures electric pressure.

Wainscoting Matched boarding or panelwork covering the lower portion of a wall.

Wale Horizontal beam.

Wallboard Flat sheets made of composition, used for partitions, interior walls, built-ins and other light carpentry.

Warp To sag or bend from original shape or line; often happens to lumber not carefully seasoned or dried.

Wash Slant upon a sill, capping and so forth to allow the water to run off easily.

Water table Finish at the bottom of a house that carries the water away from the foundation.

Weld To attach pieces of metal together by means of heat.

White lead Pigment in paint.

Wind ("i" pronounced as in "kind") Term used to describe the surface of a board when twisted (winding) or when resting upon two diagonally opposite corners, if laid upon a perfectly flat surface.

Window frame Wood part all around window that holds the sashes.

Window sill Bottom of window frame; usually projects farther than rest of frame.

Wooden brick Piece of seasoned wood, made the size of a brick, and laid where it is necessary to provide a nailing space in masonry walls.

Wood screw Metal screw made for use in wood.

ABBREVIATIONS AND SYMBOLS USED IN BUILDING TRADES

IT IS WELL to acquaint yourself with the abbreviations and symbols that are in standard use in the building trades, so that when you receive an estimate or a bill, or need to study a blueprint, you will be able to understand the items. In addition to the following lists, the glossary at the back of this book gives the meanings of words and terms commonly used in these trades.

A.C.	Alternating current
A.D.	Air-dried
a.l.	All length
a.v.	Average
a.v.l.	Average length
a.v.w.	Average width
Bbl.	Barrel (or barrels)
bd.	Board
bd. ft.	Board foot (or board feet)
bdl.	Bundle
bev.	Beveled
Bgs.	Bags
b.m.	Board (foot) measure
btr.	Better
B.T.U.	British thermal unit (or units)
clg.	Ceiling
clr.	Clear
CM	Center matched; that is, tongue-and-groove joints are made along the center of the edge of the piece
Com.	Common
Csg.	Casing
Ctg.	Crating
Cu. ft.	Cubic foot (or cubic feet)
Cu. in.	Cubic inch (or cubic inches)
Cu. yd.	Cubic yard (or cubic yards)
d.	Denarius, or penny (nail size)
D & CM	Dressed (one or two sides) and center matched
D & M	Dressed and matched; that is, dressed on one or two sides and tongued-and-grooved on the edges. The match may be center or standard
D 2S & CM	Dressed two sides and center matched
D & SM	Dressed (one or two sides) and standard matched
D 2S & M	Dressed two sides and (center of standard) matched

D 2S & SM	Dressed two sides and standard matched
D.C.	Direct current
Deg. (or °)	Degree (or degrees)
Dia.	Diameter
Dim.	Dimension
D.S.	Double strength
D.S.	Drop siding (lumber)
E.	Edge
Fahr. (or F.)	Fahrenheit
FAS	Firsts and seconds, a combined grade of the two upper grades of hardwoods
f. bk.	Flat back
fcty.	Factory (lumber)
F.G.	Flat grain
Flg.	Flooring
f.o.k.	Free of knots
Frm.	Framing
ft.	Foot (or feet)
Gal.	Gallon (or gallons)
Hdl.	Handle (stock)
Hdwd.	Hardwood
H.P.	Horsepower
Hrt.	Heart
Hrtwd.	Heartwood
in.	Inch (or inches)
KD	Kiln-dried
k.d.	Knocked down
lbr.	Lumber
lgr.	Longer
lgth.	Length
Lin.	Linear (or Lineal)
lin. ft.	Linear foot; that is, twelve inches
L.R.	Log run
Lr. MCO	Log run, mill culls out
M.	Thousand (1,000)
Manuf.	Manufacturer
M.b.m.	Thousand (feet) board measure
Merch.	Merchantable
M.R.	Mill run
m.s.m.	Thousand (feet) surface measure
m.w.	Mixed width
No.	Number
Nt. Wt.	Net weight
1s & 2s	Ones and twos, a combined grade of the hardwood grades of first and seconds
Ord.	Order

158

Oz.	Ounce (or ounces)
P.	Planed
Pat.	Pattern
Pky.	Picky
Pln.	Plain (as in plain sawed)
Pn.	Partition
Qtd.	Quartered (with reference to hardwoods)
rd.	Round
rdm.	Random
res.	Resawed
rfg.	Roofing
Rfrs.	Roofers
Rip.	Ripped
r.l.	Random length
R.P.M.	Revolutions per minute
r.w.	Random width
S & CM	Surfaced one or two sides and center matched (referring to lumber)
S & E	Surfaced one side and one edge
S1E	Surfaced one edge
S2E	Surfaced two edges
S & M	Surfaced and matched; that is, surfaced one or two sides and tongued and grooved on the edges. The match may be center or standard
S4S	Surfaced four sides
S2S & CM	Surfaced two sides and center matched
S1S1E	Surfaced one side and one edge
S1S2E	Surfaced one side and two edges
S2S1E	Surfaced two sides and one edge
S & SM	Surfaced one or two sides and standard matched
S2S & M	Surfaced two sides and standard or center matched
Sap.	Sapwood
SB	Standard bead
Sd.	Seasoned
Sdg.	Siding
Sel.	Select
S.E. Sd.	Square-edge siding
s.f.	Surface foot; that is, an area of one square foot
Sftwd.	Softwood
Sh.D.	Shipping dry
Ship.	Shiplap
Sм.	Standard matched
s.m.	Surface measure
s.n.d.	Sap no defect
snd.	Sound
sq.	Square
sq.E.	Square edge
sq.E. & S.	Square edge and sound
sqrs.	Squares
S.S.	Single strength

Std.	Standard
Stk.	Stock
S.W.	Sound wormy
T & G	Tongued and grooved
TB & S	Top, bottom and sides
tbrs.	Timbers
V.G.	Vertical grain
w.a.l.	Wider, all length
wdr.	Wider
wt.	Weight
wth.	Width
x	Multiplied by (or times by)
Yd.	Yard (or yards)

Fractions and decimal equivalents

If you get estimates or bills marked with either fractions or decimals, the following is a table of equivalents:

1/64	= .015625	33/64	= .515625
1/32	= .03125	17/32	= .53125
3/64	= .046875	35/64	= .546875
1/16	= .0625	9/16	= .5625
5/64	= .078125	37/64	= .578125
3/32	= .09375	19/32	= .59375
7/64	= .109375	39/64	= .609375
1/8	= .125	5/8	= .625
9/64	= .140625	41/64	= .640625
5/32	= .15625	21/32	= .65625
11/64	= .171875	43/64	= .671875
3/16	= .1875	11/16	= .6875
13/64	= .203125	45/64	= .703125
7/32	= .21875	23/32	= .71875
15/64	= .234375	47/64	= .734375
1/4	= .25	3/4	= .75
17/64	= .265625	49/64	= .765625
9/32	= .28125	25/32	= .78125
19/64	= .296875	51/64	= .796875
5/16	= .3125	13/16	= .8125
21/64	= .328125	53/64	= .828125
11/32	= .34375	27/32	= .84375
23/64	= .359375	55/64	= .859375
3/8	= .375	7/8	= .875
25/64	= .390625	57/64	= .890625
13/32	= .40625	29/32	= .90625
27/64	= .421875	59/64	= .921875
7/16	= .4375	15/16	= .9375
29/64	= .453125	61/64	= .953125
15/32	= .46875	31/32	= .96875
31/64	= .484375	63/64	= .984375
1/2	= .50	1	= 1.00

Architectural symbols

Tile		Brick		Shingles (siding)	
Earth		Firebrick		Wood, rough	
Plaster		Concrete		Wood, finished	
Sheet metal		Cast concrete block		Cased or arched openings	
Built-in cabinet		Insulation: Loose fill		Single casement window	
Outside door: Brick wall		Board or quilts		Double-hung windows	
Frame wall		Cut stone		Double casement window	
Inside door: Frame wall		Ashlar			

Electrical symbols

Pull switch	P.S.	Floor outlet		Single convenience outlet	
Single-pole switch	S_1	Bell		Double convenience outlet	
Double-pole switch	S_2	Drop cord		Ceiling outlet, gas and electric	
Triple-pole switch	S_3	Ceiling outlet		Motor	
Buzzer		Wall bracket		Light outlet with wiring and switches indicated	

Plumbing symbols

Bath tubs:		Lavatories:			
Corner		Pedestal		Laundry trays	
Free standing		Wall-hung		Built-in shower	
Floor drain		Corner		Shower	s⊙—⊙s
Shower drain		Toilets: Tank		Sinks: Single drain board	
Hot-water tank	H.W.T.	Flush valve		Double drain board	
Grease trap		Urinals: Stall-type			
Hose bibb or sill cock		Wall-hung			